# TRUMP
## UNIVERSITY

# MARKETING
# 101

# TRUMP
## UNIVERSITY

# MARKETING
# 101

## How to Use the Most Powerful Ideas in Marketing to Get More Customers and Keep Them

### DON SEXTON, PhD

FOREWORD AND CHAPTER 1 BY DONALD TRUMP

WILEY

JOHN WILEY & SONS, INC.

To my terrific family,
Laura, Mitra, Matt, Daniel, Jonathan, and Nan
who are patient with me most of the time.

# CONTENTS

# CONTENTS

CONTENTS

## PART III
### IMPLEMENTING YOUR STRATEGY 141

## PART IV
### UNDERSTANDING THE NUMBERS 251

# CONTENTS

## PART V
### MAKING SURE YOUR MARKETING STRATEGY SUCCEEDS 287

# FOREWORD TO THE TRUMP UNIVERSITY 101 SERIES

People often ask me the secret to my success, and the answer is simple: focus, hard work, and tenacity. I've had some lucky breaks, but luck will only get you so far. You also need business savvy—not necessarily a degree from Wharton, but you do need the desire and discipline to educate yourself. I created Trump University to give motivated businesspeople the skills required to achieve lasting success.

The Trump University 101 Series explains the most powerful and important ideas in business—the same concepts taught in the most respected MBA curriculums and used by the most successful companies in the world, including the Trump Organization. Each book is written by a top professor, author, or entrepreneur whose goal is to help you put these ideas to use in your business right away. If you're not satisfied with the status quo in your career, read this book, pick one key idea, and implement it. I guarantee it will make you money.

DONALD J. TRUMP

# ACKNOWLEDGMENTS

Much appreciation to many people: Donald Trump for his marketing passion, demanding standards, and ongoing support; many executives in the Trump Organization who generously gave their time to provide examples and answer questions—George Ross, Jill Cremer, Tom Downing, Cathy Hoffman Glosser, Susan James, Virginia McDowell, Meredith McGiver, and Melissa Nicchitta, as well as Babs Harrison of Sheila Donnelly & Associates; Michael Sexton, the president of Trump University, for his stimulating vision and entrepreneurial energy; my other colleagues at Trump University—Ian Cohen, Jamie Pietras, Bob Kaeding, David Highbloom and Doug Blum—for their many ideas and insights and all our great discussions; and Richard Narramore, senior editor at Wiley, who always knew what to do and how to do it best. Thanks to all.

# I

## How to Build a Powerful Marketing Strategy

# 1

---

## TRUMP ON MARKETING

*by*

*Donald Trump*

I believe passionately in my products and the high quality I provide my customers. That is the foundation for all my marketing. That passion should be the foundation for anyone in marketing. You must truly believe in your product and its ability to satisfy your customers if you are going to succeed in marketing.

Ultimately, marketing always starts with a product. It is rare that you'll see somebody market something really well that isn't good. The best advice for anybody looking to do a good job in marketing is to have a good product. It makes your life a whole lot easier.

You need a great product—one that your customers want and will pay for. I think a great example of marketing is what I did with *The Apprentice*. From a show that everyone said would not be on the air long, I made it the number one show in television. I had a product I believed in and I marketed it. How do you make a strong product? A lot of it is in the details, a lot of it is in the quality—whether it's super high-end or low-end—attention to details really can make the difference.

You build great products by paying attention to all the details that customers care about. Some people seem to confuse marketing with

3

promotion. I recently built a $300 million building. It was very tough to build because I needed zoning changes, I needed financing, I needed the construction, I needed to make deals with unions—I had to go through all of this. I ended up building something that was a great success and everybody said, "Oh, what a great promotion job he did." It had nothing to do with promotion. The project became a success because it was a *great building*. Many people who don't know me think that I'm a great promoter but the fact is that what I do best is build. I build a great product and then it sells and everyone gives me credit for being a good promoter. To me a great promoter is a person who can take a piece of garbage and sell it. That's not me. I build really high-quality buildings. I think I do well in promotion because I start with a great product.

Promotion works—but only if you start with a great product. I see many people who do things wrong in marketing. I know one developer who can never understand why I get so much more per square foot than he does. He just finished this building where he has tiny little windows and a terrible color brick. It's an unattractive building both from the outside looking in and the inside looking out. And he goes around telling people he doesn't understand why Trump gets higher prices than he does. The guy doesn't have a clue. The mistakes in marketing often have to do with mistakes in the product.

---

**Promotion works—but only if you start with a great product.**

---

Your brand is your reputation—and comes from the strength of your products over time. Branding is an important part of marketing. The Trump brand stands for very high quality and very high confidence. People feel secure in the brand. That's why my building in Las Vegas is so successful. Other builders are not doing well and I'm doing very well.

It's the same story in Chicago. My Chicago building has been a great success. We've raised the prices way above anything they've seen. Because of the Trump brand, people buy in my buildings without ever having seen the units. They don't do that with other builders. My customers know the building's going to be the highest quality, the best architecture, and the best location.

A strong brand gives customers confidence—and leads to higher prices and higher demand. Great marketers are born with a marketing instinct. While I have known people who developed into good marketers, I think that, like an athlete, it helps to be born with a marketing sense. If you don't have

Trump World Tower Skyline and the Manhattan Waterfront.
Photo credit: The 7th Art, 1998. Photo courtesy of the Trump Organization.

that intuition, you'll never be great in marketing. You can make yourself good, but you'll never make yourself great.

**A strong brand gives customers confidence—and leads to higher prices and higher demand.**

You have in your hands a powerful introduction to all the most important ideas in marketing from a top marketing professor and consultant. If you don't have that marketing instinct, this book will help you learn it—and become a good marketer. If you were lucky enough to be born with it, this book will help you become a great marketer. Read on!

# 2

## WHAT IS MARKETING?

Marketing is about people. It is about understanding what people want, then trying to give it to them at a price that they are willing to pay and a price that will provide you with an acceptable profit.

Marketing is about targeting. It is about strategically choosing which customers you want to try to satisfy.

Marketing is about positioning. It is about designing a product or service that has benefits that people want and can't get elsewhere then building your reputation—your brand—based on those things that you do well.

Marketing is also about advertising and pricing and promoting and distributing and other marketing programs. But foremost it is about people and targeting and positioning—the strategic aspects of marketing. Without knowing to whom you want to sell and what you want to give them, you really can't know how to advertise or price or promote or distribute effectively. Stop right now and ask yourself these three questions:

1. What do my customers want from my product or service?
2. Am I targeting the right customers?
3. What is the unique benefit of my product or service that my customers can't get elsewhere?

## POSITIONING TRUMP INTERNATIONAL HOTEL & TOWER

Trump International Hotel & Tower, New York City.

Photo credit: Jon Ortner, 2002. Photo courtesy of the Trump Organization.

The Trump Organization is a leader in building and marketing luxury hotel/condominiums in many locations, including New York City, Chicago, Las Vegas, and Fort Lauderdale. The positioning of each Trump International Hotel & Tower is the same as all Trump endeavors: "best of the best" and "exclusivity." For example, the Trump International Hotel & Tower in New York City, which has a five-star rating, was voted the best hotel in New York City by *Travel & Leisure* magazine.

Trump International Hotel & Tower is also an example of great marketing. Each building is designed with targeted high-end customers clearly in mind and terrific attention to all the details that those customers want. According to George Ross (co-star of *The Apprentice,* and executive vice president for the Trump Organization), the building design philosophy is "put your money where it can be seen." As a result, Trump condominiums are known for their smart layouts, impressive views, and top-tier fixtures and appliances.

Besides marketing to hotel guests, Trump International Hotel & Tower also targets buyers who want an apartment in the city, but not necessarily for full-time use. To reach these customers, Trump uses a creative new financial incentive, which is also a key marketing feature. Owners can use their units any time they wish and enjoy the exclusive services of the hotel and the security and privacy of the most exclusive apartment buildings in the city, but they also have the option to let Trump International Hotel rent out their units to hotel

8

> guests—and share in the income—whenever they are not occupying the unit. So owners enjoy rental income without the headaches of landlording.
>
> At the New York City property, the owner-investors are from many parts of the world. In Chicago, the investors are often from the suburbs and looking for a pied-à-terre, while in Fort Lauderdale, they are more likely to be retirees. Besides the hotel's amenities and services they enjoy when they stay at the International Hotel & Tower, these customers also share financially in the success of the property.

This book will help you sharpen and improve your answers to these questions.

## MARKETING FAILURES

Many large and famous disasters in business were failures in marketing. The Edsel was a car with styling no one wanted. Both the RCA VideoDisc and Polaroid's Polavision were products technologically inferior to competing products. The U.S. Air Force and U.S. Navy did not purchase the Northrup Tigershark fighter aircraft because it was designed without important input from them.

What all these disasters had in common were managers who *thought* they knew what their customers wanted when in fact they did not. Unfortunately for those managers, their mistakes of not knowing what their customers wanted cost millions or billions of dollars and perhaps their jobs.

## SMALL BUSINESS MARKETING MISTAKES

The mistakes of large companies are repeated every day—with much less publicity—by owners and managers of small businesses.

Many small businesses don't think about marketing. They do not target their efforts to specific customers or position their services on specific benefits. They simply open up their doors and hope for the best.

Think about the dry cleaners in your area—are they known for anything special? Think of the mom-and-pop grocery stores—are they known for anything special? Think of the auto repair shops—are they known for anything special? Think of the hardware stores—are they known for anything special?

If they are known for anything special, then they know something about marketing—whether by instinct or by training. If not, then they are offering the world *commodities*—the worst word in marketing. A product or service that has nothing special about it is a commodity and can compete only on price. You need luck to survive if you are selling commodities.

Any business can be special to its customers. A dry cleaner can be known for its ability to remove any stain. A mom-and-pop food store can be known for stocking healthy foods. An auto repair store can be known for finishing work when promised. A hardware store can be known for providing do-it-yourself advice.

As I was growing up, my family's business consisted of installing water systems—pumps and pipes for housing developments, farms, and country clubs. Some times I worked with my father. He was known for something special—honesty, integrity, and willingness to go out anytime someone was without water—not always to my mother's delight.

When I was growing up, I had no clue what marketing was and what my father was doing. Today I understand.

Every business needs to have a way to make itself special to customers—a way to differentiate itself—and every business needs to focus on certain customers. In marketing "You can't be everything to everyone"—you have to focus your efforts on those customers you wish to attract.

This book is designed to help anyone develop marketing strategies that target customers—in attractive markets, with products or services that have great appeal, and which are implemented with well-designed programs such as pricing and advertising. In short, this book teaches marketing success.

## Marketing Strategy/Marketing Tactics

Unfortunately, many people think of marketing too narrowly—as a bag of "tactics" and not central to their business strategy. Many marketing textbooks perpetuate this narrow view of marketing by defining marketing as the "4 Ps": Product, Price, Place, and Promotion.

What is wrong with defining marketing as the "4 Ps"?

The "Ps" are not all equal. One of them, Product, is really a strategic choice, and must come before the other "Ps." The three other "Ps"—Price, Place, and Promotion—are tactics. If the product is not designed to meet customer needs, then a terrific price, a convenient place, and an exciting promotion will not save it.

What is missing in the "4 Ps" are many important strategic decisions, such as targeting markets and targeting competitors, which are addressed in this book. The tactical bias represented by the use of the "4 Ps" definition tends to marginalize marketing and remove marketers from discussions of strategy. Marketing is first about strategy, then about tactics.

To help get past this belief that marketing is just about tactics, when I'm conducting a workshop, I start by asking participants: "What kinds of actions, decisions, and responsibilities do you think of when you think of marketing?"

I write their answers on two flip charts, sorting them into two lists— those answers dealing with strategy and those dealing with tactics. The typical responses I obtain are shown in Exhibit 2.1.

Marketing includes both strategy and tactics but keep in mind that strategy must come before tactics. If the strategy is wrong—wrong target market, wrong positioning, and wrong target competitor—then it really does not make much difference how great the advertising or selling or distribution or pricing is, the product or service will fail eventually. In fact, the more effective the tactics the quicker a poor product will disappear. There is a saying in advertising: If the product is poor, great advertising will cause it to fail even faster—as more people are persuaded to use it, more people will find out that they don't like it.

**Exhibit 2.1  Selected Marketing Actions, Decisions, and Responsibilities**

| Strategic Areas | Tactical Areas |
| --- | --- |
| Understanding customers | Advertising |
| Identifying segments | Packaging |
| Targeting segments | Sales promotion |
| Designing the product or service | Personal selling |
| Positioning product or service | Public relations |
| Establishing the brand | Internet marketing |
| Understanding organization capabilities | Pricing |
| Understanding competitors | Distributing |
| Understanding the macroenvironment | Customer service |

*Source:* "Arrow Guide—The Marketing Challenge," The Arrow Group, Ltd.®, New York, 2004. Used with permission.

## How Marketing Has Changed

Back in the 1950s and 1960s, marketing was mainly about tactics. If you examine the marketing textbooks from that era, most of the chapters were devoted to tactics such as pricing, advertising, and sales force decisions. Tactics were emphasized because the competitive environment of the 1950s and 1960s in the United States was what you might call a "quiet time" when—at least in comparison to today—competition was less intense and technology seemed to be moving more slowly. During the quiet time, well-implemented tactics could lead to success.

However, the competitive environment today is a "noisy time"—intense, widespread competition, fast-changing technologies, and ever more well-informed customers searching for deals on the Internet. During the noisy time, you need *both* well-developed strategies *and* well-implemented tactics to succeed. If you look at a marketing text today, you will see how marketing has changed—current marketing texts devote a considerable amount of space to customers, competitors, targeting, and positioning—they emphasize strategy before tactics.

## Customers and Their Perceptions

When Paul Simons took over a troubled Woolworth in Australia, he said, "If we were going to revitalize Woolworth, we had to start with understanding the customer." All marketing strategy starts with understanding your customers and prospective customers and how they perceive your products and your services. Customers behave according to their perceptions of products and services, *not* according to managers' opinions of the products and services they are trying to sell.

Customers' perceptions can be summarized as *perceived value*. Perceived value is not some fuzzy theoretical concept. In this book, perceived value is defined in a very practical way:

> *Perceived Value:* The maximum a customer or prospective customer will pay for your product or service.

Perceived value is not the price you charge—it is the ceiling on the price you can charge:

- Perceived value can be estimated and measured in monetary terms. In fact, an entire chapter, Chapter 5, is devoted to just that.
- Perceived value varies across customers according to their needs and priorities. These groups are called *market segments*. (See Chapters 9 and 10 for more on this.)
- Perceived value can be managed with both strategy and tactics.
- The higher the perceived value of your product or service, the higher your sales, profits, and cash flow will be.

## A NEW DEFINITION OF MARKETING

Everything you do in marketing affects perceived value. All the decisions, actions, and responsibilities in Exhibit 2.1 affect perceived value.

That is why the definition of marketing is definitely *not* just what is covered in the 4 Ps.

Marketing is managing perceived value. To manage perceived value, you must understand your competitive environment, target markets, position products and services, build strong brands, satisfy customers, set price, develop advertising, organize sales efforts, arrange distribution, forecast results, and motivate your people—and do all those things extremely well.

**Marketing is managing perceived value.**

That's what successful marketers do well. That's what this book is about.

## CONCLUSIONS

Marketing consists of both strategy and tactics. Over time, marketing has moved from tactical decisions to both strategic and tactical decisions. Understanding the customer's needs and perceptions is the foundation of marketing. Marketing is managing the value perceived by the customers.

For review questions for this chapter, log on to www.trumpuniversity .com/marketing101.

# 3

---

# BUILDING A
# MARKETING STRATEGY

A marketing strategy is the blueprint for how you will allocate your resources to achieve your business objectives. Without a marketing strategy, there is no clear focus on which customers you will pursue. Without a marketing strategy, there is no clear definition of what is special about your organization's products or services and why the target customers should buy them.

You need a marketing strategy to organize all your marketing efforts over time. You also need a marketing strategy because people you will ask for money—lenders, investors, donors—want to know what you will be doing with their money.

Organizations of any size need a marketing strategy. In fact, small organizations especially need a strategy since they may need to concentrate whatever resources they have against much larger opponents.

An effective marketing strategy can be summarized in just one page (Exhibit 3.1). In this chapter, we describe exactly what goes on that page. In the chapters that follow, we move step-by-step through every element of the marketing strategy.

**Downloadable Exhibit 3.1    The Product or Service Market Strategy***

Product or Service: _____          Market Segment: _____

| | | Year | | | |
|---|---|---|---|---|---|
| | | **1** | **2** | **3** | **4** |
| **Objectives** | Share | | | | |
| | Profitability | | | | |
| | Cash flow | | | | |
| **Positioning** | Target DMU† member | | | | |
| | Target competitor | | | | |
| | Benefit advantage | | | | |
| | Competitive advantage | | | | |
| **Programs** | Design | | | | |
| | Advertising | | | | |
| | Identifiers | | | | |
| | Promotion | | | | |
| | Selling | | | | |
| | Public relations | | | | |
| | Pricing | | | | |
| | Distribution | | | | |

†DMU: Decision-Making Unit (Chapter 4)
*Source:* "Arrow Guide—Market Strategy Analysis," Copyright © 2004, The Arrow Group, Ltd.®, New York. Used with permission. ***A blank version of this page can be downloaded from www.trumpuniversity.com/marketing101 and customized for your personal use.*** For any other use, contact Don Sexton at Marketing101@thearrowgroup.com.

## WHAT A STRATEGY SHOULD DO FOR YOU

A good strategy delivers the three Cs—the main reasons for preparing a strategy:

1. Coordinate.
2. Concentrate.
3. Communicate.

A strategy *coordinates* all your organization's resources and actions so that they are intended for the same goals. People you work with all may have different views as to how they should run their functions. For example, a production manager may want just one version of the product to lower costs

## TARGETING AND POSITIONING: TRUMP INTERNATIONAL HOTEL & TOWER, NEW YORK CITY

Breakfast Overlooking Central Park, at Trump International Hotel & Tower, New York City.
Photo courtesy of the Trump Organization.

The two most crucial components of a marketing strategy are the target market and the positioning. The strategy of the Trump International Hotel & Tower in New York City illustrates how they are defined and how they are intertwined.

Trump International Hotel & Tower provides high-income hotel guests and residents the Trump attention to detail and impeccable service that they demand. George Ross, executive vice president of the Trump Organization, says that in their construction, they use only perfect mirrored steel and only the finest marble (and each piece must match). The New York City Trump International Hotel & Tower includes the five-star restaurant Jean Georges (which provides room service) and unparalleled food for guests.

Overall cleanliness is given high priority—windows and carpets are cleaned much more often than in the properties of others.

> The entire staff is extraordinarily attentive to customer needs. Tom Downing, general manager of the New York City Trump International Hotel & Tower, recalls one incident of typical beyond-the-call-of-duty service where "A guest, a musician, had checked out of our hotel and was already at the airport before realizing he had left his prized guitar behind in his suite. He was on his way to a concert and could not perform without it, and did not have time to return to the hotel himself for fear of missing his flight. Our security staff located the guitar and a bellman personally brought it in a car to the airport to reunite it with the guest before he boarded his flight. The concert went on as planned!"

while a sales manager may want many versions to please customers. A marketing strategy provides the opportunity for all these views to be balanced so that all the functions of an organization are coordinated.

Achieving goals requires that efforts be *concentrated* on specific products, services, and markets. A long-time military precept is "concentrate your firepower." The precept holds in marketing as well. If you think everyone is your customer then no one is your customer. If you never say no to anyone, you do not have a marketing strategy because you have not focused your efforts.

Finally, a strategy must *communicate* to all the members of an organization what they are supposed to do. If your employees do not understand the marketing strategy, how can you expect them to implement it?

## Marketing Strategy—Restaurant Example

Suppose you are running an Italian restaurant. You have done well so far without any special marketing strategy because yours is the only Italian restaurant in the neighborhood. However, recently a national chain of Italian restaurants opened a new restaurant in your geographical area. What are you going to do?

You need a marketing strategy!

Before developing your strategy, you might consider what you know about your customers and potential customers. Perhaps there are many young families in your area or perhaps there are many seniors in your area. You would want to think over what type of restaurant each of these groups might prefer.

You also need to imagine how the chain restaurant will compete. You would certainly go there and look over its menu. You would also probably anticipate that it will use some form of promotion to acquire new customers.

After you have collected your thoughts on your market and competition, you can then begin to consider different options. A useful way to do that is to imagine scenarios if you were to target particular groups of customers (known as *target market segments*—see Chapters 9 and 10). For example, you might choose to focus your efforts on young families because you think they are becoming more numerous in your area. If so, what items should be on your menu? How should your restaurant look? How should your waitstaff treat your customers? For what should your restaurant be known? All these decisions concern what is known as the *positioning* of your product or service (see Chapter 11).

As you go through this analysis, you should also be thinking how the chain restaurant might react to your actions. You'd like to find a scenario where it will be at a disadvantage. For example, you would not want to engage it in a price war because it likely has more financial resources than you do.

Your marketing strategy begins with your choice of target market, for example, young families, and your positioning, perhaps the tastiness of your food and the friendliness of your waitstaff. You may communicate this strategy by establishing your brand as "your favorite local Italian restaurant—we've known you for years." In turn, the target market, positioning, and branding would guide your advertising, promotion, and pricing. You would advertise in local newspapers read by members of these young families, aim promotions toward their children, and price accordingly.

Whether you defeat the national chain depends on how well you execute your strategy. But, if you and your employees follow your strategy, you will coordinate, concentrate, and communicate your efforts so that you are making the best use of your resources and will have the highest chance of defeating the competitor.

## COMPONENTS OF A PRODUCT/MARKET STRATEGY

A marketing strategy has four major components (Exhibit 3.2):

1. *Target market:* The specific group of customers who will be the focus of your strategy.
2. *Business objectives:* The reason you are in business. Usually stated in terms of financial results such as revenue, profits, or cash flow, but also stated as units sold or market share.

**Exhibit 3.2    Components of a Market Strategy**

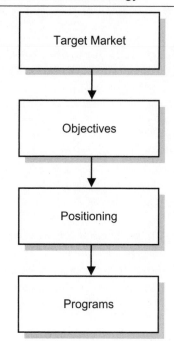

*Source:* "Arrow Guide—Market Strategy Analysis," The Arrow Group, Ltd.®, New York, 2004. Used with permission.

3. *Positioning:* The one or two key benefits of your product or service selected to be the core of the strategy. The positioning serves to coordinate all the programs.
4. *Programs:* The actions you pursue to implement the strategy. Sometimes called tactics or *the marketing mix*, these actions concern activities such as advertising, personal selling, pricing, and distribution.

Target market and positioning are the heart of the marketing strategy. Without specifying your target market and positioning, your strategy cannot coordinate, concentrate, or communicate.

In the course of consulting with Fortune 500 companies, I have been asked to review countless marketing plans and provide comments. Half of the plans I reviewed did not clearly set forth their target market or positioning. These plans did not describe marketing strategies—they described tactics. They did not represent strategic marketing, they represented tactical marketing—an inadequate and likely dangerous approach during a noisy competitive environment. If you do nothing else about marketing strategy, make sure you determine your target markets and your positioning!

---

**If you do nothing else about marketing strategy, make sure you determine your target markets and your positioning!**

---

## HIERARCHY OF STRATEGIES

In many organizations—even small ones—there are often many levels and many strategies at each level. This is called the *hierarchy of strategies* (Exhibit 3.3).

The broadest strategy in your business is your corporate or organization strategy. That is the strategy for all the activities and all the products and services and all the markets in which the organization is involved. Not only is it the broadest strategy, it should also be the strategy that looks the furthest into the future because it should indicate how and where the entire organization should grow.

Below the organization strategy is the strategy for what are often called *strategic business units* or SBUs. A strategic business unit is a collection of businesses that have something in common—resources, technologies, raw materials, customers, or competitors. General Electric (GE) has strategic business units such as Industrial, Infrastructure, and Consumer Finance. However, much smaller organizations may have strategic business units as well. For example, a restaurant may provide catering services and a dry cleaner may provide tailoring services.

Strategic business units typically consist of collections of products or services—product groups. For example, GE Infrastructure has businesses that deal with aviation, rail, and energy and each would have its own strategy. MasterCard has groups that deal with consumers and groups that deal with companies. Universities have marketing departments and finance departments. A restaurant may provide catering for children's birthday parties and catering for adult dinner parties.

Product groups in turn consist of specific products or services. The GE aviation business has several engines, each for different types of aircraft. A university marketing department may have courses in pricing and in advertising. A restaurant may have numerous meat entrees or fish entrees. Each of the products and services may be targeted to different groups of customers. For

**Exhibit 3.3   Hierarchy of Strategies**

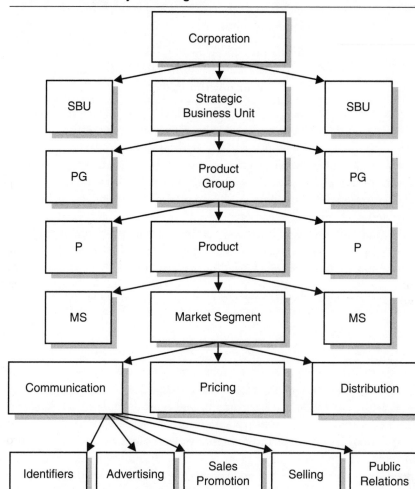

*Source:* "Arrow Guide—Formulating the Product/Market Strategy," The Arrow Group, Ltd.®, New York, 2004. Used with permission.

example, the GE 90 engine was specifically designed for the Boeing 777. Advertising courses might be targeted to students interested in careers marketing consumer products. Fish entrees might be targeted to health-conscious diners.

A strategy for a specific product or service focused on a specific target market is known as the *product/market strategy.*

## The Role of the Product/Market Strategy

Whether you are in a large organization or a small organization, the product/market strategy is the atom of strategic planning. It is the basic unit of planning for marketing and is not divisible.

More to the point, the effectiveness of your product/market strategies determines whether or not you make money. Organization strategies should be built from the product/market strategies. Objectives may be set from the top down, but to achieve those objectives, organizations must win customers—that is what the product/market strategy does.

The product/market strategy is the strategy for marketing a specific product or service to a specific group of customers. For example, a computer manufacturer might focus on universities or a glass manufacturer might focus on breweries. Among smaller organizations, a dentist might focus on children, a food store on seniors, and a dry cleaner on customers who go to work early and need to find the cleaner open at those hours. These specific groups of customers are the *target markets*.

---

**The product/market strategy is the strategy for marketing a specific product or service to a specific group of customers.**

---

The *positioning* for each target market is the reason the marketer gives the potential customers in that group to buy their product or service. The computer manufacturer might provide proprietary software to the university and the glass manufacturer might provide fast delivery time to the breweries. The dentist might provide a child-friendly environment with toys and other diversions, the food store might have a broad selection of single-serving foods desired by seniors, and the dry cleaner might open earlier than its competitors.

Whether the organization is large or small, the product/market strategies must make clear the target markets and the positioning. How well they do that determines whether the organization succeeds or fails.

## PROGRAM STRATEGIES

Programs include design, advertising, promotion, selling, public relations, Internet marketing, pricing, customer service, and all other actions involved in implementing the strategy. Overall, the programs are typically known as the *marketing mix*.

Each program has a strategy that is discussed in later chapters.

Your target market and positioning decisions described in your product/market strategy coordinates all your programs. For example, Neiman-Marcus and Wal-Mart have different marketing strategies that are reflected in their merchandise selection, advertising, and price points. Ritz-Carlton Hotels and Motel 6 have different marketing strategies that are reflected in their design, services, and price points.

## How to Develop a Product/Market Strategy

Developing a product/market strategy requires several related steps (Exhibit 3.4). As you pull together your strategy, sometimes you must return to an earlier step and redo a particular analysis or change a particular decision. Real life is messy—not as simple and linear as the diagram in Exhibit 3.4. Developing a marketing strategy may require you to repeat some steps several times until everything fits together.

Each step is covered in later chapters. This chapter provides you with an overview of the process of developing the product/market strategy.

The first stage is known as the *situation analysis*. The situation analysis is when you develop a foundation for the product/market strategy by evaluating your competitive environment. You define *customers* and examine their needs. You identify *competitors* and predict their actions. You evaluate your *organization* with respect to its capabilities. You explore changes in the *macroenvironment* such as demographic, technological, economic, social, or political trends that might affect you.

For example, to develop a strategy in the Italian restaurant example, you considered customers, the new chain competitor, and your own restaurant, as well as possible changes in the demographics of the area—more young families moving in.

The situation analysis usually produces three to five *key planning assumptions* (KPAs) on which the strategy will be based. If any of those KPAs change, you need to review your strategy.

*Segmentation* consists of two activities: *Identifying* market segments and *selecting* market segments. At this point, you make a tentative choice of a target market.

*Assembling the strategy* involves setting objectives, determining positioning, and outlining programs. All decisions are tentative until you finalize the product/market strategy.

**Exhibit 3.4   Developing a Product/Market Strategy**

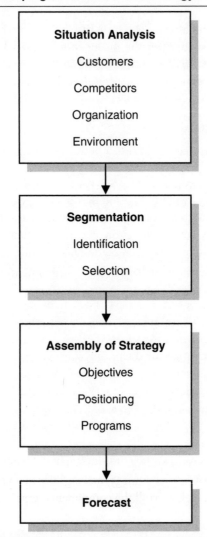

*Source:* "Arrow Guide—Formulating the Product/Market Strategy," The Arrow Group, Ltd.®, New York, 2004. Used with permission.

The final step is *forecasting* the outcomes of the strategy—especially the business objectives. If the forecasts based on the strategy at least meet the business objectives, then this strategy is a viable strategy. If they do not meet the business objectives, then it is necessary to go through the process again—and again—and maybe again—until a viable strategy is found.

## FINDING A MARKETING STRATEGY THAT YOU LIKE

Sometimes you can't find a strategy that delivers the business objectives you need. One option is just to lower the business objectives. While sometimes you may have to do that, it is usually not the first option you want to consider.

Even if you find a strategy that you think will achieve your business objectives, you still should consider going through the strategy development steps again because you may find another strategy that is superior to the one you already found.

To improve your strategy or to find a better one, reverse the steps of the development process.

You first might want to review your marketing programs. Perhaps you can improve your communications or your pricing. If that doesn't work, then you might examine your positioning. Perhaps you might focus on a different benefit or a different target competitor. If changing positioning doesn't help, then you might reconsider your target market or even how you segmented the market.

If you were trying to improve the strategy in the Italian restaurant example, you might first reevaluate your advertising plans or your pricing. Next, if necessary, you might reconsider your positioning on taste and friendliness and, perhaps, focus on portion quantity and friendliness instead. If that doesn't help improve your strategy, then you might try to avoid the national chain and compete with another restaurant, perhaps the local pizzeria. Finally, you might decide to target young singles or even try an entirely new segment of the market. Each of those changes will change your marketing strategy and have an impact on the objectives you can expect to achieve.

You can change any part of your marketing strategy to find one that might be more successful. However, a product/market strategy is like a complicated piece of machinery. All the components must work together. You need to be systematic about any changes in your strategy, making sure that your target market and positioning are always clear so all the components remain coordinated.

## CONCLUSIONS

The product/market strategy coordinates all efforts of the organization to get and keep customers, concentrates the organization's efforts on specific markets, and communicates to all involved what must be done to get and keep customers. The heart of the strategy is the target market and the positioning.

For review questions for this chapter, log on to www.trumpuniversity .com/marketing101.

# 4

---

# UNDERSTANDING
# YOUR CUSTOMERS

Understanding customers is the heart of marketing. All the major failures in the history of marketing can be traced to a lack of knowledge about customers' needs and wants. If you don't know the needs and wants of your customers, how can you possibly satisfy them? This chapter focuses on how to think about customers so you can be successful in marketing to them.

## WHY MANAGERS FORGET TO TALK TO CUSTOMERS

Why do some managers neglect to talk to their customers when they develop a marketing strategy? Here are a few of the reasons:

- *Pressure to get short-term results:* Some organizations demand that their managers obtain profits in a very short period of time. Often this can lead to major marketing mistakes that end up killing profits in the long term.
- *Belief that they already know what the customer wants:* Customers are not always easy to figure out. They may see product advantages or disad-

vantages of which the marketing manager is unaware. Managers sometimes believe customers behave the same way as they do—not likely.

- *Unwillingness to contact customers:* When customers have nice things to say about your product or service, it is a pleasure to talk with them. However, when they have complaints, it is less pleasant. Customer complaints, in fact, should be treated as gold by organizations because they reveal ways in which performance can improve. Some companies, such as Xerox and Procter & Gamble, require their managers to read or listen regularly to complaints from customers.
- *Belief in the product or service:* Some managers believe that their product or service is so terrific that every customer will demand it. On occasion that can be true—certain pharmaceutical products or certain electronic products, for example, may represent dramatic technological breakthroughs that provide benefits that everyone will want. However, even breakthrough products do not always succeed.

  Even when a product succeeds, you can expect competitors to imitate the pioneer product and improve on it. If you want to stay ahead of those competitors, then you need to be close to your customers and know their needs, especially if they are changing. One of the main reasons for a pioneering product to fail is not evolving the product or service to keep pace with the customers' changing concerns and preferences.
- *Belief that it is not necessary to target customers:* There is a marketing joke where a sales representative gets into a taxi and says to the driver, "Take me anywhere. I have customers all over." It's a joke because the reality is that customers differ dramatically. While everyone might be a potential customer, it is important to focus on the customers you want and the customers you feel you can satisfy better than your competitors can.

## BENEFITS

Benefits represent the size of a customer's problem. Note that in marketing, a *customer problem* represents a golden opportunity—a customer need you hope to satisfy.

If you have an allergy, then your problem is how to feel better. Several benefits come to mind: getting rid of your headache, cough, or stuffy nose; getting rid of them quickly; and getting rid of them with no unpleasant side effects. All of these are dimensions of your problem.

## WHY YOU NEED TO TALK TO YOUR CUSTOMERS: TRUMP CASINOS AND RESORTS

Trump Taj Majal, Atlantic City.
Photo courtesy of the Trump Organization.

Las Vegas and Atlantic City are the two largest destination markets for gaming in the United States, and both cities feature billion dollar properties where no expense was spared to create an atmosphere of upscale elegance. The Trump Taj Mahal Casino Resort is joined in Atlantic City by Trump Plaza, and Trump Marina, with its sweeping views of the bay and million dollar yachts. James B. Perry, chief executive officer of Trump Entertainment Resorts, says that the secret to managing these properties is simple—find out what is important to customers; then exceed their expectations.

While this may sound simple, Perry maintains that most companies never really invest the time or the resources to truly understand their customers, and make the serious mistake of assuming they know what customers want. For example, many gaming companies making significant capital investments in their facilities in an effort to improve results, when what is really needed are operational changes.

When you listen to customers, you sometimes get surprising results. In a recent comprehensive research study, Trump Casino customers were surveyed, as well as customers loyal to competitors in the Atlantic City market, Connecticut, and Delaware. The survey required customers to rank 19 different casino and service attributes in order of importance, then to rank each of the surveyed casinos on delivery or satisfaction.

The results? Customers' top priority was not headline entertainment, or free rooms, or free food. Not restaurants, or trendy retail shops, or the selection of slots and table games. The attribute most important to the loyal customers who were surveyed was cleanliness! This was a surprise to many who assumed that it was primarily the offers and amenities that customers wanted. "If you think about it, you won't be comfortable visiting any facility that is not clean, whether it is a movie theater, or a shopping mall, or a casino," explained James Perry. "We know what is most important to our customers, quite simply because we asked them. And we listened to what they said." This gives us a competitive advantage in a very competitive market.

If you are a working parent, then your problem may be finding a place to care for your young children while you are at work. The benefits you look for might include competence, responsiveness, and friendliness, as well as a pleasant environment, convenient location, and convenient hours.

## TYPES OF BENEFITS

You can classify benefits into three types:

1. *Economic:* This includes anything to do with money. The price, of course, but economic benefits would also include costs of supplies or costs of maintaining a product or service.
2. *Functional:* Does the product or service do what it promises to do? Clear up a stuffy nose. Make millions of calculations with accuracy. Remove stains from a garment. Provide nutritious food in a restaurant. Help you find a home at a reasonable price in an area with good schools.
3. *Psychological (or emotional):* The feelings or beliefs associated with a product or service. These might include feelings of status from a luxury automobile or fashionable clothing but might also include many other kinds of feelings, such as feelings of reliability that a drug will work, of friendliness and courtesy in a restaurant, or confidence that a tax matter or a bad tooth will be handled correctly.

## MEETING CUSTOMERS' NEEDS: DREYER'S LOW-FAT ICE CREAM

Good marketers listen to their customers. Dreyer's found out through marketing research that many consumers much preferred the taste of premium ice cream to that of low-calorie ice cream. In response, they developed Dreyer's Grand Light Slow-Churned Ice Cream—50 percent less fat and 30 percent fewer calories. Chris Deyo, vice president of marketing/business development for Dreyer's observed: "We've reinvented light ice cream with our patented process. . . . Consumers are skeptical. But once they try it, they won't be able to tell the difference between it and full-fat."

*Source:* Sonia Reyes, "Dreyer's Has the Scoop to Please Ice Cream Skeptics," *Brandweek,* May 10, 2004, p. 5.

## FEATURES VERSUS BENEFITS

While a benefit is a dimension of the customer's problem, a feature is a specification of a product or service. For example, the seat on an airplane may be a certain number of inches wide—that is a feature. However, the width of the seat leads directly to a functional benefit, *comfort* for the passenger on the flight.

In 1999, Westin Hotels and Resorts introduced the Heavenly Bed into their rooms—providing such a good "bed experience" that guests wanted to buy them. The bed was the feature; a good sleep was the benefit.[1]

Managers control *features,* but customers buy *benefits.* There are many famous one-liners in marketing regarding features and benefits. For example: "Last year a tool manufacturer sold hundreds of thousands of drills that people did not want." They did not want the drills (feature)—they wanted the holes the drills could make (benefit).

**Managers control *features,* but customers buy *benefits.***

## WHO IS THE CUSTOMER?

To develop a marketing strategy, you must focus on the customer, and it is not always easy to know who your customer really is.

The customer is anyone involved in the purchase decision. In most instances, several people may be involved in the purchase decision. You must think through how the purchase decision is made to identify who might be involved.

Effective sales representatives are very good at discovering who will be involved in the purchase decision. The sales representative may not be able to or need to call on everyone involved in the purchase decision, but he or she must decide where to allocate his or her selling time to maximize the chance of obtaining the sale.

## Decision-Making Unit

All the people involved in a purchase decision in any way comprise the *decision-making unit*. Different individuals may play different roles in the decision-making unit:

- *Gatekeeper:* Controls access to the members of the decision-making unit. "Look at this automobile ad I saw in the newspaper."
- *Initiator:* Starts the purchase decision process. "We do need a new car."
- *Influencer:* Has an interest in the outcome of the purchase decision and will contribute opinions. "I'd really like to buy a minivan so each of the children can have a seat."
- *Decider:* Makes the final decision ("signs off") but may not be the most important member of the decision-making unit. "I'll see what money we have in the bank."
- *Vetoer:* Stops the purchase. "I won't drive a car unless it has side air bags."
- *User:* Uses the product or service. "I need to have space for our children and the neighbor's children."

Some decision-making unit members may have more than one role. A teenager may suggest the need for a new car and may provide information about cars. A cat is the user of cat food but may be a vetoer by refusing to eat a specific brand.

## Components of Perceived Value

As a marketer, you need to know how customers perceive your product or service. How they value your product or service overall is known as *perceived value*—the maximum they are willing to pay for your product or service.

Perceived value depends on four components:

1. The benefits you provide.
2. The actual performance of those benefits by you and by your competitors.
3. The performance of those benefits by you and by your competitors *as perceived by the customer.*
4. The relative importance of each of those benefits to the customer.

How all of these components are related may vary by customer but you can evaluate them systematically by applying one of my planning techniques, a *Perceived Value Analysis.*

## Perceived Value Analysis

There are six steps to analyzing the perceived value of your product or service:

1. Select a target segment.
2. Select a target member of the decision-making unit.
3. List the main competitors.
4. List the benefits associated with the product or service.
5. Estimate the relative importance of each benefit to your target customer.
6. For your company and for each competitor, evaluate the performance on each benefit *as perceived* by your customer.

One very important point: The benefits, the relative importance estimates, and the perceived evaluations of performance must come from your *customers.* Although you can guess at what your customers want—and sometimes perhaps make pretty good guesses—it is always important to find out what your customers are thinking and feeling. The greatest disasters in marketing occurred because no one asked the customers their thoughts and feelings about a product or a service.

## Perceived Value Analysis—Dry-Cleaning Example

To illustrate how the analysis works, suppose you were operating a small dry-cleaning establishment, DES Cleaners. You have four local competitors: Al's Cleaners, Barbara's Cleaners, Carol's Cleaners, and Dan's Cleaners.

Your current customers are mainly professional women and men—they will be your target customers for the analysis. Based on your experience, you make a list of the benefits you think your customers want from a dry cleaner and estimate how important each benefit might be. You also talk to some of your customers, show them the list, and obtain their opinions as to what benefits they want and how important those benefits are to them. This information is shown in Exhibit 4.1. (You can also download and customize a blank version of this worksheet to analyze the perceived value of your own product or service. See the source note in Exhibit 4.1 for details.)

*Warning:* When making lists of benefits, avoid words like quality that are general and vague.

Everyone knows what quality means to them but everyone's definition of quality may not agree. Think of an automobile brand that you would consider a "quality" automobile. There are many such automobiles, but some are quality automobiles because of their reliability, some because of the luxuriousness of their interior, some because of their safety. Rather than use the word *quality*, you should provide the specific benefit that you have in mind. Quality is not an actionable word—only in a very broad sense. In marketing, you need to know the specifics of what makes a product or service quality.

**Downloadable Exhibit 4.1   Perceived Value Analysis—Dry Cleaners***

| Relative Importance | Benefits | DES | Al's | Barbara's | Carol's | Dan's |
|---|---|---|---|---|---|---|
| 10 | Clean clothes | 4 | 3 | 2 | 5 | 3 |
| 10 | Stain removal | 5 | 3 | 4 | 3 | 2 |
| 7 | Quick turnaround | 5 | 5 | 3 | 1 | 4 |
| 3 | Courtesy | 2 | 4 | 3 | 4 | 4 |
| 6 | No damage | 4 | 4 | 4 | 4 | 3 |
| 5 | Convenient location | 2 | 3 | 2 | 5 | 4 |
| 8 | Convenient hours | 4 | 3 | 5 | 2 | 4 |
| 4 | Cleaning knowledge | 2 | 3 | 3 | 5 | 3 |
| 5 | Pressed neatly | 3 | 3 | 3 | 4 | 3 |
| 4 | Ability to make repairs | 2 | 5 | 4 | 4 | 3 |

*Note:* Relative importance: 1—Not important, 10—Very important
Perceived performance: 1—Poor, 5—Excellent
*Source:* "Arrow Guide—Perceived Value Analysis," Copyright © 2004, The Arrow Group, Ltd.®, New York. Used with permission. ***A blank version of this page can be downloaded from www.trumpuniversity.com/marketing101 and customized for your personal use.*** For any other use, contact Don Sexton at Marketing101@thearrowgroup.com.

**Everyone knows what quality means to them
but everyone's definition of quality may not agree.**

Next consider how well customers think DES Cleaners provides benefits as compared to its competitors.

How do you find this information? You probably already know a fair amount about how you are perceived by your customers just by listening to your friends and your customers. However, you can also ask people or have your friends ask people what they think of your competitors. This is called a survey.

A larger company would likely commission a formal survey to discover the perceptions of their customers. Even though a small company, such as a neighborhood dry cleaner, would usually not have the money and time to commission a survey, the principle is the same: Learn how you are perceived by your customers relative to your competitors.

Your estimates of the perceptions of your customers for the various benefits can be gathered and recorded by downloading the blank version of Exhibit 4.1. When complete, the information can provide many insights.

In the example, notice how the dry cleaner, DES Cleaners, is perceived by customers. It does best on "stain removal" and "quick turnaround." Stain removal is one of the two most important benefits for customers so that is very good news. Quick turnaround is very important to customers although not one of the two most important benefits.

Based on the estimates in Exhibit 4.1, you might want to examine why customers do not perceive performance on "clean clothes" to be at the highest level. Another area you might consider improving is "convenient hours."

In fact, if you could raise your perceived performance in both "clean clothes" and "convenient hours," you would be a formidable competitor and likely very successful.

If you look at the competing dry cleaners, you see that only Carol's received a score of 5 for "clean clothes" and its performance on other important benefits such as "stain removal," "convenient hours," and "quick turnaround" was weak. Barbara's really has only "convenient hours" as a benefit that is perceived to be high; Al's has only "quick turnaround"; and Dan's doesn't have any benefit at all that is perceived to receive a high score.

None of these competitors can be assumed to be standing still and each one of them may be trying to improve their perceptions among customers.

While Exhibit 4.1 contains a lot of helpful information, keep in mind:

- The list of benefits, the relative importance estimates, and the perceived evaluations of performance must come from *customers*.
- Generally, perceived value is not additive, so resist the temptation simply to multiply all the perceived performance evaluations by the importance ratings.
- All the benefit rows are usually not equally important, so focus first on the benefits with the highest importance ratings—often they will determine the winners and losers.

## Customers You Need to Know

You should know the needs and benefits sought by all your customers but you should keep in mind what you can learn from different types of customers and be in contact with them on a regular basis. The kinds of customers include:

- *Current customers* let you know how you are doing now. You need to be in touch with them to monitor your current actions. You can also get ideas for new products and services by asking them about their future needs and how they will be satisfied.
- *New customers* give you important information about what is attracting people to your products and services and the ways in which you are perceived to be superior to your competitors.
- *Lost customers*—those who defect—are very important to contact. They have valuable information for you, namely, where you fell short in satisfying them. It may be a benefit not delivered. It may be a negative interaction with someone in your organization. It may be a price thought to be too high. Whatever it is you need to know about it before another customer leaves for the same reason.
- *Heavy users* or *high-tech users* are the experts on your product or service and those of your competitors. They can advise you of trends in the product category. They can guide you to problems that need to be solved. In addition, the heavy users probably comprise the majority of your sales.
- *Potential customers* are your growth opportunities. You need to know their needs and how those needs may differ from the needs of your current customers so you can redesign your product or service if necessary and so you can communicate to them the information they need if you are to persuade them to buy from you.

## CONCLUSIONS

What customers pay must cover all the costs—and profits—of an organization. You must understand the needs and wants of your customers, not just now, but in the future. You must use customer information to identify and select target markets and to position your product or service.

For review questions for this chapter, log on to www.trumpuniversity .com/marketing101.

# 5

---

## MEASURING AND MANAGING
## YOUR PERCEIVED VALUE

Perceived value depends on your customer's needs and wants and how those customers evaluate your product or service relative to all your competitors. Perceived value is the maximum that a customer is willing to pay for a product or service.

The price you can charge and the amount of units you can sell both depend on perceived value. For example, if you allow customers to perceive that the value you give them is just above your costs, then your margins will be razor thin. Worse, if they perceive the value you give them is below your costs, you go out of business.

Alternately, if your customers perceive the value you give them is much higher than your costs, then you either have high margins, high unit sales, or some combination of both—your choice.

Marketing is managing perceived value. It is important to know that perceived value is not some kind of fuzzy abstract concept. It can be measured. It can be managed. Here's how.

---

**Marketing is managing perceived value.**

---

## THE POWER OF PERCEIVED VALUE: TRUMP INTERNATIONAL HOTEL & TOWER, CHICAGO

Trump International Hotel & Tower, Chicago.

Photo credit: Skidmore Owings & Merrill, 2005.

Photo courtesy of the Trump Organization.

High perceived value allows you to charge high prices because you are providing high value to your customers. For example, the selling price of units in the Chicago Trump International Hotel & Tower is very high. According to Tracy Cross, whose firm tracks the prices of housing in the Chicago area, prices in this Trump building are so high, they were a major cause of a 30 percent increase in the average price of new town home and condo units in the whole Chicago area during the last quarter of 2003. Prices in the Trump building at that time started at about a half million dollars—top units were selling for over $11 million. In contrast, the average price for all town home /condo units in the Chicago area during the quarter was $340,000.

The Trump Organization estimates the Trump name on a building results in a price lift of 50 percent to 60 percent. As one reporter observed, "Call it the Donald effect."

*Source:* Alby Gallun, "City's Average Home Price Gets a Bump from Trump," *Crain's Chicago Business* (February 2, 2004).

## MEASURING PERCEIVED VALUE

To manage perceived value (or anything) you first must be able to measure it. If you cannot measure something, it is impossible to manage it.

Four common ways to estimate perceived value are:

1. Value-in-use.
2. Direct customer response.
3. Indirect customer response.
4. Subjective estimation.

### Value-in-Use

The value-in-use approach estimates value to customers by looking at what their costs are while using their current product or service and calculates the price of a new product or service that would make them indifferent between their current product and the new one.

For example, suppose an office building used 500 light bulbs and changed all of them every four months (Exhibit 5.1). Current price per bulb is $1 but the major cost is the labor cost of changing all the bulbs, amounting to $4,000 three times per year. Suppose a new bulb has a longer life that would mean that the bulbs would need to be changed only twice a year. What would be the perceived value of that new bulb?

**Exhibit 5.1   Value-in-Use Example**

Light bulbs:
- Currently change every four months @ $4,000
- Current price is $1
- 500 light bulbs

Current cost:

$(500 \times 3 \times \$1) + (3 \times \$4,000) = \$13,500$

Cost with new light bulb:

New light bulb requires change every six months.

Price = ?

$(500 \times 2 \times (?)) + 2 \times \$4,000 = 1,000 \times (?) + \$8,000$

Implies max price = $5,500/1,000 = $5.50

Their total costs with the current bulb are $13,500. Their total costs with the new bulb would be $8,000 plus the cost of buying 1,000 bulbs. If the new bulbs were priced at $5.50, then the office manager would be indifferent between purchasing the current bulb and the new bulb. That means the perceived value—maximum price willing to pay—is $5.50 per bulb.

Said another way, if the producer of the new bulb charged $5.50, it would provide no economic incentive for the office manager to buy the new bulb.

The value-in-use approach to estimating perceived value is especially useful in situations where the economic impact can be estimated. The value-in-use approach is less helpful in situations where emotional benefits or brand reputation are major components of perceived value.

## Direct Customer Response

You can try to estimate how your customers will react to prices by asking them directly. If they are honest with you, this approach can provide you with useful information. However, often customers will give you artificially low answers whenever you ask them questions such as, "How much are you willing to pay?"

Rather than asking them, you might try different prices and see what happens. This is known as doing a pricing experiment. (Be careful—in some situations laws prohibit charging different prices to different customers so check with your lawyer first.) If you are able to charge different prices, then you can examine the impact on your sales which will provide you with information about the perceived value for your product or service.

## Indirect Customer Response

There are a set of marketing research tools called, "constrained choice models." If you have a budget for marketing research, you might want to consider using one of these techniques to estimate perceived value for your key product or service.

How these techniques work is simple to understand. Exhibit 5.2 shows an example for a motel room. Suppose that a manager of a motel in a chain is considering two price levels ($200 and $300 per night) and whether or not to offer breakfast for free. They also want to understand the influence of their brand name on the customer's perceived value.

**Exhibit 5.2   Conjoint Analysis Example—Motel Room**

| Order of Preference | Well-Known Chain Brand | Free Breakfast | Room Rate per Night ($) |
|---|---|---|---|
| 5 | Chain brand | Free | 300 |
| 7 | No brand | Free | 300 |
| 6 | Chain brand | Not free | 300 |
| 8 | No brand | Not free | 300 |
| 1 | Chain brand | Free | 200 |
| 3 | No brand | Free | 200 |
| 2 | Chain brand | Not free | 200 |
| 4 | No brand | Not free | 200 |

A customer is offered eight choices that cover all the possible combinations of price, breakfast, and brand name and is asked to rank them in order of preference. What this means is that customers must give up something each time they make a choice. For example, suppose a $200 room rate, free breakfast, and a well-known brand name comprises their first choice. Then, when they choose the combination they rank second, if they want to stay at a $200 room rate, they must give up either the free breakfast or the brand name. If they want to keep the brand name, they must give up the $200 room rate or the free breakfast. If they want to keep the free breakfast, they must give up the $200 room rate or the brand name.

Because the customer must give up benefits and cannot always choose the lowest price, this technique may yield more realistic responses and more accurate pricing information than the direct response approach.

The particular technique illustrated in the motel room example is known as *conjoint analysis* or, sometimes, *trade-off analysis*. There are other methods of constrained choice models but they all provide similar types of information.

The information they provide is an estimate of the overall perceived value—in monetary terms—for any bundle of benefits offered to the customer. Savvy marketers such as DuPont, Marriott, and Ford often use these techniques to help develop their product design and pricing strategies.

These techniques also furnish organizations with estimates of what specific benefits are worth to the customer. For example, if a customer thought a "free" breakfast was worth $6 and it cost only $2 to provide it, the motel should consider offering the free breakfast since the value to their customer would increase more than their costs. Similarly, these techniques can be used to evaluate the worth of a brand in the eyes of the customer.

## Subjective

If you don't have a marketing research budget and cannot afford a lot of data collection and some of the fancier statistical techniques like conjoint analysis, what do you do?

You do what marketers have done for centuries—make a subjective estimate of perceived value. However, it need not come from thin air. You can develop a subjective estimate of perceived value *systematically*.

The first thing to keep in mind is that you are trying to estimate perceived value—not price. You will use perceived value to help you set price (Chapter 24) but perceived value is the ceiling on price, not price. Where you price is up to you.

Discussions with customers still can provide you with some idea of their perceived value for your product or service. You can also "try out" a few prices for their reaction and that will help narrow what perceived value might be. Finally, you can survey the prices charged by your competitors and make allowances for how their products or services (and strategies) differ from yours to obtain some idea of what perceived value for your offering might be.

Putting all that information together, you can then make a subjective estimate of what you think the maximum target customers might pay—their perceived value.

## ROLE OF PERCEIVED VALUE IN COMPETITION

Organizations compete in two ways—value or costs—and these are called *strategic themes*. Organizations can be located on the grid in Exhibit 5.3 according to how they perform on the two strategic themes. Both are important. You can't focus on just one theme.

The *value theme* is perceived value—the maximum a customer is willing to pay for a product or service. Note that perceived value is not the price charged the customer but is the ceiling on that price.

The *cost theme* is incremental cost per unit—the cost of getting the product or service in the hands of the customer. This cost includes all costs such as production, communications, and transportation. Note that incremental cost is *not* the price charged the customer but is the floor on price.

**Downloadable Exhibit 5.3   Strategic Themes\***

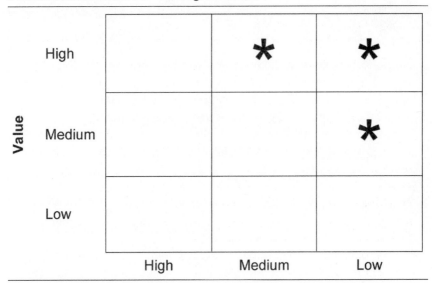

Note: * = Winning positions
Source: "Arrow Guide—Strategic Theme Analysis," Copyright © 2004, The Arrow Group, Ltd.®, New York. Used with permission. **A blank version of this page can be downloaded from www.trumpuniversity.com/marketing101 and customized for your personal use.** For any other use, contact Don Sexton at Marketing101@thearrowgroup.com.

Winning strategies are found in the upper right corner of the matrix:

- High perceived value/low incremental cost
- High perceived value/medium incremental cost
- Medium perceived value/low incremental cost

The strongest of all strategies of course would be high perceived value/low incremental cost, as then one could pursue either a high or low price strategy against any competitor and win. However, the other two strategies are often winning strategies because very few organizations are able to achieve a high perceived value/low incremental cost strategy. (One organization that has been able to provide highest perceived value at lowest cost is Southwest Airlines.)

Where you do *not* want your organization to be is low or medium perceived value coupled with high or medium incremental cost. Those cells are what Harvard Business School Professor Michael Porter has referred to as "stuck in the middle." Organizations stuck in the middle lose customers interested in high perceived value to organizations in the top row of the matrix

HIGH PERCEIVED VALUE AND LOW COST:
SOUTHWEST AIRLINES

In 2003, Southwest Airlines earned $442—more than all the other U.S. airlines combined. Its market capitalization of $11.7 billion is larger than all competitors combined. In May 2003, Southwest boarded more domestic passengers than any other airline.

Southwest Airline's cost per available seat mile (CASM) is 7.60 cents versus between 9 cents and 13 cents for the large carriers. Southwest uses much lower fares, flies "point-to-point" (no hubs), flies only 737s, serves no meals only snacks (peanuts mainly), charges no fees for changing same fare tickets, has no assigned seats, no electronic entertainment on board but does have "relentlessly fun flight attendants" and high satisfaction ratings from their customers.

To see the power of combining low cost with high perceived value, consider the success of Southwest Airlines versus that of U.S. Airways: In the late 1980s, U.S. Airways had a 58 percent share of the San Francisco-Southern California routes, by the mid-1990s, Southwest had driven U.S. Airways out of them. In the early 1990s, Southwest entered Baltimore Washington International Airport where U.S. Airways had a major hub—by 2004, U.S. Airways had 4.9 percent of the traffic there while Southwest had a leading 47 percent share.

*Source:* Andy Serwer, "Southwest Airlines: The Hottest Thing in the Sky," *Fortune,* vol. 149 (March 8, 2004), pp. 86–90.

and lose customers interested in lower prices to organizations in the right-hand column of the matrix.

## STRATEGIC THEMES—DRY-CLEANER EXAMPLE

In the dry-cleaner example discussed in Chapter 4, suppose that Dan's Cleaners and DES Cleaners had the lowest costs while Al's, Barbara's, and Carol's had average costs. Then DES Cleaners would likely be in the upper right corner of the grid because it provided high performance on the two benefits of most importance to the customers. Carol's would be in the upper middle cell because they also provided high value but did not have the lowest cost. Al's and Barbara's would be stuck in the middle with no special benefit. Dan's would probably use low prices to attract customers because they did not offer high value on any benefit.

## INCREASING PERCEIVED VALUE

Suppose you would like to move your position on the matrix toward the upper right corner. One way to do this of course, is by decreasing costs. The other way is by increasing perceived value.

Perceived value depends on many things: the benefits the product or service provides, how well they are provided, whether the customer correctly perceives how well they are provided, how important the benefits are to the customer, and the brand reputation.

Perceived value can be increased several ways but note that they all typically involve communications (Exhibit 5.4).

*Add benefits and then inform the customer about them.* A magazine publisher once changed their format in a very striking and attractive way. When asked how and when they informed customers about the change, they replied that they thought the customer would see the changes when they purchased the magazine. Such thinking, of course, is backward—you need to inform customers about new benefits so that they might be persuaded to purchase.

**Exhibit 5.4   Increasing Perceived Value**

| Perceived Value Depends On | Increase Perceived Value by Communicating |
| --- | --- |
| Benefits | Current or new benefit offered |
| Actual performance on benefits | Close gaps between actual performance and perceived performance |
| Improved performance on benefits | Inform customer of improvements |
| Importance of benefits | Persuade customer of importance of selected benefits |
| Brand reputation | Build brand with consistency on important benefits |

*Source:* Don Sexton, "Pricing, Perceived Value, and Communications," *The Advertiser,* April 2006, pp. 56–58. Used with permission.

*Close gaps between customer perceptions of benefit performance and actual performance.* One of the most famous and respected advertising campaigns ever—the Doyle Dane Bernbach introduction of the Volkswagen Beetle to the United States in the 1950s—faced the problem of customer skepticism about the quality and value of "foreign cars" (hard to believe today, but true). Volkswagen closed the gaps between perceived and actual benefits with fact-based, distinctive black-and-white magazine ads about availability of spare parts, engine reliability, and resale value. So effective were these Volkswagen ads in managing perceived value that Kawasaki motorcycles ran an ad imitating the Volkswagen ads, saying, "Think even smaller."

*Improve performance, then tell the customer—in that order.* In the telecommunications industry, sometimes companies have done this backward, telling customers that their service has improved before that has happened. Banks and fast-food chains sometimes have made the same mistake—touting their customer service before the service was improved. In contrast, both British Air and Continental Airlines improved their customer service, then communicated the improvements to customers with great positive impact on sales.

*Persuade the customer that certain benefits are especially important.* The certain benefits would be those that the company does well. To persuade customers to change their priorities is not always easy. Land Rover Discovery focused on the family market and emphasized their seating capacity (at the time greater than most of their competitors'). Seating capacity may not have been a priority benefit until Land Rover pointed it out. Some SUV manufacturers are currently trying to emphasize their (relatively) more efficient fuel consumption—a growing concern when gasoline prices increase.

*Build the brand consistently on key benefits.* Consistency is Branding 101. Campaigns as diverse as those from IBM, Visa, MasterCard, Foster's, GE, Mountain Dew, Samsung, Dow Corning, Pfizer, The Hallmark Channel, and Nokia have employed consistency over time and markets to build strong brands.

## Increasing Perceived Value: Dry-Cleaner Example

You can add services that your customers might value. For example, perhaps you want to guarantee free repair of any minor damages you find like missing buttons.

You can improve your performance on a benefit. If "convenient hours" is important to a significant number of your customers, then perhaps you should consider opening your cleaning establishment earlier in the day or keeping it open later in the day.

You can be sure your customers know how well you deliver the important benefits. For example, if your dry cleaner is open at 7 A.M. and people do not know that, then they may perceive your operating hours not to be as convenient as in fact they are. This is what we call a "communications gap" and it is easily fixed by communicating to your customers your hours of operation with signs, handouts, or even advertising.

You can try to alter the relative importance of the benefits to the customers. If you attempt this, you are of course trying to persuade the customers to consider the benefits on which you perform well to be more important to them. If your dry-cleaning establishment consistently returns clothes that are undamaged, you might try to explain to the customers that such consistency is an important benefit that should not be taken for granted. Their clothes can be expensive and they certainly do not want to take a chance on them being destroyed. Altering the relative importance of benefits to customers usually takes time so it should be pursued only after due consideration.

You can also raise perceived value by increasing the positive impact of your brand. Once you have identified the main benefits for which your dry cleaner is to be known (e.g., "We get out the toughest stains"), you repeat that consistently in all your communications with customers—advertising, signs, stationery, bills, everything.

## Conclusions

Customers behave according to their perceptions of the value they receive, not according to the actual value they receive. Managing those perceived values is what marketing is about. Perceived Value—the maximum a customer is willing to pay for your product or service—can be measured and can be managed.

For review questions for this chapter, log on to www.trumpuniversity .com/marketing101.

# 6

---

# UNDERSTANDING
# YOUR COMPETITORS

You rarely have the good fortune to market in a vacuum where there are no competitors. You must assume that there are or will be competitors and that they will be tough competitors.

You should treasure tough competitors—they keep *you* tough. When you are developing your marketing strategy, you should be clear who your target competitors are—the ones from whom you expect to win business. You don't need to take on everyone. Your target competitors will influence your targeting and positioning decisions. Keep in mind that you may be able to choose your competitors, but sometimes competitors will choose you.

---

**You should treasure tough competitors—
they keep *you* tough.**

---

In this chapter, you learn the four key questions you need to ask about your competitors and how to answer them.

# DOING WHAT YOUR COMPETITORS CAN'T: THE DONALD J. TRUMP SIGNATURE WATCH COLLECTION

The Donald J. Trump Signature Watch Collection.

Photo courtesy of the Trump Organization.

Ideally, you want to have a strategy that is difficult for your competitors to imitate. One way to do that is to use a unique branding position. Keep in mind that branding is most powerful when it is the most simple—focusing on a few special attributes. Donald Trump is associated with attributes such as business success, high expectations, and demanding that the people with whom he works are prepared and committed to their goals. In short, at several levels his brand embodies the idea that "time is money."

The Donald J. Trump Signature Watch Collection was introduced by the Trump Organization and the E. Gluck Corporation to exploit that brand position. The Trump Organization provides the brand, the E. Gluck Corporation provides the timepiece expertise.

The watches feature solid stainless steel cases and bracelets, diamonds, mother-of-pearl dials, and Italian leathers, reflecting Donald Trump's reputation for style and elegance.

The combination of the Trump brand with luxury styling and performance is a difficult combination for a competitor to copy.

## ANALYZING COMPETITORS

To analyze your competitors, you need to answer four questions:

1. Who are your competitors?
2. What do they want?

3. What can they do?
4. What will they do?

## Who Are Your Competitors?

A *competitor* is any organization that can satisfy the needs of your customers—either now or in the future. Identifying current competitors is usually not so difficult. You consider the choices currently open to your customers—those are the current competitors. If you have a family restaurant, you can observe many of the current competitors simply by looking around. You can also ask your customers, what else or who else they are considering as they make their purchase.

If you are a sales representative, one of the most important questions to ask a customer is who else the customer is considering. You should not denigrate competitors, but if you know who your competitors are, then based on the benefits the customers want, you should be able to determine whether your product or service is superior. Those benefits should be emphasized in your sales call.

More generally, knowing your competitors allows you to make more precise positioning decisions. For example, Visa had low penetration—only 20 percent—among small businesses in the United Kingdom. In 2003, Visa launched a campaign targeted at small businesses. Even though the American Express Business card was the market leader, Visa considered its target competitor for small businesses to be cash and checks so it positioned and promoted the Visa card with benefits that cash and checks could not match—all transactions shown on monthly statements and use of cash without interest for 50 days[1]

## What Do They Want?

Different competitors may have different business objectives. For example, some may be focusing on short-term profits, some on long-term market share. Business objectives affect behavior. In the early 1980s, a survey was made of managers in U.S. companies and managers in Japanese companies. The U.S. managers ranked return on investment and stock price as their most important objectives while the Japanese managers ranked market share, return on investment, and new products—each nearly the same—as their top three objectives. Many people interpreted the findings of this survey to indicate that during that time period Japanese companies had much longer-term business objectives than did U.S. companies. If true, that would explain the very aggressive pricing strategies used by many Japanese companies to gain shares in the automotive and consumer electronics industries in the United States during the 1970s and 1980s.

---

**Different competitors may have different business objectives.**

---

You may not be competing with a U.S. or Japanese multinational company, but if you know your competitors place priority on market share or sales volume, then you can expect them to be very aggressive—perhaps with low prices and special promotions.

## *What Can They Do?*

*To evaluate what your competitors might be able to do, you need to evaluate their capabilities and determine their strengths and weaknesses.* For example, if you are running a restaurant, does your competitor have a great chef or well-trained waitstaff? Or does the competitor have a low-cost source of food or beverages?

You should list your competitors and, for each of them, identify what you think are their strengths and weaknesses and the implications for the benefits they can offer customers (Exhibit 6.1). (See also Exhibit 7.1.)

Understanding your competitors' strengths and weaknesses not only can help you predict what they may do next, but can also help you determine your own response or—better—your own preemptive actions.

If a competing restaurant has a well-trained waitstaff, for example, maybe you need to improve the training of your staff or attract more skilled people by offering higher compensation. Or perhaps you need to do something else such as add items to your menu that may have appeal to specific target customers such as seniors, children, or health-conscious diners.

## ACTUAL VALUE ANALYSIS

You can summarize the implications of your competitors' capabilities on the benefits they can provide with what I call an *Actual Value Analysis* (See Exhibit 6.2). There are six steps:

**Downloadable Exhibit 6.1    Competitors' Strengths and Weaknesses\***

| Competitor | Strengths | Weaknesses | Implications for Benefits |
|---|---|---|---|
| | | | |
| | | | |
| | | | |
| | | | |
| | | | |

*Source:* "Arrow Guide—Strengths and Weaknesses Analysis," Copyright © 2004, The Arrow Group, Ltd.®, New York. Used with permission. *A blank version of this page can be downloaded from www.trumpuniversity.com/marketing101 and customized for your personal use.* For any other use, contact Don Sexton at Marketing101@thearrowgroup.com.

1. Select a target segment.
2. Select a target member of the decision-making unit.
3. List the main competitors.
4. List the benefits associated with the product or service.
5. Estimate the relative importance of each benefit to your target customer.
6. For your company and for each competitor, evaluate the actual performance on each benefit.

This analysis parallels the Perceived Value Analysis you performed in Chapter 4 (Understanding Your Customers). Both analyses have the same format—competitors, benefits, priorities, and evaluations. The major difference between the two is that in this analysis you will try to evaluate the *actual* performance of each competitor on each benefit, not the value as perceived by the customer.


## *Actual Value Analysis—Dry-Cleaning Example*

Suppose you are managing DES Cleaners as you did in Chapter 4. Recall that your current customers are primarily professional women and men and you assume that they are your target customers. The competitors are Al's, Barbara's, Carol's, and Dan's.

The benefits are shown in Exhibit 6.2 as well as the relative importance of each one to your target customer. Remember that information regarding the benefits to be included on the list and the relative importance of each to your target customer should be gathered from the target customers themselves by asking them directly or by surveying them.

The last step in the analysis is to estimate the actual performance on each benefit by you and by each of your competitors.

How do you get this information?

First, notice that such information is easier to get for functional benefits than for emotional or psychological benefits. Functional benefits, such as "quick turnaround" and "convenient hours," can typically be measured. Emotional benefits, such as "courtesy," are really perceptions and need to be measured by having objective individuals do the evaluations for those benefits. For example, in the restaurant business and in the film business, people who evaluate benefits are professionals known as *critics*. If possible, you need some objective individual acting as a critic to provide the evaluations of the emotional benefits.

You can collect information on your competitors' performance by trying their services yourself or by having a friend, family member, or employee do so. Many banks ask some of their employees to open accounts with competing banks. As faculty director of several executive education programs for a university, I made sure that I was on the mailing lists of my competitors—other universities providing programs similar to the ones I was managing.

In the dry-cleaning situation, it would be relatively simple to have someone check out the competing dry cleaners for you. That would allow you to complete the actual value analysis (Exhibit 6.2).

**Downloadable Exhibit 6.2    Actual Value Analysis—Dry Cleaners***

| Relative Importance | Benefits | DES | Al's | Barbara's | Carol's | Dan's |
|---|---|---|---|---|---|---|
| 10 | Clean clothes | 4 | 3 | 2 | 5 | 3 |
| 10 | Stain removal | 5 | 2 | 4 | 3 | 2 |
| 7 | Quick turnaround | 4 | 5 | 4 | 2 | 3 |
| 3 | Courtesy | 4 | 4 | 3 | 4 | 3 |
| 6 | No damage | 4 | 3 | 3 | 3 | 3 |
| 5 | Convenient location | 2 | 3 | 2 | 5 | 4 |
| 8 | Convenient hours | 5 | 3 | 5 | 3 | 2 |
| 4 | Cleaning knowledge | 3 | 4 | 3 | 4 | 3 |
| 5 | Pressed neatly | 4 | 3 | 2 | 4 | 2 |
| 4 | Ability to make repairs | 3 | 4 | 3 | 4 | 3 |

Note: Relative importance: 1—Not important, 10—Very important
Actual performance: 1—Poor, 5—Excellent
Source: "Arrow Guide—Actual Value Analysis," Copyright © 2004, The Arrow Group, Ltd.®, New York. Used with permission. ***A blank version of this page can be downloaded from www.trumpuniversity.com/marketing101 and customized for your personal use.** For any other use, contact Don Sexton at Marketing101@thearrowgroup.com.

## What Will They Do?

If you have listed your competitors and evaluated them, you have one last task—predict what they will do next. If you don't try to predict what they will do next, then you have wasted your time considering them.

Predicting competitor actions is the outcome of analyzing competitors. It is a key planning assumption for developing the marketing strategy.

How do you predict competitors' actions?

First, generate some scenarios. *Scenarios* are possible strategies and actions that you think your competitors might do. For example, if you own a restaurant, you might expect a competitor to try a special promotion, perhaps giving discounts to families, or the competitor might add new items to its menu. If you have a real estate office, you may consider the possibility that one of your competitors may try to enlarge its presence by adding more agents, perhaps by hiring some of your people.

Second, evaluate which one of the scenarios may be more likely. You can do this by considering what your competitors have done in the past or what they are doing now. You can even try to put yourself in their shoes and determine what strategy you might follow if you were them.

The last step is to select what you consider is the most likely scenario for the behavior of that competitor. That becomes a key planning assumption when you build your marketing strategy.

If there is more than one scenario that you think is likely, then you may want to develop more than one strategy to deal with each possibility or you may want to develop a strategy that allows you flexibility to deal with whichever scenario actually occurs.

## Predicting Actions—Dry-Cleaning Example

In the dry-cleaning illustration, it looks like one of the more formidable competitors to DES Cleaners might be Carol's because they already have a relatively high score on the very important benefit "clean clothes." A possible scenario would be Carol's improving their stain removal capabilities so they could compete directly against our strength. If they were to do so, then DES Cleaners might need to improve their performance on cleaning clothes (which probably they should be doing anyway).

In contrast, Dan's Cleaners does not excel relatively in any of the benefits except perhaps convenient location. To be a more effective competitor on value, Dan's would need to improve their performance on several benefits at the same time, which might prove very difficult. A more likely scenario for Dan's might be that they would cut prices. If they do so, then DES Cleaners might have to consider how to respond—possibly with coupons to retain their customers versus Dan's lower prices.

## Competitor Information

Information on competitors is usually considered some of the most difficult information for a manager to obtain. Actually the problem is not in finding competitor information—it's plentiful—the problem is in organizing the information.

There is much information about competitors that is available without any need for approaches that might be considered unethical or illegal.

The simplest type of information to obtain is observation. Look at their place of business. Go there. Buy their products or services. See firsthand what they are like.

You can also ask your customers their opinions of your competitors and what they hear about their plans.

Newspapers and other publications may have information about competitors. Competitors' ads may be very revealing of their intentions regarding markets or products or services. Visit their web sites—often they will be rich in information.

Suppliers may talk about your competitors—but if they do they are probably talking about you also.

Overall, you can find competitor information from:

- Print media
- Broadcast media
- Internet
- Information services
- Marketing research providers
- Government
- Customers
- Resellers
- Suppliers
- Your employees
- Competitors (e.g., speeches by their managers, advertisements)

The most important suggestion for competitor information is to have someone in charge of gathering this information. It may be yourself. However someone needs to put all the information together, just like a jigsaw puzzle. Then you can use it to develop your planning assumptions regarding competitors.

## CONCLUSIONS

Competitors' possible actions are often ignored in marketing strategies, but, as one general observed, "The best plans do not survive engagement with the enemy." What the general meant was that plans need to be flexible in ways that allow you to deal with whatever your competitor throws at you. To do that, you need to go beyond merely listing competitors. You need to confront what competitors are able and likely to do, the consequence to you, and what you can do about it—before it happens.

For review questions for this chapter, log on to www.trumpuniversity .com/marketing101.

# 7

---

# UNDERSTANDING YOUR
# ORGANIZATION'S CAPABILITIES

Once you have identified the needs of the customers in your target market, you must evaluate whether you can provide a product or service that will meet those needs. Just because you understand the customer's desires does not mean that you can satisfy them—especially at a profit. Everyone would like a device that would teleport them from one location to another with no discomfort and at a very low price but that does not mean such a device will be available soon.

Your customers may want your haircutting establishment to be open every day, your automobile mechanics to be knowledgeable about every make of car, and your chef to be able to prepare every dish all the time—with no calories, but those expectations may or may not be met for a variety of reasons.

Customers tell you what they want. Your organization's capabilities determine what you can do for them. The stronger your capabilities, the more options you have and the more likely you will win. When you look at your capabilities, you first have to see them as they are. You need to look in the mirror with honesty, not wishful thinking. Then you can set about improving your capabilities.

---

**Customers tell you what they want. Your organization's capabilities determine what you can do for them.**

---

Many years ago, Komatsu, the Japanese manufacturer of earthmoving equipment, looked in their mirror and realized that they were weak in technology and that their costs were too high—especially with Caterpillar as their main competitor. They developed a systematic plan to improve their capabilities, step-by-step. They worked on technology, on product design, on lowering costs—but they never tried to do too much at any one time. After several years of hard work, they emerged as a worthy opponent of Caterpillar.

You may not face as sizable a challenge as that faced by Komatsu but the idea is the same, evaluate your capabilities and improve them where you need to.

## CAPABILITIES AND YOUR MARKETING STRATEGY

You need to evaluate your organization's capabilities—determine what your organization does well—*before* you target markets and determine the positioning for your product or service.

Selecting target markets depends in part on your relative strengths in satisfying the needs of customers in a given market. For example, if you are considering opening a haircutting salon in an area with many trendy young people, then your staff should include stylists who are up-to-date on the latest trends—and who look like they are up-to-date. If you don't have such employees, either you recruit them or you should consider a different market.

Positioning your product or service depends on your capabilities. If you want your health club to be positioned as a full-service health club, then you need both the equipment and staff to cover all those services. If you don't have such equipment and staff, either you find that equipment and staff or you need to describe your health club as something other than full-service.

If your capabilities are not sufficient to win the market you want, either you need to improve your capabilities or change your target market. If your capabilities do not support your desired position, either you need to improve your capabilities or find a different position.

## Capabilities and Customers: Mar-a-Lago

In his book *Trump Strategies for Real Estate,* Trump Organization Executive Vice President George Ross describes the history of Donald Trump and Mar-a-Lago—an excellent example of how capabilities can lead directly to satisfied customers.

Mar-a-Lago is a magnificent oceanside estate of 118 rooms and 62,500 square feet, built in Palm Beach, Florida, in the 1920s by Marjorie Merriwether Post. After her death, the property was managed by a trust but it was unsuccessful as a museum and put up for sale. The property was purchased by Donald Trump who turned it into an elite, luxurious country club.

The transformation of the former mansion into an elegant club is an example of applying the Trump Organization's core capabilities—refurbishing and managing luxury property.

Refurbishing Mar-a-Lago required spending millions of dollars to modernize the kitchen; expand the dining areas; add luxury suites and cottages, a cabana and pool, championship caliber tennis courts, a spa and top-level fitness facility, and a grand ballroom. All materials, such as stonework and marble, used in the restoration were of the highest grade and selected to be consistent with the aesthetics of the property.

The ongoing management of Mar-a-Lago includes a world-class chef and well-trained staff. Well-known entertainers are brought in on weekends. Donald Trump himself regularly walks through the property to ensure that every detail is in order. The result is a world-class country club with an initiation fee of $250,000—a testimony to the high perceived value created.

## Strengths and Weaknesses

You can start evaluating your organization's capabilities by performing an analysis of your strengths and weaknesses (similar to what you did when evaluating competitors in Chapter 6).

When you do a strength/weakness analysis, try to focus primarily on the *capabilities* of your organization. Sometimes in a strength/weakness analysis, people tend to throw in everything that they can think of about the organization. Besides capabilities, they often include business outcomes such as market share or sales growth. Positive business outcomes are certainly important but they are *not* strengths. Business outcomes are the *results* of strengths (or weaknesses).

Similarly, try to avoid including benefits in the same list with capabilities. Benefits and capabilities are quite different from the viewpoint of marketing. Benefits are what your customers want; capabilities produce benefits and are what managers manage.

Suppose, for example, you provide services for people who get their water from wells since the municipal water supply is not available to them. Your capabilities might include a large inventory of spare parts and several knowledgeable employees. One of the benefits that those capabilities allow you to provide is prompt response if a customer calls because they are not able to get water.

Suppose you ran a small regional bus service. You have acquired buses that have suspensions superior to most other buses. Suspension is a feature of your product—a capability, but that capability allows you to provide your customers with a smoother, more comfortable ride—a benefit.

Capabilities are important because they provide benefits. You will find it very helpful to keep capabilities and benefits separate in your strength/weakness analysis.

## Types of Capabilities

Capabilities consist of:

- Skills
- Resources
- Features

A *skill* is usually expertise associated with a person. The haircutting talents of a stylist in a salon. The breadth of repair knowledge of an automobile mechanic. The cabinetry abilities of a carpenter.

A *resource* is something inanimate. The spare parts inventory of a company that fixes water pumps. The equipment in a health club. The parking lot of a shoe store.

A *feature* is a characteristic of a product or service. The suspension of a bus. The caffeine content of a drink. The hours that a delicatessen is open.

## Evaluating Capabilities

You can determine your organization's strengths and weaknesses with a Capability Analysis (Exhibit 7.1):

- List capabilities of your organization.
- Determine your target competitors.
- Evaluate performance on each capability relative to competitors on a 1 through 5 scale, where 1 is poor and 5 is excellent.
- Note any implications for providing benefits.

Any capability with a score of 4 or 5 is a strength; any capability with a score of 1 or 2 is a weakness. (You can download a blank version of the worksheet in Exhibit 7.1 to simplify this exercise.)

**Downloadable Exhibit 7.1    Capability Chart***

| Capability | Evaluation | Implications for Which Benefits |
|---|---|---|
| Modern equipment | 3 | Cleaning |
| Equipment on premises | 4 | Quick turnaround |
| Cleaning expertise | 3 | Cleaning and cleaning knowledge |
| Stain-removal expertise | 5 | Stain removal |
| Tailor available | 3 | Ability to make repairs |
| Order information system | 4 | Quick turnaround |
| Skilled staff | 4 | Cleaning, pressing, and no damage |
| Courteous staff | 4 | Courtesy |
| Number of staff | 4 | Convenient hours and quick turnaround |
| Accessible location | 2 | Convenient location |

Note: 1—Poor, 5—Excellent
Source: "Arrow Guide—Capability Analysis," Copyright © 2004, The Arrow Group, Ltd.®, New York. Used with permission. ***A blank version of this page can be downloaded from www.trumpuniversity.com/marketing101 and customized for your personal use.** For any other use, contact Don Sexton at Marketing101@thearrowgroup.com.

## CAPABILITY EVALUATION— DRY-CLEANING EXAMPLE

Capabilities of a dry cleaner might include: modern equipment, equipment on premises, cleaning expertise, stain-removal expertise, tailor availability, order information system, skilled staff, courteous staff, number of staff, and accessible location. These would be entered in Exhibit 7.1.

Next, you would evaluate your capabilities—in this case the capabilities of DES Cleaners. It is important to be honest when making these evaluations, otherwise they will not be helpful. You should also evaluate yourself *relative* to your target competitors.

According to Exhibit 7.1, the main strength of DES Cleaners, a 5-rating, seems to be stain-removal expertise. However, other capabilities such as equipment on premises, order information system, courteous staff, skilled staff, and number of staff also received strong evaluations (4s).

## COMPETITIVE ADVANTAGE AND BENEFIT ADVANTAGE

Keep in mind that capabilities—skills, resources, and features—are not important by themselves. They are important if they enable your organization to produce a product or service that is superior to that of competitors in one or more ways. There was a time when some 747 aircraft featured piano bars. For most of the flying public, the presence of a piano bar is likely not a major attraction so even if an airline had that capability, it would not be valuable in attracting customers from the general flying population. Having a piano bar would be a unique capability but it would not be a useful competitive advantage:

> A *competitive advantage* is a capability that allows an organization to provide one or more benefits to customers in the target market at a level superior to that of their competitors.

In turn, competitive advantages lead to benefit advantages—the heart of positioning:

> A *benefit advantage* is a benefit to which customers in the target market assign a high priority and which the organization provides at a level superior to that of their competitors.

**Exhibit 7.2   Actual Value Analysis—Dry Cleaners**

| Relative Importance | Benefits | DES | Al's | Barbara's | Carol's | Dan's |
|---|---|---|---|---|---|---|
| 10 | Clean clothes | 4 | 3 | 2 | 5 | 3 |
| 10 | Stain removal | 5 | 2 | 4 | 3 | 2 |
| 7 | Quick turnaround | 4 | 5 | 4 | 2 | 3 |
| 3 | Courtesy | 4 | 4 | 3 | 4 | 3 |
| 6 | No damage | 4 | 3 | 3 | 3 | 3 |
| 5 | Convenient location | 2 | 3 | 2 | 5 | 4 |
| 8 | Convenient hours | 5 | 3 | 5 | 3 | 2 |
| 4 | Cleaning knowledge | 3 | 4 | 3 | 4 | 3 |
| 5 | Pressed neatly | 4 | 3 | 2 | 4 | 2 |
| 4 | Ability to make repairs | 3 | 4 | 3 | 4 | 3 |

*Note:* Relative importance: 1—Not important, 10—Very important
Actual performance: 1—Poor, 5—Excellent
*Source:* "Arrow Guide—Actual Value Analysis," The Arrow Group, Ltd.®, New York, 2004.
Used with permission.

## Competitive Advantage and Benefit Advantage—Dry-Cleaner Example

The benefit implications of the capabilities of DES Cleaners are shown in Exhibit 7.1 and in Exhibit 7.2, the Actual Value Analysis (discussed in Chapter 6). The benefits that DES Cleaners provides relatively well as compared to their competitors are clean clothes, stain removal, quick turnaround, courtesy, no damage, convenient hours, and pressed neatly—all have scores of 4 or more in Exhibit 7.2 and all are possible benefit advantages for DES Cleaners to use in their positioning. Each benefit is supported by a competitive advantage—a capability where DES Cleaners is strong relative to their competitors.

In Chapter 11—the chapter on positioning, you will learn how to systematically identify competitive advantages and benefit advantages.

## CONCLUSIONS

To succeed, an organization should have capabilities that allow them to provide benefits to their target customers that no competitor can provide as well. Such capabilities are known as competitive advantages and hopefully are sustainable over some reasonable length of time. The benefits they produce are known as *benefit advantages* and are the candidates for the benefits used for the positioning of the product or the service. Without competitive advantages and benefit advantages, you have a commodity—you will need to have the lowest costs if you are going to succeed with a commodity.

For review questions for this chapter, log on to www.trumpuniversity .com/marketing101.

# 8

---

# Understanding Your
# Overall Competitive
# Environment

One of the first lessons of marketing is *know your market.* That means know your customers, know your competitors, know your organization, and know the overall competitive environment.

The competitive environment is complicated so it is not necessarily easy to understand what is going on now, much less in the future. However, you can be *systematic* in examining your competitive environment and that can help you determine what might happen in the future.

Statements about the future are the *key planning assumptions* on which any strategy must rest. Analyses of your competitive environment generates these planning assumptions.

These assumptions are the foundation for your marketing plan—if you see that any of them might be incorrect, you should revisit your marketing plan and change it as necessary. This chapter provides you with a systematic framework to look at what's in your competitive future.

---

**These assumptions are the foundation for your marketing plan.**

---

## WATCHING THE ENVIRONMENT: DONALD J. TRUMP DRESS SHIRTS AND NECKWEAR

The Donald J. Trump Signature Collection.

Photo courtesy of the Trump Organization.

The Trump Organization licenses the Phillips-Van Heusen Corporation to manufacture and distribute dress shirts and neckwear with the Donald J. Trump label. In this brand alliance, the Trump Organization provides the brand positioning—power boardroom dressing—and the Phillips-Van Heusen Corporation provides the manufacturing and distribution know-how.

The Donald J. Trump Signature Collection is following two trends in the competitive environment—a trend by some males to dress more formally at work and an increase in the demographic group of aspiring executives likely to purchase Donald J. Trump shirts and neckwear. (Sales of men's suits increased by over 30 percent in 2004 after eight years of sales declines.)[1] It also involves another trend—the growing importance of resellers. The shirts and neckwear were launched exclusively in Federated Department Stores (including the Macy's chain), throughout the United States.

## THE COMPETITIVE ENVIRONMENT

There are a number of approaches for examining the competitive environment. The method followed here—the Situation Analysis—is based on an approach suggested by Michael Porter but adapted significantly to make it more relevant to marketing decision making.

Consider your organization to be in the center of the diagram shown in Exhibit 8.1. There are six *forces* that can directly affect the performance of your organization:

1. Current competitors.
2. Potential entrants.
3. Substitute products or services.
4. Suppliers.
5. Resellers.
6. End-users.

**Exhibit 8.1   Forces Affecting Organization Performance**

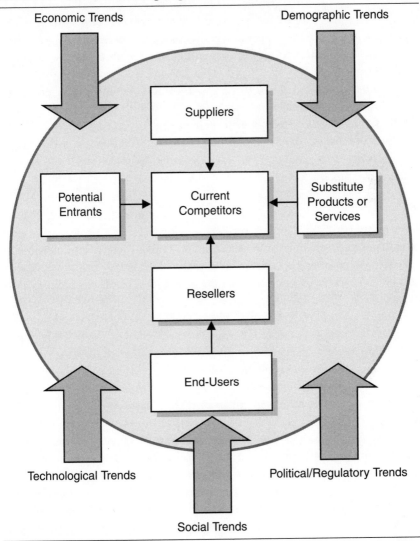

Economic Trends

Demographic Trends

Suppliers

Potential Entrants

Current Competitors

Substitute Products or Services

Resellers

End-Users

Technological Trends

Political/Regulatory Trends

Social Trends

*Source:* "Arrow Guide—Situation Analysis," The Arrow Group, Ltd.®, New York, 2004. Used with permission.

The horizontal axis of the diagram is the *competitive axis*. Current competitors are your short-term competitors—the competitors that will likely have the most impact on your current performance during the coming year. Potential entrants are competitors likely to enter the market soon and so are usually thought of as your middle-term competitors. Substitute products or services may be short-term, middle-term, or long-term, depending on whether they currently exist. For example, for some people tea is a substitute for coffee and that means although it is a substitute product, it is a short-term competitor for coffee. If you were developing a new type of caffeine drink, that drink might be a middle-term or a long-term competitor for coffee, depending on the time when it would be launched.

The vertical axis is the *distribution chain* axis. It begins with your suppliers. In turn, your products and services may be sold through various levels of resellers. The end-users are your final customers.

Each of these six players may have an impact on your financial performance.

## Current Competitors

These are organizations that currently produce and market products and services that look like your products and services and provide the same benefits as your products and services. Generally, the more numerous the current competitors and the more capacity they have—the more intense will be short-term competition. Often such competition takes the form of price wars.

You can avoid price wars with moves such as adding value and targeting markets and these are explored in later chapters; however, the best advice may be to try to avoid markets susceptible to price wars if at all possible.

Two aspects of a market that affect the likelihood of a price war are *exit barriers* and *entry barriers*. *Exit barriers keep you in a market* and include long-term contracts and legal constraints that prevent organizations from leaving.

*Entry barriers keep you out of a market.* Examples of entry barriers include capital requirements, special expertise, existing brand positions, transportation costs, and required permits or licenses.

Markets that are most likely to have price wars have low entry barriers and high exit barriers. It's easy to get in the market but difficult to get out. Conversely, markets where you might be able to avoid price wars often have high entry barriers and low exit barriers—hard to get in and easy to get out.

## Potential Entrants

Potential entrants include what are often referred to as *followers*, organizations that have been thinking about and working on a product or service similar to that of your organization but are just now coming into the market. Followers may help develop the market.

Potential entrants may be imitators—producing products and services nearly identical to what is already on the market. Imitators typically set off a price war when they enter a market as they have no differentiation from existing products and therefore no specific reason to offer the customer to buy their product besides price.

## Substitute Products or Services

Existing substitutes should have been taken into consideration when our product/market strategy was developed so usually they are not the main problem in this category.

The substitute products or services that often are a concern are ones that are likely superior to your product or service. While they are not currently in the market, they are expected in the future. Such products can "overhang" the market which means that customers may not buy your product or service while they wait for the substitute to appear. For example, suppose you are in the catering business and have a catering hall. If a new hotel is about to open in your area, then prospective customers may want to wait and see what the facilities of the new hotel will be like before committing to you.

Even if they do not cause market "overhang," superior substitutes will obviously have an impact on the performance of your organization when they are launched—unless, of course, your organization also owns the superior substitute products.

## Suppliers

If there are only a few suppliers of a critical raw material or component of your product or service, then they will likely have power over your organization. Such power is often translated into negotiation power as regards pricing and other terms.

Other issues with suppliers concern the quality of their product—that is, how it performs on the benefits of concern to us—and how reliable they are as a source. Reliability is a very important benefit for a package delivery company to provide. FedEx, for example, located their main U.S. sorting operation in Memphis, Tennessee, because the airport there is closed relatively few days each year—it's a reliable source of "good weather"—a very important resource to FedEx.

## Resellers

Organizations may sell direct to end-users and which is fairly common in business-to-business marketing of products such as chemicals, computers, and telecommunications equipment. However, even in those industries, smaller customers may be served by distributors.

Most consumer products and services are still sold through resellers even if some of the levels of distribution or some resellers are disappearing due to Internet marketing. In some product or service categories, there may be several levels of resellers.

Resellers have power over our organization if they "own" markets or customers; that is, if they are the main routes to those markets or customers. They may have built up a base of clients that trusts them and relies on them for their needs in certain product or service areas. For example, consumers may trust an electronics store or a health-food store for their expertise and integrity. That means to reach those customers you must use the services of the reseller.

## End-Users

These are your final customers—they use the product or service for themselves. The price they pay must pay for everything that happens in the distribution chain. The profits of the suppliers, producing and marketing organizations, and resellers all depend on whether the end-user purchases the product or service and at what price.

In any marketing situation, knowledge of the end-users is absolutely crucial, even if you do not sell to them directly. DuPont, for example, has had many successful products such as Stainmaster carpet fiber and Teflon coating because of its attention to the needs of the end-user—even though it does not sell directly to that final customer.

## MACRO TRENDS

The competitive environment is also affected by macro trends. These include:

- Economic trends
- Demographic trends
- Technological trends
- Social trends
- Political/regulatory trends

It is important to examine these trends not just for the sake of curiosity or history but because they may have an *impact* on some or all of the players in your competitive environment. For example, changes in the age distribution of a county's population can have enormous implications for the health-care market and for physicians and dentists in particular. Decreases in home construction activity in an area affect all those providing building supplies. Changes in food handling regulations can affect how a restaurant does business.

In looking at macro trends, you should constantly ask the question: "If this trend persists, who will it affect and how will it change their behavior in ways that might affect the markets in which I am selling my product or service?"

For example, because baby boomers are "demanding great tasting foods that fit their healthy lifestyle and help them proactively manage their health," Kellogg launched potassium-rich Corn Flakes *with Real Bananas*.[1] For similar reasons, Pizza Hut introduced a lower fat pizza called "Fit 'N Delicious" with lower calories per slice.[2]

As regards technology, in the video game market, Nintendo was slow to change from cartridges to CD-ROMs and from 1992 to 2002 that oversight caused Nintendo's share to decrease from 90 percent to 15 percent.[3]

Suppose you are a dentist—how might the growth in the number of children in your area affect your revenue? How would a protective coating for teeth affect you? If you own a restaurant, how might trends toward health consciousness affect you? Suppose you own a video rental store. What changes in video technology might affect you?

## KEY PLANNING ASSUMPTIONS

After you have worked through an evaluation of the competitive environment, then you should step back and consider what changes or trends have the potential to have the largest impact on your marketing efforts. Those changes or trends are known as the *key planning assumptions.*

Normally, there should be just three to five key planning assumptions. The temptation is to make a long list of planning assumptions so that every possible event is covered. Unfortunately, such long lists are not very useful since they do not spotlight the most important assumptions.

Examples of key planning assumptions for a restaurant:

- In the next two years, the number of young couples in our geographical area will increase by 20 percent.
- A new Italian restaurant from a national chain will try to attract customers with discount coupons.
- Local supermarkets will offer precooked Italian meals.

The product/market strategy is built on the key planning assumptions. Those assumptions need to be checked regularly. If you have reasons to believe that one of them is no longer realistic, then you should replace that assumption with a new one that is correct and then reevaluate your product/market strategy and, if necessary, redo the strategy.

## CONCLUSIONS

Before developing any marketing strategy, you should immerse yourself in what you know about the markets in which you are interested. You should read all you can about those markets. Look at what competitors are doing in those markets. Talk to customers or potential customers in those markets. Consider any trends that affect those markets.

Once you have reviewed and sifted through all that information, then try to summarize it with a few key planning assumptions. Then you are ready to start assembling your marketing strategy.

For review questions for this chapter, log on to www.trumpuniversity.com /marketing101.

# 9

---

# IDENTIFYING YOUR
# POSSIBLE MARKETS

If you think everyone is your customer, then no one is your customer. Marketing is about meeting the needs of targeted customers. Customers are different. They have different needs and different priorities. If you do not focus on specific customers, then you will not have customers because competitors will target their efforts on specific customers—the most profitable ones—and win their business.

If every customer were the same, then there would be no need for this chapter. But customers are different and marketers must always keep that in mind.

There are two distinct stages for determining your target market: identifying possible target markets and selecting your target market. This chapter shows you how to *separate* a market into market segments. The next chapter explains how to *choose* which segments on which you want to focus your efforts.

## FAILURE TO TARGET MARKETS

Once I was teaching a course in which students worked in teams to develop marketing strategies for luxury products. One team had the assignment of

## TARGETING THE VIP SEGMENT: TRUMP CASINOS AND RESORTS

Mark Juliano is the chief operating officer at Trump Entertainment Resorts in Atlantic City. Juliano's extensive experience in the gaming industry taught him how to make every customer feel special—but this is no easy feat when dealing with a customer base that numbers in the millions. Technology plays a role; data warehousing and yield management systems enable the company to identify the most profitable customers, and to build programs around their identified needs and preferences.

VIP customers—guests who are accustomed to preferential treatment at the finest resorts around the globe—require extra care. According to Juliano, "It's not the suites or the gifts that matter most to these customers, it is the personal attention and recognition. We retain their business because of exemplary service." For example, Trump Entertainment Resorts employs highly trained butlers dedicated to taking care of the most elite guests. "We know what specific linens they prefer on their beds, the brand of imported tea to serve with their breakfast. We know what flowers to place in the suite upon their arrival, and more importantly, what flowers they may be allergic to," Juliano said.

Sometimes, the butlers even know the customers better than they know themselves. A butler at Trump Taj Mahal Casino once noticed that a guest he knew very well looked particularly pale. The butler insisted that the woman seek medical attention, and she eventually agreed. When she was examined, a serious medical condition was diagnosed and treated. And now she's doing fine.

"We do understand how important it is to make our guests smile," Juliano explains. "In some cases, it may be a promotion in the middle of the winter where we give our guests portable snow shovels. For the higher level of customer, we even may give them a snow blower. But the difference at Trump Entertainment Resorts is that, for a VIP customer, we also know when to hire a crew, send them to the VIP customer's house, and plow their entire driveway."

assembling a launch strategy for very expensive stationery. Halfway through the semester, a member from each team gave an oral report on their progress. One member of the stationery team said their target market was composed of men and women between the ages of 18 and 80!

That market choice was unacceptable. The student was saying that their team believed that an 18-year-old man and an 80-year-old woman looked at writing paper the same way. That is difficult to believe. Their strategy had no target market.

Does this happen often in business? Unfortunately, yes.

Half the marketing plans from well-known companies that are submitted to me for review and feedback lack clearly stated target markets and positioning. Why does that happen? Here are my theories:

- *Concept too simple:* Market segmentation is not very difficult to understand. Conceptually, it is simple. Because it is simple, managers may skip over market segmentation, not realizing how important it is.
- *Hard work:* While simple to understand, market segmentation can be hard to do. Developing a market segmentation scheme is not easy. It may require several weeks and a lot of thought and, hopefully, a lot of information about customers.
- *Belief that everyone is their customer and there is no need to target customers:* It may be a laudable goal to *want* every customer (although that may strain the resources of any organization). However, even if you want every customer, you still need to think of them as individuals with different needs and you need to group them into target markets of similar customers.
- *No information:* Some segmentation efforts falter because no data have been collected on which to base segmentation decisions. Segmentation questions are among the most important to include in surveys of customers.

## ROLE OF SEGMENTS AND TARGET MARKETS IN MARKETING STRATEGY

Determining target markets provides marketers with a basis for concentrating their efforts—and concentration is one of the main purposes for developing your marketing strategy. If you never say no to a customer—exclude no one from your efforts, then you do not have a strategy.

By focusing efforts on a target market, it becomes possible for you to develop a precise positioning. Without a target market, you may have a product or service designed for everyone, which means it is designed for no one in particular.

## Determining a Target Market

You need to go through two stages to determine your target market: Identify possible market segments, then select a target market from those segments you have identified. As mentioned, this chapter focuses on identifying your possible market segments; the next chapter on selecting your target markets.

Notice that just because a segment has been identified does not mean that you need to use it as a target market. Identifying segments allows you to see the market opportunities you have and compare them.

There may be many ways to segment a market. In general, there is no "right" way to segment a market. However, for a given organization and a given competitive situation, some segmentation approaches will be superior to others.

## Market Segmentation

A *market segment* is a group of customers or potential customers who have a similar problem *or* seek approximately the same benefits. The word *problem* signifies the needs that the customers are trying to fill. The word problem is being used positively, in the same way a sales representative would use it: "You have a problem—I can help you solve it." The word problem here is not a negative—it refers to unmet needs.

For example, a manager who travels often may need her clothes cleaned immediately so that they will be available for her next trip. A parent may need an automobile he considers safe for transporting his children. A writer may need an attorney familiar with law governing intellectual property. A design engineer for a manufacturer of jet aircraft engines may need a metal with specific properties.

All of these situations are examples of customer problems and benefits are the dimensions of problems. For example, each problem suggests specific benefits that the customer with that problem may be seeking: a dry cleaner with fast turnaround, an automobile with a very effective braking system, an attorney with expertise in copyright law, and a metal with certain strength/weight ratios.

## Characteristics of Market Segments

Any segmentation system requires you to know benefits customers want *and* customer characteristics. To define a market segment, you need to know the benefits that customers are seeking to enable you to group customers together. You also need to be able to describe or label customer groups in some way so you can find the customers in the segment. For consumer products or services, such labels are often demographics such as age, gender, and income, but may also include other characteristics such as lifestyle (e.g., single, young family) or psychographics (personality descriptors). For industrial products or services, segmentation labels may be industry, organization size, location, and, if you are considering the decision maker, descriptors such as job title or function.

---

**Any segmentation system requires you to know benefits customers want *and* customer characteristics.**

---

Benefits define the segments and provide the foundation for positioning. Labels describe the segments and provide the basis for targeting marketing efforts toward them.

## Segment Identification Analysis

Four steps will help you identify market segments:

1. List the benefits that might be sought by the customers.
2. List possible segments defined with appropriate labels.
3. For members of each segment, estimate the importance or priority for each benefit.
4. Combine the segments if their priorities are similar.

Please always remember that both the list of benefits and the priority estimates should be collected *from customers*. While a team of managers can make preliminary estimates based on their own knowledge of customers, any final analysis should be based on the opinions of the customers themselves.

## Segment Identification—Realty Example

Suppose you are attempting to segment the market for a small real estate company.

Benefits sought by real estate customers might include financing expertise, knowledge of area schools, accessibility of realtor, and realtor's ability to match homes with the customers' needs. These benefits would be obtained by talking with the customers.

Possible segments would include singles, young couples, young families, mature families, and empty nesters. Keep in mind that your possible segments need not cover everyone in the market. Also, it is fine if some of the segments overlap.

The importance ratings for each benefit also come from the customers. For example, singles may be especially concerned with how well the realtor knows the rental market and young families may be interested particularly in financing expertise and knowledge of school systems.

When the segment identification grid is completed you may find that some segments are very similar to others. For a sample grid, see Exhibit 9.1. In the real estate illustration, singles and empty nesters value similar benefits. Except for interest in school knowledge, young couples and young families are very similar. If segment members are similar, you may be able to combine them—at least as regards designing the services you will provide. You still may need to communicate to them differently—singles will likely be reading different magazines or listening to different radio stations than seniors.

**Downloadable Exhibit 9.1    Identifying Real Estate Segments\***

| Benefits | Descriptors of Possible Segments | | | | |
|---|---|---|---|---|---|
| | Singles | Young Couples | Young Families | Mature Families | Empty Nesters |
| Financing expertise | 7 | 9 | 10 | 5 | 6 |
| Rental expertise | 10 | 7 | 5 | 2 | 8 |
| Small home expertise | 8 | 9 | 9 | 1 | 9 |
| Large home expertise | 1 | 3 | 2 | 9 | 1 |
| School expertise | 3 | 6 | 9 | 7 | 1 |
| Match homes with needs | 7 | 8 | 8 | 6 | 7 |
| Accessibility | 5 | 6 | 5 | 4 | 6 |

*Note:* Benefit importance ratings: 1—Not important, 10—Very important
*Source:* "Arrow Guide—Segment Identification Analysis," Copyright © 2004, The Arrow Group, Ltd.®, New York. Used with permission. *A blank version of this page can be downloaded from www.trumpuniversity.com/marketing101 and customized for your personal use.* For any other use, contact Don Sexton at Marketing101@thearrowgroup.com.

## SEGMENTS AND THE DECISION-MAKING UNIT

You can sometimes add another level of precision to the segmentation identification analysis.

In a given segment, consider who might be involved in making the purchase decision. For example, in the real estate example, with a young couple you would imagine that both the wife and the husband will have a significant role in the choice of a new home. However, in their choice of realtor, each may not want exactly the same benefits. Perhaps the wife is somewhat more concerned with financing issues while the husband is somewhat more concerned with obtaining small home expertise. If so, then you can amend the segment identification grid by placing two columns under the heading "young families" (Exhibit 9.2). One column is for the male, the other for the female. Then you can put the benefit priorities for each of them in the respective column.

Sometimes this extra detail will not make a difference in your marketing strategy, but sometimes it might. For example, if the wife were much more concerned with financing issues than the husband, then you might run ads that emphasize your ability to help with financing and place them in sections of the newspaper more apt to be read by the wife.

A similar situation occurs in automobile showrooms. Automobile salespeople are very sensitive to the benefits sought by the various members of a family decision-making unit, which may involve not only the wife and husband but perhaps children, especially teenagers, as well. The salesperson will

**Exhibit 9.2  Identifying Real Estate Segments with Decision-Making Unit Members**

| Benefits | Description of Possible Segments | | | | |
|---|---|---|---|---|---|
| | Singles | Young Couples | Young Families | Mature Families | Empty Nesters |
| Decision-making unit member | M  F | M  F | M  F | M  F  C | M  F |
| Financing expertise | 8  7 | 8  10 | 10  10 | 5  6  1 | 6  7 |
| Rental expertise | 10  10 | 7  6 | 6  4 | 2  1  1 | 7  9 |
| Small home expertise | 7  9 | 10  8 | 8  10 | 1  1  1 | 9  9 |
| Large home expertise | 1  1 | 3  4 | 1  3 | 8  10  2 | 1  1 |
| School expertise | 2  4 | 5  7 | 9  10 | 7  7  6 | 1  1 |
| Match homes with needs | 7  8 | 8  7 | 8  8 | 5  8  6 | 7  7 |
| Accessibility | 4  6 | 6  5 | 4  5 | 6  4  3 | 6  7 |

*Notes:* M = Male, F = Female, C = Child
Benefit importance ratings: 1—Not important, 10—Very important

*Source:* "Arrow Guide—Segment Identification Analysis," The Arrow Group, Ltd.®, New York, 2004. Used with permission.

be attentive to all those involved and try to position the automobile to satisfy the different needs of the different family members—not always an easy task.

## Issues to Keep in Mind

Segments consist of *people*—not products or services. Often marketing plans define segments as products such as hot versus cold ready-to-eat cereals or large versus small copiers. Such analyses are not ways to segment markets, they are product line descriptions.

Because market segments are made up of people, segmentation can be a difficult process. If the segments were the same as the products, then there would be no reason to consider the customers.

What people in a market segment have in common is a problem—therefore they seek similar benefits, have similar priorities, and expect similar performance on each benefit.

Segment members seek only approximately the same benefits. There is not necessarily one way to segment a market—there may be many ways to segment a market. Segmentation requires both creativity and the ability to interpret data. Often the winner is the marketer who is able to segment a market in ways that allow them to use their organization's capabilities to the best advantage.

Segments need to be identifiable *and* accessible. This is why labels must be part of any segmentation scheme. If you cannot find the members of a segment, then you cannot focus advertising, promotion, or personal selling efforts to persuade them to buy your products or services.

## Market Segments and Strategy

Remember the reason you are segmenting—to *focus* your marketing efforts. Each segment you choose to go after requires and deserves its own special marketing strategy. Once a manager said to me, "I really like your segment identification process. We did something like that a couple months ago. We reviewed our segmentation and reduced our number of market segments from 12 to just 5." I replied, "Good for you. How many marketing strategies do you employ?" He said, "Just one—we treat everyone the same."

---

**Each segment you choose to go after requires and deserves its own special marketing strategy.**

---

The reason you segment is because you cannot treat everyone the same. Examples of targeted strategies:

- Verizon Wireless targeted its instant-message service to the lucrative and high-growth 18- to 24-year-old market in part because of those customers' comfort level with technology. An analyst for Yankee Group, commented: "Carriers recognize that this group [18- to 24-year-olds] is extremely tech savvy, reliant on wireless services and frequently influence phone usage within their family . . . [and they] are already familiar with IM lingo, and thus more willing to adapt to the complexity of cellphone IM-ing."[1]
- Campbell's focused their strategy toward juice drinkers in the Hispanic segment by using bilingual packaging and launching three tropical flavors that research showed were favorites among Hispanic consumers: guava-passion fruit, mango-peach, and tropical colada.[2]

## CONCLUSIONS

Market segmentation is the first strategic choice you make in developing a marketing strategy. You can certainly revisit how you segmented a market and change it later if a particular segmentation scheme is not working for you. However, market segmentation—understanding customers and potential customers—is the logical starting point for developing a marketing strategy. Who is out there? What do they want? How can I find the customers I can satisfy?

In the next chapter, you will learn how to select the market segments that will be your target markets.

For review questions for this chapter, log on to www.trumpuniversity.com /marketing101.

# 10

---

## SELECTING YOUR
## KEY TARGET MARKET

After you have identified potential market segments, you face the crucial choice of selecting which of those segments will be the target of your marketing strategies. The target market choice is one of the most important decisions you make in developing your marketing strategy. If your target market decision is wrong, you may not be able to find any marketing strategy that will work. You should spend a lot of time, effort, and thought on selecting your target markets.

If you do make a mistake in selecting your target market, keep in mind that *you can change your choice* and refocus your marketing efforts on another target market. That can be expensive because you may have already committed resources to the target market that is not working out. However, it may be better to change your target market than to continue to throw resources at a situation that will not improve.

The best approach is to get your target market choice right the first time—*before* you spend money on a losing market choice. It's a lot easier (and cheaper) to change your strategy before you implement it. In this chapter, you learn how to make your target market choices right the first time.

## TARGETING A MARKET: TRUMP'S WEST SIDE APARTMENTS

Trump Place on Manhattan's Upper West Side, 180 Riverside Drive.
Photo credit: Jon Ortner, 2002. Photo courtesy of the Trump Organization.

The Trump Organization has several buildings on the Hudson River in New York City. They are targeted especially for young professionals who want to live on the West Side of Manhattan. Some buildings consist of rental units and some of condominiums. Each unit has the great views and layouts expected of Trump properties. But to reach the target market, each building also has a superb health club because members of this market segment tend to be very interested in health and fitness.

## MARKET SELECTION CRITERIA

You may not be a gambler but, for a moment suppose you are. You arrive at the door of a room filled with poker tables. Each table has one empty seat. How would you decide where to sit down?

Your eye would be attracted to the amount of money on the table. Assuming that you are looking for a large return for your evening's efforts, you would be tempted to sit at a table where the winnings might be attractive. However, before you sat down you might want to take a look at the other players already sitting at the table and assess their abilities. You would like your abilities to be superior relative to theirs.

The two dimensions you would use to decide where to play poker—attractiveness of opportunity and relative ability versus competitors—are the same dimensions you should use in selecting business opportunities and target markets. Ideally, you would like to find a target market that is quite attractive and where the competition is not strong. That may take work because attractive opportunities tend to attract strong competitors just like high-stakes poker games attract the most skilled players.

---

**The two dimensions you would use to decide where
to play poker are the same dimensions you should use
in selecting business opportunities and target markets.**

---

*Attractiveness* refers to how important winning this market is to your organization. Measures of market attractiveness include size of market, growth rate, cost of serving customers, price sensitivity (or insensitivity) of customers, and stability. For example, Verizon Wireless has found the youth market (18- to 24-year-olds) attractive in part because of their high involvement with cell phones—77 percent penetration versus 56.3 percent for the rest of the U.S. population.[1]

Relative ability refers to the chances that your organization can win this market. The chances of your winning a market depend on your organization's capabilities in areas such as operations, customer service, logistics, branding, and finance. Overall, your chances of winning the customers in a market depend on how well your product or service meet those customers' needs versus the products or services of your competitors. Through marketing research, Toyota found that their Solara convertible appealed to women and so focused their communications toward women in their late 30s and early 40s.[2] Kellogg targeted healthy cereals to baby boomers as research showed that they are especially concerned with health issues (and also happen to have the highest cereal consumption) and focused their marketing even more precisely by promoting Corn Flakes with Bananas to Hispanic consumers based on research findings on the role of bananas in the Hispanic diet.[3]

## SYSTEMS FOR SELECTING
## BUSINESS OPPORTUNITIES

Many consulting firms have developed systems for selecting among business opportunities. Most use these same two basic dimensions of attractiveness and relative ability but have varied in the specific measures they employ to evaluate each dimension. For example, one of the first such approaches was developed by the Boston Consulting Group. The initial BCG system was quite straightforward—long-term market growth rate was used to evaluate attractiveness and relative market share to evaluate relative ability. In contrast, McKinsey developed a system that used long lists of measures to evaluate attractiveness and relative ability, then applied a complex weighting system to develop attractiveness and relative ability scores for a specific business opportunity.

The Segment Selection Analysis I developed applies the two basic dimensions of attractiveness and relative ability in a very straightforward way so that they can be used by you or your employees in a relatively short time.

## Segment Selection Analysis

There are six steps in this approach to selecting target markets:

1. List the characteristics of a market that would make it attractive to you.
2. List the capabilities of any organization that would make it strong in a market.
3. List the product or service/market segments that you are considering.
4. Evaluate each product or service/segment with regard to how attractive it is to you.
5. Evaluate each product or service/market segment with regard to your organization's relative ability to win that segment.
6. Graph each product/market segment or service/market segment on a segment selection chart.

## TARGET MARKET SELECTION—REALTY EXAMPLE

In the real estate office example from Chapter 9, there were five segments under consideration: singles, young couples, young families, mature families, and empty nesters.

Attractiveness for each segment is rated on a 1 to 5 scale, where 5 means very attractive. Relative ability is also rated on a 1 to 5 scale, where 5 means you have high relative ability. These evaluations are based on your experience and are estimated subjectively. However, any manager should be able to say how attractive a market segment is and rate how strong or weak their organization is.

Young couples and young families would likely be attractive market segments because of their potential for several sales over the years (Exhibit 10.1). Mature families—families with precollege children—would also be attractive because of the relatively larger homes they might buy. Singles and empty nesters might be less attractive segments because they would likely prefer rentals or smaller homes.

Suppose that the real estate office rated high on expertise regarding small homes. That would give them relatively high ability to sell to young couples,

**Downloadable Exhibit 10.1   Evaluation of Real Estate Segments***

| Segments | Attractiveness | Relative Ability |
|---|---|---|
| Singles | 1 | 2 |
| Young Couples | 4 | 4 |
| Young Families | 5 | 4 |
| Mature Families | 5 | 2 |
| Empty Nesters | 2 | 4 |

*Note:* Attractiveness: 1—Not attractive, 5—Very attractive

Relative ability: 1—Weak, 5—Strong

*Source:* "Arrow Guide—Segment Selection Analysis," Copyright © 2004, The Arrow Group, Ltd.®, New York. Used with permission. ***A blank version of this page can be downloaded from www.trumpuniversity.com/marketing101 and customized for your personal use.*** For any other use, contact Don Sexton at Marketing101@thearrowgroup.com.

young families, and empty nesters. Knowing less about larger homes might be a disadvantage for them with customers in the mature family segment and so their relative ability would be rated lower for that segment.

The evaluations in Exhibit 10.1 allow you to plot the different segments in the Segment Selection Chart (Exhibit 10.2).

## TYPES OF MARKET SEGMENTS

Each quadrant in the Segment Selection Chart poses a different strategic question.

Opportunities in the upper left (often called "Stars" from the Boston Consulting Group system) are market segments that are attractive and which your organization serves well. The question here is how much growth is enough? In the long-term, all marketing efforts will have diminishing returns as it becomes more and more difficult to persuade the next customer to buy. At some point, even attractive target markets become saturated and resources need to be allocated elsewhere.

In the real estate illustration, you are doing well with the young families and young couples segments. Is there enough growth left in those markets to satisfy you or do you want to consider entering other markets?

Opportunities in the upper right (often called "Problem Children") are market segments that are attractive to you but where you may need to invest to improve your capabilities. The strategic question here is on which markets

**Downloadable Exhibit 10.2   Segment Selection Chart with Real Estate Segments***

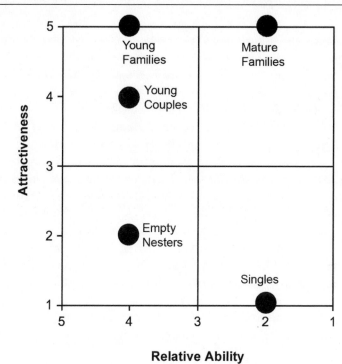

**Relative Ability**

---

*Note:* Attractiveness: 1—Not attractive, 5—Very attractive

Relative ability: 1—Weak, 5—Strong

*Source:* "Arrow Guide—Segment Selection Analysis," Copyright © 2004, The Arrow Group, Ltd.®, New York. Used with permission. ***A blank version of this page can be downloaded from www.trumpuniversity.com/marketing101 and customized for your personal use.*** For any other use, contact Don Sexton at Marketing101@thearrowgroup.com.

should you focus? If you try to focus on all of them, you may spread your resources too thin and you may not succeed in any of these market segments.

The mature families segment is a good example of a Problem Child in the realtor example. The question for the realtor is whether or not it is worthwhile to improve their performance in those capabilities that provide benefits of importance to customers in the mature families segment. For example, mature families are looking for larger homes—perhaps there is something the realtor can do to improve their knowledge of larger homes, perhaps set up an information base similar to the one they already have on smaller homes.

Opportunities in the lower left (often called "Cash Cows") are market segments where you can do well or where you perhaps have done well in the past. The strategic question here is how much current support should you give them? These markets are perhaps not as attractive as others to which you could devote resources. However, if these segments receive too little support, they may fail.

Empty nesters are in the Cash Cow segment in the real estate example. Customers in that segment may provide steady revenue but they may displace effort from more lucrative market segments. Perhaps they can be served with lower cost efforts.

Opportunities in the lower right ("Dogs") include the widest range of market segments. In general, these businesses are not attractive and do not match well with your organization's capabilities. However, that does not necessarily mean that you should ignore them or discard them. Some of these businesses can provide you with necessary windows to new markets or new technologies. Others are needed to provide products or services that complement your more attractive products or services. Some "Dog" businesses are profitable or provide a positive cash flow that is worthwhile given the resources involved. Finally, some of these businesses do represent cash drains on the organization—"the Junkyard Dogs." The strategic question is what role should each of these businesses play within your organization?

In the example, suppose that our realtor does not consider the singles market very attractive as many of them are looking for rentals and does not feel that it is worth any special efforts to win their business.

## SEGMENT SELECTION CHART

The Segment Selection Chart is a very useful tool for developing your strategy, and you can make it even more valuable by adding more information. You can conduct the same analysis for each of your products and services and summarize them all on the same chart. For example, if the realtor was interested in expanding to services for commercial buyers involving, for example, office buildings or factory buildings, then those market segment opportunities could also be graphed on the same chart (Exhibit 10.3). That would provide an overview of all the market opportunities the realtor might pursue and information for allocating their resources.

Rather than just locate a market segment on the Segment Selection Chart, you can provide more information by making the circle bigger or smaller in proportion to the sales (or profits) you think that market segment represents over the next year or the next few years. Then you have an even more comprehensive picture of the choices available to you. For example, if

**Exhibit 10.3   Segment Selection Chart with Real Estate Segments—Residential and Commercial**

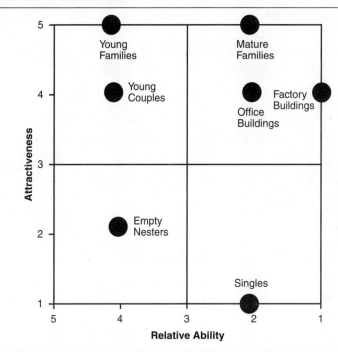

*Note:* Attractiveness: 1—Not attractive, 5—Very attractive

Relative ability: 1—Weak, 5—Strong

*Source:* "Arrow Guide—Segment Selection Analysis," The Arrow Group, Ltd.®, New York, 2004. Used with permission.

the opportunities open to our realtor were those shown in Exhibit 10.4, it would be a major strategic decision to decide what to do about the market opportunities in the upper right-hand corner—all of them are very attractive and all would need resources if they were to be pursued.

The approach described in this chapter allows you to see all your opportunities at once and that is its power. What you next need to do is choose those market segments that you think have potential for your organization. You can't choose them all so you need to choose the ones you think make sense.

Then for the segments you select you need to develop a product/market strategy, including positioning and programs. You make the final selection of whether to go ahead or not when you forecast the sales and profits from your strategy (covered in Chapters 26 and 28).

**Exhibit 10.4  Segment Selection Chart with Real Estate Segments—Residential and Commercial (Circles Sized in Proportion to Expected Sales of Total Market)**

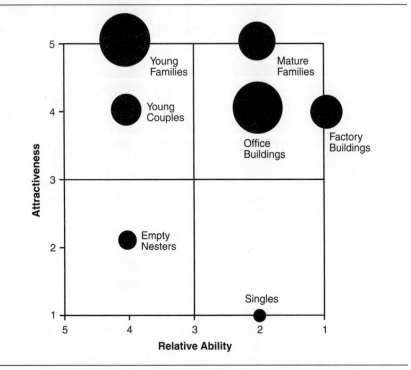

*Note:* Attractiveness: 1—Not attractive, 5—Very attractive

Relative ability: 1—Weak, 5—Strong

*Source:* "Arrow Guide—Segment Selection Analysis," The Arrow Group, Ltd.®, New York, 2004. Used with permission.

## CONCLUSIONS

If you do not select a market segment, then your marketing strategies will have no focus.

Concentration of effort is one of the main purposes of any strategy. Selecting segments is a process that involves evaluating how attractive a market segment is but, just as important, it involves evaluating how strong your abilities are to win that market segment.

For review questions for this chapter, log on to www.trumpuniversity .com/marketing101.

# 11

---

## POSSIBLY THE MOST IMPORTANT CHAPTER IN THIS BOOK

*Positioning Your Product or Service*

Positioning is the heart of your marketing strategy. Positioning is the reason your target customer should buy from you rather than from a target competitor. The stronger your positioning, the more effective is your marketing strategy.

Determining your positioning and your target market are the two most important decisions you make when you put together a marketing strategy. Both decisions depend on how well you understand the needs of your customers and how well you understand your capabilities and those of your competitors.

To determine your positioning, you must know your customers and know your own capabilities. Your positioning should be sufficiently strong to win customers and defeat competitors. In this chapter, you learn a powerful and efficient process for determining the most effective positioning for your marketplace.

## POSITIONING WITH EMOTIONAL BENEFITS: DONALD TRUMP, THE FRAGRANCE

Donald Trump, The Fragrance.
Photo courtesy of the Trump Organization.

You have wide latitude for positioning fragrances because they are very much about emotional benefits. The marketing power of fragrances usually comes from the brand—which may be built from scratch; may reflect a place, object, or characteristic; or may be based on the personality of a celebrity such as a designer, an actor or actress, or a business executive. Donald Trump, The Fragrance, is positioned to reflect the personality of Mr. Trump, in particular the traits of confidence, success, and character. The Trump Organization contributes the brand and Estée Lauder the production and distribution expertise.

The challenge for the fragrance designers at Estée Lauder was to develop a product that would capture the personality of Donald Trump. They sought ingredients that would communicate different aspects of his personality, using the language of aromas to create a physical product with the required emotional benefits.

A key aspect of Donald Trump's personality that they wished the fragrance to communicate was *confidence*—reflecting a man who is commanding, stimulating, and coolly assured. The fragrance communicates those attributes in part with "bright citrus notes . . . sparked with hints of refreshing mint." They showed *success*—depth of experience and knowledge—with "select green and aromatic notes rounded out by spicy, peppery accents." *Character*—strength and power, elegance, masculinity, and sex appeal—was expressed with "luxurious, exotic woods" and "earthy, herbaceous, and spicy notes." The result—a product formulated to provide the emotional positioning of the brand.

## WHAT IS POSITIONING?

Positioning consists of one, two, or perhaps three benefits that customers want and that you can provide at a level superior to your competitors. The benefits might be functional, emotional, or economic. A print shop might offer the fastest turnaround. A hardware store might offer the widest selection of merchandise. A delicatessen might be open the longest and most convenient hours. A health club might offer the most expert and supportive personal training advice. A restaurant might offer the friendliest atmosphere. An art supply store might offer the most generous student discounts.

---

**Positioning consists of one, two, or perhaps three benefits that customers want and that you can provide at a level superior to your competitors.**

---

Positioning should consist of only a few benefits because if you try to communicate all the wonderful things you do for customers, you may overwhelm them and most likely they will remember, if at all, only a few of the benefits you cited. Resist the temptation to mention all your benefits. Be selective and choose for your positioning those benefits that the customers want the most and that you provide at the highest level. Be known as the dry cleaner that always gets the stains out, the auto repair shop that always can fix the problem, the furniture store that always provides sound decorating advice, or the restaurant that always welcomes children.

Positioning is tailored to the needs of your target segment. For example, a car rental service targeted for business travelers might position itself as providing the quickest check-in service at airports. A car rental service targeted toward people who need the use of another car because theirs is being repaired might position itself as offering the convenience of bringing a car to your home. Walk into any restaurant—the positioning and target market should be clear just from their décor, their menu, and the appearance and attitudes of their waitstaff since all should be tailored to the needs of their target customers.

### COMPONENTS OF POSITIONING

There are four questions you need to answer to determine your positioning for customers in a given market segment (Exhibit 11.1):

1. Who is your target member of the decision-making unit?
2. Who is your target competitor?

**Downloadable Exhibit 11.1    Positioning Description***

| Product or Service: _____ Target Market Segment: _____ | |
|---|---|
| Target member of decision-making unit | |
| Target competitor | |
| Benefit advantage | |
| Competitive advantage | |

*Source:* "Arrow Guide—Formulating the Product/Market Strategy," Copyright © 2004, The Arrow Group, Ltd.®, New York. Used with permission. ***A blank version of this page can be downloaded from www.trumpuniversity.com/marketing101 and customized for your personal use.*** For any other use, contact Don Sexton at Marketing101@thearrowgroup.com.

3. What is your benefit advantage?
4. What is your competitive advantage?

## Target Decision-Making Unit Member

Most marketing books describe positioning as being focused on a market segment. Such thinking falls a bit short. Positioning needs to be done at the level of the individual customer since they are the ones who make decisions. That is why you should define your positioning in relation to an individual member of the decision-making unit—the target DMU member (see Chapter 4 for more discussion of the decision-making unit).

Successful salespeople understand this point about positioning very well. Salespeople do not sell to segments, they sell to individuals. A real estate agent working with a couple will be aware of what the wife and husband both want in a home, but the agent will also be very aware of what each wants as an individual. The agent will position any home to both wife and husband but will also be careful to position the home to satisfy the needs of each as individuals.

## Target Competitor

What competitors is your target customer considering? From whom are you trying to get business or trying to defend against?

If you are a salesperson, to know who else your customer is considering is gold because it allows you to more precisely position the product or service you are selling.

Positioning depends on your target competitor. If you do better on a specific benefit of importance to your target customer, you may need to point that out. For example, if your dry-cleaning service offers the fastest turnaround, then you may offer that as your positioning. If your competitor has even faster turnaround, then you may need to offer superior performance on another benefit such as home delivery.

Be careful that however you communicate your positioning, you do not denigrate your competitor. Criticizing your competitor directly rarely works.

## Benefit Advantage

This is the reason your target customer should buy from you rather than someone else. It should consist of just a few benefits, be easy to understand and easy to communicate, be important to your target customer, and be something you do better than your competitors. The child-care service with the most stimulating environment. The dental practice with the most flexible scheduling. The motel with the most comfortable beds. Another term for the benefit advantage is the *product/market fit*—how well your product or service meets the needs of the target market.

## Competitive Advantage

You would like your benefit advantage to be sustainable—for as long as possible. That is why you need to evaluate your competitive advantage. The competitive advantage is a capability that allows you to provide the benefit advantage. Another term for competitive advantage is *organization/product fit*—how suited your organization capabilities are to provide an appealing product or service.

A competitive advantage may be a skill associated with people, a resource, or a feature of your product or service. For example, a child-care service may provide a stimulating environment for children because of the expertise of people who work with children who designed the space. A dental practice may provide flexible service by setting up a partnership of several dentists, one of whom is always available. A motel may provide comfortable beds by installing mattresses with superior comfort.

If the competitive advantage is unique, it is more likely that it will be sustainable for a long time period. If it is not sustainable, you may need to find another positioning. For example, if all motels imitate you and install the same type of comfortable mattress, then you may have to find some other benefit to attract customers.

## COMPETITIVE ADVANTAGE ANALYSIS

Determining positioning for your product or service begins by examining your capabilities to find a competitive advantage that will in turn provide one or more benefit advantages to your target customers.

An analysis of your capabilities needs to be *diagnostic*. It must identify not only capabilities that currently are strengths but also capabilities that, while currently weaknesses, need to be transformed into strengths if the organization is to succeed. This diagnosis can be accomplished with my Competitive Advantage Analysis (Exhibit 11.2). The Competitive Advantage Analysis

**Downloadable Exhibit 11.2  Competitive Advantage Chart—Real Estate Target Segment: Young Families***

| Relative Importance | Benefits Sought | Capabilities | | | | | |
| --- | --- | --- | --- | --- | --- | --- | --- |
| | | Access to Lenders | Small Home Information Base | School Familiarity | Empathetic Personality | Location | Working Hours |
| 10 | Financing expertise | 1,0 | | | | | |
| 9 | Small home expertise | | 1,1,1 | | | | |
| 9 | School expertise | | | 1,0 | | | |
| 8 | Match homes with needs | | | | 1,1,0 | | |
| 5 | Accessibility | | | | | 1,0 | 1,0 |
| 5 | Rental expertise | | | | | | |
| 2 | Large home expertise | | | | | | |
| | | | | | | | |
| | | | | | | | |
| | | | | | | | |

*Note:* Relative importance: 10—Very important, 1—Not important
*Source:* "Arrow Guide—Competitive Advantage Analysis," Copyright © 2004, The Arrow Group, Ltd.®, New York. Used with permission. ***A blank version of this page can be downloaded from www.trumpuniversity.com/marketing101 and customized for your personal use.** For any other use, contact Don Sexton at Marketing101@thearrowgroup.com.

helps you determine all the elements of an effective positioning for your product or service.

There are seven steps:

1. Select a segment and a member of the decision-making unit.
2. List benefits sought by your target customer in descending order.
3. List capabilities that *any* organization would like to have.
4. Link benefits with the capabilities required to provide them.
5. Evaluate capabilities.
6. Identify possible competitive advantages.
7. Identify possible benefit advantages.

## Benefits and Capabilities—Realty Example

Suppose, for example, that you manage a small realty firm and have decided to focus on young families, many purchasing a home for the first time. The target members of the decision-making unit are the husband and wife. The target competitor is a large office of a national realty chain.

Benefits sought from a realtor by such a couple would likely include expertise in financing, expertise with smaller homes, and expertise on local school systems as well as the ability to find homes that match their needs and availability. These benefits are entered on the Competitive Advantage Chart in descending order of importance to the couple (Exhibit 11.2).

The capabilities you list on the Competitive Advantage Chart are capabilities that *any* realtor targeting that market would like to have. Such capabilities might include relationships with mortgage lenders, an information base on small homes, familiarity with the local school systems, agents with empathetic personalities, and an easy-to-reach location and generous working hours.

Next you link the benefits with the capabilities that are required to provide them (as you did in the Capabilities Analysis in Chapter 7). For example, relationships with mortgage lenders affect the financial advice a realtor can provide and the location of the realty office affects availability of the realtor. Note that a benefit can be associated with more than one capability. If no capability is associated with a benefit, then probably some capabilities have been left out of the analysis and you may want to consider adding to the list of capabilities. For example, rental market knowledge was not included in this analysis.

You indicate a relationship between a capability and a benefit by squaring the cell in the benefit row and the capability column. Usually you can expect to square about one-third of the cells in the chart although that percentage will vary by situation.

## EVALUATING CAPABILITIES

The most important step in this process is to evaluate your own capabilities versus those of the target competitors. You must be candid during this phase, otherwise the process will be a waste of time.

Remember that the evaluations need to be relative to a target competitor so you need to have a competing realtor in mind as you evaluate your capabilities. Usually you would want to see how you would do against your toughest competitors, so you might select them as the target competitor for your first analysis.

Capabilities should be evaluated on three dimensions. I call these questions the three Ss:

1. *Sufficient:* Do you have the capability at a level sufficient to compete for the target customer?
   1—yes
   0—no
2. *Superior:* Do you have the capability at a level superior to that of the target competitor?
   1—yes
   0—no
3. *Sustainable:* Can you sustain the capability for a given time interval?
   1—yes
   0—no

Notice that if your capability is not sufficient, it cannot be superior and it is not worth answering the question of whether or not it is sustainable. Similarly, if your capability is not superior, there is no need to ask if it is sustainable or not.

There are four possible patterns that you might see in a cell:

1. [0]—*Capability insufficient:* This is a veto. If you do not improve this capability, you will be unable to compete successfully in this market.
2. [1,0]—*Capability sufficient but not superior:* This is a neutral rating—doesn't hurt you, doesn't help you.

3. [1,1,0]—*Capability is superior but is not sustainable:* This is a competitive advantage, but short-lived. You need to take advantage of it as soon as possible.

4. [1,1,1]—*Capability is superior and sustainable:* This is a sustainable, competitive advantage and may be the foundation for your positioning.

## *Evaluating Capabilities—Realty Example*

The realtor needs to consider how their expertise and other capabilities compare to those of competitors—especially those capabilities linked to the benefits of most importance to the members of the target market.

Exhibit 11.2 shows the evaluations for the realty service. For example, suppose you have a small home information base that is unmatched by your competitors. The rating for that capability is therefore [1,1,1]—a sustainable competitive advantage. You also have agents with empathetic personalities but that could be imitated by your competitors through recruiting or training their agents so the evaluation for that capability is [1,1,0]—a short-lived competitive advantage. The other cells have neutral scores.

## IDENTIFYING COMPETITIVE ADVANTAGES AND BENEFIT ADVANTAGES

Once you evaluate your capabilities, then you can examine the chart for competitive advantages. You start with the benefits of highest importance to the members of the target market and search for any capabilities in that row that received high evaluations—either [1,1,1] or [1,1,0].

The benefit advantages are found by identifying those benefits for which the organization has one or more capabilities that are competitive advantages. These benefits are candidates for the benefits selected for positioning of the product or service.

## *Identifying Competitive Advantages and Benefit Advantages— Realty Example*

In the real estate example, there is a sustainable competitive advantage consisting of an information base of small homes that the realtor has assembled. It provides an important benefit to the young family customer—small home expertise—and is something that would be difficult for a competing realtor to copy in the near future. The short-lived competitive advantage (empathetic sales people) also leads to an important benefit—ability to match homes with buyer's needs.

## No Competitive Advantage

If you find no competitive advantage, that is a sign not to try to sell that specific product or service to customers in that particular market. A product or service with no competitive advantage (and therefore no benefit advantage) is known as a *commodity*. Commodities are sold only on price as there is no basis for differentiation on benefits.

Unless the organization has the lowest costs (or is in a protected market), it is very difficult to succeed with a commodity. However, if you do not find a competitive advantage for a specific product or service in a particular market, there are other possibilities to consider before abandoning the venture. For example:

- Can you improve your capabilities? For example, can you develop more contacts with lenders?
- Might you focus on a different target competitor? Perhaps you can avoid the strong competitors.
- Might you focus on a different decision maker? Rather than focus on both the husband and wife, might you be more successful by focusing on the husband or the wife?
- Might you focus on a different target market? If you do not have current information about schools, perhaps you might focus on families whose children are grown and who have left home.
- Should you resegment the entire market? If you cannot find a segment you think you can win, you may need to rethink your segmentation scheme.

## Other Segments, Other Members of the Decision-Making Unit, Other Target Competitors

Note that you do not have to redo this analysis if you want to evaluate other segments or other members of the decision-making unit. If you change segment or DMU member, all that you need to do is reorder the rows according to the benefit priorities of the new segment or new DMU member—you've already done all the capability evaluations.

If you change target competitor, then you do have to redo the analysis because the capability evaluations will likely change.

## DETERMINING POSITIONING

Effective positioning is based on superior performance on a benefit of importance to the target customer and the capability to sustain that benefit performance over time.

In the realty example, you might describe the positioning of your agency as "the small home experts who know how to find the home for you." Small home expertise and matching homes to needs are both benefit advantages of importance to your target market and they are supported by competitive advantages. You can summarize your positioning decision with answers to the four positioning questions in Exhibit 11.3.

## POSITIONING AND PERCEIVED VALUE

Even though you have a clear positioning with a powerful benefit advantage, remember that the customer may not know about it. The competitive

**Exhibit 11.3   Positioning Description—Real Estate Example**

| | |
|---|---|
| Product or Service: | Real Estate |
| Target Market Segment: | Young Families |
| Target member of decision-making unit | Wife and husband |
| Target competitor | Chain realtor |
| Benefit advantages | Small home expertise<br>Match home to needs |
| Competitive advantages | Small home database<br>Empathetic agents |

*Source:* "Arrow Guide—Formulating the Product/Market Strategy," The Arrow Group, Ltd.®, New York, 2004. Used with permission.

advantage analysis shows those benefits that you have which are superior to those of your competitors. These lead to *actual* value as regards the benefits you can provide your customers. You may still need to convert them into value *perceived* by the customer by effectively communicating them to your target customers.

Managing perceived value (see Chapter 5) starts with the actual value you provide. However then it requires communications to ensure that your customers correctly perceive all the value that you are providing them. You can't assume that they know—you must tell them. (See Chapter 17 on communications.)

## Conclusions

Positioning is a major strategic choice for any organization. It depends on the needs of customers in your target market and it also depends on the capabilities of your organization compared to those of your competitors. An effective position has a benefit advantage supported by a competitive advantage.

For review questions for this chapter, log on to www.trumpuniversity .com/marketing101.

# II

## IMPROVING YOUR MARKETING STRATEGY

# 12

---

# CREATING YOUR MOST
# VALUABLE ASSET

## *Your Brand*

Your brand is probably the most important and most valuable asset of your organization.

Each of the 10 most valuable brands in the world is estimated to be worth billions of U.S. dollars (Exhibit 12.1). Compare these brand value estimates to the market value of the companies owning the brands and it is easy to see how powerful brands are. For consumer market companies, well-managed brands typically represent about 50 percent to 80 percent of a company's total value; for industrial markets companies, well-managed brands appear to be about 10 percent to 30 percent of a company's total value.

What is true for large organizations is true for small organizations: Brands represent a *lot* of money. How you manage your brand has a tremendous impact on the return you will obtain from your business.

There are a few basic principles for building your brand and keeping it strong. You learn those principles in this chapter.

---

A number of the ideas in the "Components of a Brand" section on pages 108-110 were stimulated by the work of Peter Farquhar, a colleague and friend.

**Exhibit 12.1   Brand and Company Values (in Billions of U.S. Dollars)**

|  | Brand Equity[a] | Market Value[b] |
|---|---|---|
| Coca-Cola | $67.5 | $103.1 |
| Microsoft | 59.9 | 273.7 |
| IBM | 53.4 | 152.8 |
| GE | 47.0 | 372.1 |
| Intel | 35.6 | 149.4 |
| Nokia | 26.5 | 73.1 |
| Disney | 26.4 | 57.2 |
| McDonald's | 26.0 | 41.6 |
| Toyota | 24.8 | 140.9 |
| Marlboro | 21.2 | 134.8 |

[a] *Business Week,* August 1, 2005.
[b] *Forbes,* April 18, 2005.

## How Are Strong Brands Built?

Brands are built with *relentless consistency*—over time and over markets. From 1974 through 1994, Burger King changed their advertising and brand position nearly every year. Their themes during this time period included: "Have It Your Way," "Best Darn Burger," "Aren't You Hungry for Burger King Now?" "Search for Herb," "Sometimes You Gotta Break the Rules," and "I Love This Place." Constantly changing brand communications does not build a brand. Over the same 20-year period, McDonald's brand communications were much more consistent. Burger King has returned to what might have been their most powerful brand position, "Have It Your Way," and appears now to be following a consistent brand-building strategy.

> **Brands are built with *relentless consistency*—over time and over markets.**

In credit cards, Visa's "Everywhere You Want to Be" position was extraordinarily consistent for many years and was constantly renewed through different but consistently "on-brand" creative executions. Only after many

## THE POWER OF THE TRUMP BRAND

Label for the Donald J. Trump Signature Collection.

Photo courtesy of the Trump Organization.

A New York company called Brand Keys conducted a survey of 500 adults and asked them to evaluate 1,200 brands in a wide variety of product categories such as clothing, banks, and fast-food restaurants. In the clothing category, the brands with the highest ratings were Chanel, Ralph Lauren, Isaac Mizrahi, Victoria's Secret, and Donald Trump. At the time of the survey, the Donald J. Trump Signature collection of men's clothing had been sold at Federated Department Stores for only about a year. To build a brand in such a short time is unheard of. Normally, it takes five to seven years to build a brand. The Chanel brand, for example, has been built with decades of marketing and publicity. The participants in the survey found the Trump brand to be associated with "comfort, style, and fit." In addition, the Trump brand also has strong associations with business success. These functional and emotional benefits worked together to form a strong new clothing brand with amazing speed.

*Source:* Cathy Horyn, "Fashion & Style," *New York Times* (November 24, 2005).

years of success did Visa move to the "Life Accepts Visa" campaign. For many years, MasterCard branding was inconsistent until the debut of their brilliant "Priceless" campaign.

The brand generally conceded to be the most valuable brand in the world is Coca-Cola. One Coca-Cola executive has attributed some of their success to their long-term consistent focus on a very specific group of customers—18- to 25-year-olds—who appear to have a lot in common around the world.

The same principles companies like McDonald's, Visa, and Coca-Cola use can be used to build the brand of your organization. Building a brand requires a clear understanding of what your brand stands for and the discipline to build and maintain it.

## WHAT IS A BRAND?

How would you define a brand? Take a moment and write down your definition:

_____

_____

_____

_____

In executive seminars I conduct on managing brands, I often ask the participants to write down their brand definitions. Here are some:

"Distinguishable logo or name that creates a preference."

"Trust, promise."

"Association that identifies brand and is worth paying for."

"Nature and strength of relationship consumer has with brand."

"How strongly consumers link your name to a personality."

"Ownable difference that allows producer to charge a premium."

Was your response similar to any of theirs? There is a surprising degree of unanimity among how people think of brands. Even though the details of their definitions vary, the individuals who provided these definitions would likely not dramatically disagree with any of the other definitions. Some definitions focus more on names and logos, some more on attributes, some more on values, and some more on the customer/brand relationship, but all of these definitions are all quite consistent with each other.

## THE COMPONENTS OF A BRAND

A brand has three main components:

1. *Identifiers:* Name, logo, color, shape, aroma, taste, feel—anything that cues the customer to the brand's attributes.
2. *Attributes:* Anything connected in the customer's mind to the brand. Attributes include the product or service itself, features, benefits, and needs.
3. *Associations:* The connections between the identifiers and the attributes.

## Identifiers

Your identifiers signal your brand position to your customers. Diageo planned an increase of 50 percent in their marketing spend to rejuvenate Smirnoff by emphasizing its Russian heritage. To accomplish that change, they developed a new identifier—a label with a silver-and-white color scheme and a Cyrillic translation of Smirnoff.[1] The identifiers need to be clearly visible as they are the cue that leads to associations in your customers' minds. Texas Instruments persuaded television set manufacturers to put a DLP logo on the face of every set that has their DLP technology—similar to Intel's "Intel Inside" campaign.

When you change any of the identifiers, you are changing the brand. Over the years, Prudential Insurance Company has used the Rock of Gibraltar as its logo. There were many changes since 1902 but in 1984 the logo was changed so much it resembled a bar code more than the Rock of Gibraltar. The next year it was changed back to a more recognizable Rock.

## Attributes

Generally, when you mention a brand, the first attribute that people mention is the product or service itself. There is nothing wrong with that—people should know what product or service your brand stands for. However, a brand should lead to attributes beyond the product or service. A brand should make your customers think of benefits or needs.

Most brands are built with attributes that consist of functional benefits. Holiday Inn has tried to win back customers who have gone to cheaper mid-scale hotels or slightly more upscale hotels by adding functional benefits such as high-speed Internet access—wireless and land-line—bigger workspaces, and an ergonomic chair. They also are paying attention to their identifiers—redesigning their sign to recall the iconic Holiday Inn sign of the past and bringing back the green-striped Holiday Inn towel.[2]

If possible, you should try to build your brand on emotional benefits. Emotional benefits are more difficult for competitors to copy and may have more impact on customers' purchasing decisions than functional benefits alone. For example, in the middle of the nineteenth century, when steam engines and ocean liners created demand for good-looking trunks, Louis Vuitton developed trunks that were stackable and waterproof—functional benefits. He also had the good sense to cover the trunks with canvas stamped with his logo. Later, his trunks and brand extensions became the foundation of an empire, built on the emotional benefits of style and fashion and the support of famous, well-respected people like Coco Chanel.[3]

Your benefits must be delivered consistently over time. Texas Instruments' DLP specialists visit retailers at least once a month to check that TVs are tuned properly and deliver video clips that show their high picture quality.[4]

Your brand should be associated with market needs, not with a product or a service. If technology changes and that product or service disappears, then the brand will suffer if its main association is with the old technology. For example, Kodak has long had a strong association with film. According to one reporter, "While the 115-year-old company's heritage is unrivaled in the photography market, what is more debatable is whether the brand has the cut-through to appeal to a younger, techno-savvy generation of consumers."[5] During one five-year interval, some publicly available brand equity estimates show the value of the Kodak brand falling U.S.$7 billion—a loss of about half the brand's value. Managing their brand remains a crucial concern for Kodak.

## Associations

The associations are the "wiring" in the customer's mind that leads him or her from the brand identifiers to the attributes. Because it takes time to build associations in a customer's mind, it takes time to build a brand.

If you do not maintain the currency of your brand's associations over time, then your brand may founder. Sales of Levi's jeans slid from a peak of $7.1 billion in 1996 to about $4 billion in 2003. Levi's were popular in the 1960s but did not sustain their positioning for jeans buyers in later generations. According to Lew Frankfort, CEO of Coach, Inc., "Levi's did not create the 'emotional associations' that lead to brand loyalty. . . . Levi's managers saw themselves as a jeans company making great jeans as opposed to part of the American landscape." Their distribution through stores such as J.C.Penney and Sears did not appear to help reinvigorate their brand position. Shoppers looking either for economy or for style did not buy Levi's—a classic example of what was called being "stuck-in-the-middle" in Chapter 5.[6]

Building associations for a brand requires consistency. Once a brand position has been selected, then all your contact points with customers must be orchestrated to deliver a consistent brand message. Especially important is that all your employees know the brand position and why it is important to maintain a consistent brand position.

## Creating a Brand Position

The brand position derives from the product or service position (see Chapter 11).

The product or service position should consist of those benefits that are of high priority to your target customer and that your organization can provide better than any of your competitors. The brand position should consist of just a few benefits—ideally just one, two, or possibly three benefits.

Why only a few benefits? Because customers cannot remember a long list of benefits. They will remember some benefits but perhaps not the ones you want them to remember. It is imperative that you make your brand position very clear so it can be communicated effectively and the target customer will learn it quickly and remember it.

Marketing and branding are intertwined. Where marketing and branding may differ is *discipline*. A strong brand requires discipline to select only a few benefits as a brand position and the discipline to communicate that position consistently over markets and over time. Some managers are reluctant to choose just a few benefits. However, without that discipline, there is little chance of building a strong brand.

When Helmut Panke, CEO of BMW, was asked how they keep the BMW brand consistent, he replied, "the biggest task is to be able to say 'No.' Because in the end, authentic brand management boils down to understanding that a brand is a promise that has to be fulfilled everywhere, at any time. So when something doesn't fit, you must make sure that that is not done." For example, BMW said "no" to producing a minivan since they did not feel it was consistent with the BMW brand position they desired at the time.[7]

## Building a Brand

To build a brand you must:

- Select a target market.
- Choose the key benefits in the positioning of your product or service.
- Determine the attributes currently perceived to be associated with your brand by customers in your target market (the association audit).
- Identify any differences between the attributes the customers perceive to be associated with your brand and the attributes you wish them to associate with your brand.
- Develop a communications strategy to build the desired associations.

## BUILDING A BRAND—REAL ESTATE EXAMPLE

In the real estate example in prior chapters, the best positioning for the realtor seemed to be the "small home expert" for young families and young couples. That might be a viable positioning for their brand.

Suppose that an association audit (Exhibit 12.2) showed that many customers associated "small home expertise" with the realtor. That would be good news but they would still want to repeat that message in all that they do.

To maintain that brand position, the realtor would want to make sure that *every* contact point with customers reinforced that position. Certainly, any advertising would repeat that position. In addition, any signs, stationery, and promotional giveaways should all reinforce that position.

It would be especially important that all the employees know the brand position and why it is crucial for them to support it. The realtor may explain

**Exhibit 12.2   Association Audit—Real Estate**

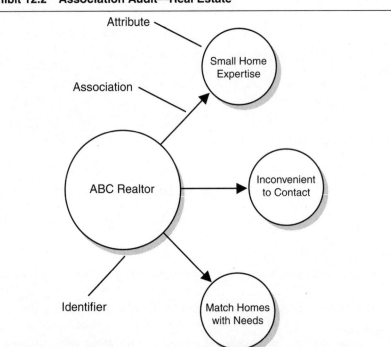

*Source:* "Arrow Guide—Brand Attribute Analysis," The Arrow Group, Ltd.®, New York, 2004. Used with permission.

the brand position for them and also provide them with material describing the brand position and the implications for their contacts with customers. In particular, all the employees should always mention the small home expertise of the agency.

Attributes associated with a brand may be negative. For example, if the association audit discovered that "inconvenient to contact" was an association of the realtor (Exhibit 12.2) and was an important concern to their target customers, then they should try to change that situation. That could be done by showing how easy it is to reach their agents and the large number of hours their offices are open.

Any benefit claim that is part of the brand position needs to be true because it will receive a lot of attention and scrutiny. If brand claims are not true, customers usually find out very quickly and then they may not believe the next claim you make.

## COMMUNICATING THE BRAND TO MEMBERS OF THE ORGANIZATION

Studies by the Conference Board and by the American Productivity and Quality Center suggest that two of the most important drivers for building strong brands are support by top management and support by employees.[8]

Many organizations have what they call a "style guide"—information as to how their name and logo should be portrayed. Organizations that are more sophisticated in their branding efforts go beyond the style guide to what you might call a "brand book."

The brand book includes all the style guide information, but also explains the argument as to why it is important for everyone in the organization to understand the brand and support the branding efforts.

Exhibit 12.3 shows the general format and contents of a brand book. The first half of the brand book provides the rationale for branding; the second half provides the details as to how the brand should be communicated.

You may not need a brand book for your organization but it is important that everyone in your organization understand why it is so important to manage the brand properly and that they all have a role in managing the brand. Perhaps you can communicate the importance of the brand with a meeting, by e-mail, or perhaps with a one- or two-page explanation and description of the brand. However you do it, internal communication of the brand is essential to a strong brand.

**Exhibit 12.3   The Brand Book**

The Power of Brands
   Value to customers
   Value to organizations

How Are Brands Developed and Managed
   Consistency over time and over markets
   Brand understanding and discipline

Why Brand?

What Is a Brand?
   Identifiers
   Attributes
   Associations

What Is Our Brand?
   Logo and other identifiers
   Personality and values
   Promise

Our Brand Promise
   Significance to customers
   Keeping the promise

Who Is Our Audience?
   Their needs
   How we meets those needs

Speaking with One Brand Voice
   Tone and manner
   Logo style guide
   Graphic element style guide
   Font style guide
   Advertising style guide
   [Other style guides]

How to Be a Brand Champion

Appendices:
   Frequently Asked Questions
   Checklist for Brand Communications (Do's and Don'ts)

---

*Source:* "Arrow Guide—Brand Identity," The Arrow Group, Ltd.®, New York, 2004. Used with permission.

## CONCLUSIONS

Brands—the reputation of your organization and your products and services—represent an extremely valuable asset *if* they are managed well. The key principles of sound brand management are: positioning that is well thought out, discipline to implement brand communications programs with consistency, and understanding of your brand position by all the members of your organization.

For review questions for this chapter, log on to www.trumpuniversity .com/marketing101.

# 13

---

# DEVELOPING YOUR
# GROWTH PLAN

You want more growth for your organization. You have established your products and services with customers but you feel that you can increase your revenues and profits. Marketing can help guide you to the most attractive growth path for your organization—the growth path with superior profits and lower risk.

Organizations without growth plans are often tempted by targets of opportunity—ventures with short-term returns but which may not lead anywhere or, worse, may create risk for the organization. A growth plan provides long-run direction for an organization and discipline, so that it maintains a stable growth path. That's why you need a growth plan. That's why you need this chapter.

## THE GROWTH MATRIX

You can grow your organization through finding new customers (or new markets) or by creating new products or services (or technology). These growth

## MARKET GROWTH PATH: TRUMP INTERNATIONAL HOTEL & TOWER

Trump International Hotel & Tower, Las Vegas.

Photo credit: Bergman Walls & Associates, 2005.

Photo courtesy of the Trump Organization.

You can grow in a market direction or in a product or service direction. Trump International Hotel & Tower has moved in the market direction.

The initial property was developed in New York City. That was followed by the Trump International Hotel & Tower in Chicago, Las Vegas, and Fort Lauderdale. There is a Trump International Hotel & Tower planned for Dubai.

The positioning of each of these properties is similar—luxury hotel and condominium, but the markets are somewhat different. For example, the investors in Chicago units tend to be from the Chicago suburbs. Investors in Las Vegas units tend to be from diverse locations. Investors in Fort Lauderdale are more likely to be people who have retired. However, the strength of the product—high-end layouts and features and high-end service—appeals to all these varied target customers. Brand and product strength have carried the company to successful growth in these new markets.

paths can be systematically developed and evaluated by using the growth matrix (Exhibit 13.1), which is usually credited to Igor Ansoff, a pioneer in strategic planning.

*Current customers* are customers with whom you are conducting transactions or, better, customers with whom you already have a relationship.

**Downloadable Exhibit 13.1   The Growth Matrix***

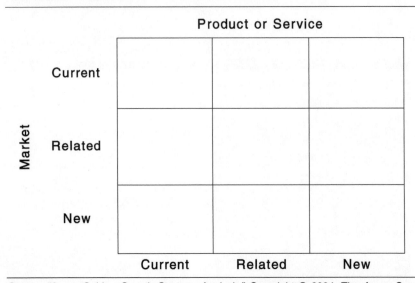

Product or Service

|  | Current | Related | New |
|---|---|---|---|
| Current |  |  |  |
| Related |  |  |  |
| New |  |  |  |

Market

Current          Related          New

*Related customers* are customers who resemble your current customers or are similar to your current customers but with whom you are not currently doing business.

*New customers* are customers with whom you are likely not familiar but you may want to target efforts toward them.

*Current products or services* are the products or services which you are currently marketing.

*Related products or services* are products or services that are similar to your current products or services but which require somewhat different expertise.

*New products or services* are products or services which would be new to your organization (but not necessarily new to the world).

Customer growth paths run from current customers to new customers or from top to bottom on the growth matrix. Product or service growth paths run from current products or services to new products or services or from left to right.

## ALTERNATIVE GROWTH PATHS—HEALTH CLUB EXAMPLE

Suppose you are running a health club catering to men in their 30s and 40s. Possible product or service growth paths would be to offer pilates classes or install a juice bar for your current customers. Possible customer growth paths would be to promote your current exercise programs to women in the same age range or to seniors.

You can also combine growth paths. For example, if you feel pilates might be especially popular with women, you might offer pilates classes to women—and grow in both the service direction and customer direction at the same time. Note though that the further you travel on the growth matrix, the higher the risk, and moving in both the service and customer direction at the same time can be tricky.

## RISK IN GROWTH

Growth usually comes with risk, so if you are considering growth opportunities you need to evaluate the possible risks as well as the possible returns. The growth matrix spotlights risk. As you move on the growth matrix—to the right or down, risk increases. In fact, the most risky growth move is thought to be the move down the main diagonal of the matrix—from current customers and current products to new customers and new products.

The reason moves on the growth matrix are considered risky is that whenever you move to a new market or to a new product or service, you need to acquire new management knowledge. A few years ago, some airlines thought that they could pursue service growth paths by adding hotel and car rental services, which they would provide to their business customers. They found it wasn't so simple. Each business requires its own expertise. In addition, it is not always easy to meld businesses—there are issues of information sharing and differences in cultures that make a business move that makes sense on paper not make sense in practice.

> **The reason moves on the growth matrix are considered risky is that whenever you move to a new market or to a new product or service, you need to acquire new management knowledge.**

Required expertise is of two kinds:

1. *New product or service expertise* consists of knowing how to produce and provide the product or service. At one point, KFC was owned by a company with little experience with restaurants. The parent company found that operating a fast-food chain required different skills than they had. Instead of the large factories they operated for their other businesses, they had to manage hundreds of small "factories" because each restaurant was relatively independent. In the restaurant business, one of the key skills is understanding real estate and traffic patterns—quite different from the skills needed to manufacture a consumer product. When they realized the problems they were facing due to their lack of restaurant expertise, they sold KFC.

2. *Customer expertise*—while it may be difficult to acquire expertise related to new products or services, many organizations have put themselves at risk because they did not have sufficient information regarding the new customers they were trying to attract. There are many instances of deficient customer information in international marketing, including well-known stories where there were problems in pronouncing a company's name or translating their slogan into the local language. (Hertz's famous "We put you in the driver's seat" supposedly became "We make a chauffeur out of you" due to mistakes in the German translation.)

More important issues about customer expertise concern knowing their expectations, attitudes, and behavior. Coca-Cola, for example, may be consumed differently in different national markets. In some countries, Coca-Cola is typically consumed with a meal and in others during breaks throughout the day. Hall's throat drops are a snack in some countries, a cough drop in others. Knowing the type of behavior to expect in a market is important in positioning the product or service and in communicating with the customers. Both Coca-Cola and Hall's, for example, tailor their advertising to match the behavior and needs of customers in their diverse markets.

Moving down the main diagonal of the growth matrix is especially risky because it requires you to acquire both customer and product information at the same time. In addition, you might need to change your organization, often in major ways.

---

**Moving down the main diagonal of the growth matrix is especially risky because it requires you to acquire both customer and product information at the same time.**

---

During the 1950s and 1960s in the United States—a relatively quiet time as regards competition—there were many companies known as conglomerates. They acquired companies in a variety of industries. Singer, for example, moved from their core sewing machine business to acquire companies such as Friden, a company that made mechanical calculators.

While the competitive environment was quiet, you could evaluate corporate acquisitions by examining the standard financial information. In the 1950s and 1960s, conglomerates tended to look at acquisitions as if they were simply buying stock. The problems came when the competitive environment became noisy—then you could not manage a company passively. During the noisy time, many conglomerates found that they did not have the product or service expertise or the customer expertise to manage their acquisitions successfully. Singer, for example, sold Friden when it became clear that electronic calculators would soon dominate the calculator market.

While conglomerates still exist, their top management understands that they need managers in charge of each of their diverse divisions who understand the products and services and customers in their markets.

## RISK AND YOUR GROWTH PATH

The concerns that large companies have about growth paths should be reflected in the way smaller organizations consider growth paths. Expansion to include new products or services requires new expertise. A restaurant adding to its menu would need a chef capable of preparing the new dishes. Expansion to new customers requires new expertise. Young couples likely want somewhat different benefits from a restaurant than do families.

In the health club example, the addition of pilates classes would require the addition of a pilates instructor and special equipment. Adding a juice bar would require knowledge of ordering and stocking beverages.

## GENERATING GROWTH ALTERNATIVES

The growth matrix is often useful for generating ideas regarding possible growth paths for an organization.

A manager or team of managers can be tasked with finding growth ideas for the different cells in the growth matrix. In turn, these ideas provide a list of business opportunities for consideration (Exhibit 13.2). Techniques such as

**Exhibit 13.2   Using the Growth Matrix—Health Club**

**Product or Service**

| Market | Current | Related | New | |
|---|---|---|---|---|
| | Professional men in their 30s and 40s— cardiovascular workouts | Free weights<br><br>Yoga<br><br>Pilates | Juice bar<br><br>Clothing or equipment store<br><br>Martial arts | Current |
| | Professional women in their 30s and 40s<br><br>Professional men in their 20s<br><br>Professional men in their 50s | | | Related |
| | Senior men<br><br>Senior women<br><br>Young mothers | | | New |
| | Current | Related | New | |

*Source:* "Arrow Guide—Growth Strategy Analysis," The Arrow Group, Ltd.®, New York, 2004. Used with permission.

the target market selection process described in Chapter 10 can be used to determine which opportunities might be pursued.

In the health club example, you might elect to provide different kinds of classes or perhaps free weights to your current customers, professional men in their 30s and 40s. You might even try to sell upscale workout clothing.

In the market direction, you might target younger men or older men or perhaps women in the same age range as your current customers. If you wanted to stretch your market further, you might try women in other age ranges.

Meeting with your managers and leading them in a discussion of possible growth paths doesn't mean that you will follow any of those growth paths. But such a discussion may provide you with ideas you can pursue and perhaps one or two of them will be successful. One successful idea is worth the time it takes to brainstorm a number of possible growth paths.

## FOCUSING GROWTH STRATEGIES

Once you have decided on a growth path, you will need to determine how your efforts will be focused on specific customer actions such as product trial or increased usage. The next chapter explains how to focus your growth strategies.

## CONCLUSIONS

Growth is the goal of many managers. Well-planned growth can lead to success but growth also leads to risk. Many organizations have tried to grow too fast or have tried to grow in the wrong directions and have failed because of those choices. An organization needs a growth plan to ensure that it is not misled by targets of opportunity that lead to risk or to dead ends.

For review questions for this chapter, log on to www.trumpuniversity .com/marketing101.

# 14

---

## DETERMINING YOUR FOCUS
## FOR GROWTH

After you have decided on your overall growth path, you need to consider exactly how you will achieve that growth and how you will approach your target customers to provide that growth.

You can grow in the product (or service) direction or in the customer (or market) direction. However, knowing the general direction you will move doesn't really give you the details you need for how you are going to go about it. You need to have a *growth focus* so that you can make decisions regarding marketing programs such as advertising, promotion, pricing, and distribution. Otherwise, your marketing programs can be inconsistent and cancel each other.

This chapter is about making the focus of your marketing strategy more *precise* so that you can coordinate your marketing programs more effectively and achieve your objectives more easily.

### A FOCUS FOR GROWTH

Exhibit 14.1 shows alternative ways to focus your growth efforts. For example, if you run a health club, you can try to attract customers away from com-

## GROWTH IN THE PRODUCT DIRECTION: THE DONALD TRUMP SIGNATURE COLLECTION EYEWEAR

Eyewear from The Donald Trump Signature Collection.

Photo courtesy of the Trump Organization.

You can grow in a market direction or in a product direction. The Trump Organization does both. For example, Trump International Hotel & Tower grows in the market direction by building similar types of buildings in new markets, while Trump licensing grows in the product direction, licensing suits, shirts, neckwear, timepieces, fragrance, and eyewear.

For example, in 2005, The Trump Organization and Eyewear Designs, Ltd. launched The Donald Trump Signature Collection—eyewear targeted toward professional men and women "who understand the importance of image." The agreement between the two companies merges their competencies. Eyewear Designs, Ltd. provides the innovative styling, high production standards, and global distribution. The Donald Trump brand provides associations with attributes such as business success, boldness, and style.

peting health clubs or you can try to sell more products and services to the customers you have now. Notice that the actions you need to take will differ depending on your focus. You may use special promotions to attract customers from the competing health clubs while you may provide more services to sell more to your current customers.

If you try to pursue several different growth focuses at the same time, they may conflict. For example, trying to increase your customers' usage of your product or service at the same time that you are trying to encourage them to pay higher prices would be counterproductive. At the least, pursuing different growth focuses will spread your resources too thin, so that none of your growth initiatives has sufficient resources to succeed.

**Exhibit 14.1   Growth Focuses**

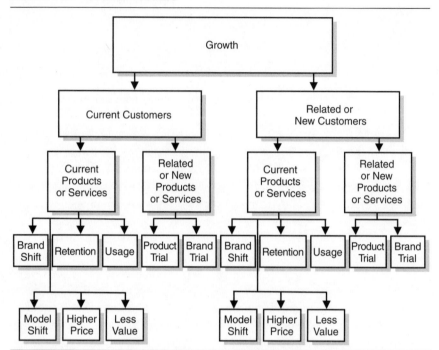

*Source:* "Arrow Guide—Strategies for Growth," The Arrow Group, Ltd.®, New York, 2004. Used with permission.

## GROWING WITH CURRENT CUSTOMERS

You can grow your organization by targeting your current customers. Growing with current customers has two main advantages. First, hopefully you know these customers well already and therefore you know their needs and priorities. Second, you are already in contact with these customers so you have opportunities to persuade them to purchase more.

You can grow with current customers with *current products* or with *related or new products*.

## CURRENT CUSTOMERS/CURRENT PRODUCTS

*Encourage customers to purchase more from you and less from your competitors.* This focus is known as a *brand shift*. You need to let your customer know why they should give you more of their business. In the health club example, you might focus on your more convenient location or more convenient hours.

## Improve Loyalty

Increasing loyalty means you are increasing the *retention* of your customers (see Chapter 15 for more on this). The most important way to increase loyalty or retention is to satisfy your customers—delight them (although remember you need to make a profit in doing so). That means you need to listen to them and find out how they like your products or services. Ask: "How did you like your workout today?" You can also encourage loyalty with various loyalty plans. For example, you may give price discounts or gifts, such as towels, to members of your health club who work out two or more times each week.

## Increase Customers' Use of Your Product/Service

There are three ways for you to persuade your customers to increase usage: Point out that their needs have increased, show them new uses for your product or service, or remind them to use it.

Over time a customer may simply *need more* of your products or services. For example, as a house appreciates in value, a policy holder may need more property insurance coverage. You might also point out to your customers that more is better for them—more workouts at your health club (within reason) may help your customers get in better shape more quickly.

*New uses* is about providing your customers with ideas for using your product or service in new ways. Many alcoholic beverage companies promote their products by publishing recipes for new mixed drinks that call for use of their product.

*Reminder* is just that—reminding the customer to use the product or service. A dentist who reminds his patients to have their teeth cleaned three times a year instead of twice a year might increase the revenue from teeth cleaning by 50 percent. "Have you worked out this week?" and "Would you like fries with that?" are both examples of reminder approaches to increasing usage, although with somewhat different effects.

## Purchase More Expensive Models or Versions

This approach is known as a *model shift* or *up-selling*. Airlines try to persuade coach passengers to fly in more lucrative classes such as business or first class.

Some car rental companies are adding special automobiles, such as convertibles, sports cars, and SUVs, to their inventory in hopes of persuading some of their customers to trade up to those models. In the health club, you might persuade customers that they need a trainer.

## Pay Higher Prices

Generally, the strongest arguments for an increased price is increased value. For example, the owner of the health club might increase the hours the health club is open or add new equipment at the same time that they raise membership fees.

## Accept Less Value

This approach may allow you to decrease your costs. Some organizations do this without letting the customers know that this is going on. For example, producers of candy may decrease the size of their packages without decreasing their price or airlines may make it much more difficult to use the frequent flyer miles that their passengers have patiently acquired. While you can likely get away with such an approach for a while, eventually your customers will notice and at that point may leave you.

A more stable approach to cutting back on costs involves what is known as *value-engineering*. Value-engineering is taking a close look at your products or services and eliminating or reducing those benefits that the customers do not really care about and which will allow you to reduce costs. For example, if health club customers rarely use certain pieces of equipment or if other equipment available provides the same type of workout, then it may be possible to remove that equipment.

## CURRENT CUSTOMERS/RELATED OR NEW PRODUCTS

You may grow your business by selling related or new products or services to your customers. Adding yoga classes to the health club would not be a stretch (sorry for that pun) and would be a related service; installing a juice bar would be a new service because it would require a number of new skills such as ordering beverages and storing them. For both related and new products or services, you must entice the target customer to try them.

## *Gain Product Trial*

Get them to try a new product or service for the first time. In the product trial, you need to inform customers that you are providing a new way to satisfy one or more of their needs and they may want to try it. If someone has not heard of pilates, for example, you may need to explain what it is and how it will help them with their fitness goals. Then they may be willing to sign up for your pilates class.

## *Gain Brand Trial*

Get them to try your version of a product or service for the first time. In the brand trial situation, your customers already know about the product or service. Your challenge is to convince them that your version of that product or service—your brand—is superior to other opportunities available to them. For example, you may point out the experience of your pilates instructors and introduce them to the customer so that they will feel comfortable with them.

## GROWING WITH RELATED OR NEW CUSTOMERS

Related customers are customers who resemble your current customers—to some extent. For illustration, if a health club caters mainly to professional men in their 30s and 40s, then related customers might be professional women in their 30s and 40s or perhaps men in their 20s or men in their 50s and 60s. While there are similarities between these markets, customers in each market likely have different needs.

New customers are customers who would be totally new to your organization. For the health club, young mothers with their babies or men or women in their 70s and 80s might represent markets with quite different needs from those you are familiar with.

## RELATED OR NEW
## CUSTOMERS/CURRENT PRODUCTS

Selling your current products or services to related or new customers is really a two-step process. First, you must get them to try your product or service. Then you would follow the same approaches described earlier for selling current products or services to current customers.

As an illustration of this two-step process, consider the health club. Suppose you wanted to sell an exercise program to young mothers with babies. First, you would want to explain to them why these services are important to them and why they might want to try the exercise programs at your health club. Once you have persuaded them to sign up at your health club, they become your current customers and all of the approaches for growth with current customers then apply.

Note that for customers who have just started their relationship with you, retention is absolutely crucial. In the first year, customer relationships tend to be very vulnerable, so it is important that special attention is paid to the newly signed-up customers and that relationships with them are managed well.

## RELATED OR NEW CUSTOMERS/RELATED OR NEW PRODUCTS

This growth focus is the most difficult of all to implement. Now you need both expertise on the customers in the related or new markets and expertise on the related or new products or services. This would be the situation where the health club owner is trying to interest men in their 80s in ballet classes. That example may be a bit extreme but it should make the point that with this situation you are trying to stretch your organization in two directions at the same time.

The process is the same as for related or new customers/current products. First you must persuade target customers to try the product or your version of the product. Then you approach them as "new" current customers.

Let's use the health club example one more time. Suppose you were trying to expand your business by offering martial arts classes to men in their 20s. You would learn about what those young men are looking for in martial arts by talking with some of them or by reading some of the magazines devoted to the martial arts. You would then consider what you would need to provide the martial arts classes—an instructor, equipment, sufficient space. When you are ready, you would need to contact young men who might be interested in such classes. Since they are not among your current customers, you would need to find ways to communicate with them. Perhaps you would use newspapers or handbills or pass the word among your current customers. For those who come to sign up for the course, you would then need to follow either a product trial or brand trial approach, depending on their prior knowledge of the martial arts. At some point, you would need to explain why your class would be superior to others. Those who enroll would then be "new" current customers and over time you would grow with them as you grow with any of your current customers.

## CONCLUSIONS

A growth plan must be implemented through your actions to change customers' behavior. That is called the *focus of the growth plan*. There are many possible focuses—some may be consistent with each other but others may conflict and even cancel each other. It is important for you to determine the focus for your growth plan to guide your actions and to evaluate the possible risks involved.

For review questions for this chapter, log on to www.trumpuniversity .com/marketing101.

# 15

---

# INCREASING YOUR
# CUSTOMER SATISFACTION

W hat is the one thing you need to have a business? Is it a product? A factory? A service? A license? Inventory? A location? Employees? The one thing you need to have a business is a *customer*. A customer is someone who thinks your product or service is worth paying for and who purchases it. Without customers, there is no revenue, no profits, and no cash flow and therefore no business. Satisfying your customers should be at the heart of your marketing efforts—although keep in mind you need to do so at a profit. Here are ways to increase your customers' satisfaction.

## HIERARCHY OF OBJECTIVES

The objectives of an organization (Exhibit 15.1) form a hierarchy and getting and keeping customers is the most fundamental objective. Customers provide revenue, profits, and cash flow that translate into value of the business. One of the founders of GE supposedly said to his salespeople, "I don't care if you burn down the factory, don't be rude to a customer." The point, of course, was that you can always rebuild a factory; you may never regain a customer who is lost.

## CUSTOMER SATISFACTION: TRUMP INTERNATIONAL HOTEL & TOWER, NEW YORK CITY

Trump International Lobby, at Trump International Hotel & Tower, New York City.
Photo courtesy of the Trump Organization.

This story, related by Tom Downing, general manager of the New York City Trump International Hotel & Tower, shows the power—and responsibility—of having highly regarded and appreciated customer service.

Our concierge received a call late one night from a guest who was distraught over having lost a shopping bag containing something very dear to him . . . so dear, that he could not travel without it. He had checked into the hotel moments before, and remembered having the bag last at the airport. The concierge alerted me and I called the airport Lost and Found Department. They knew nothing, and could find nothing. I was not going to take no for an answer because my guest was truly upset over losing this bag and I felt that something more could be done. I headed to the airport myself, to the same terminal and baggage claim area where the guest had been a short while before. I asked the Lost and Found Department manager for help and again, they had nothing to offer. I started looking around and there, lying by a garbage can, was an old plastic bag that matched the description the guest had given me. Inside was the item that held great sentimental value—an old teddy bear! I brought it back to the hotel and returned it to the guest who was so appreciative, tears were running down his face.

To provide great service, you need a culture that values great service—and that starts at the top of your organization. If you value and expect and reward great service, your people will give it.

**Exhibit 15.1   Hierarchy of Objectives**

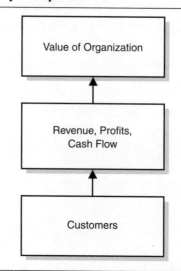

*Source:* "Arrow Guide—The Marketing Challenge," The Arrow Group, Ltd.®, New York, 2004. Used with permission.

## CUSTOMER-DRIVEN ORGANIZATIONS

Organizations that understand the key role of customers in their success are known as customer-driven organizations.

In a *customer-driven organization*, decisions are made based on the knowledge of customer needs and expectations and on the impact of those decisions on the organization-customer relationship.

## CUSTOMER SATISFACTION AND FINANCIAL PERFORMANCE

There are many management gurus who advocate that you should always satisfy customers—or always *delight* them. That is a noble sentiment but the gurus haven't gotten it quite right.

You should always strive to satisfy or delight customers—but *at a profit*. The easiest way for you to satisfy customers is to give them everything they want—at a discount—then provide liberal credit. If you do that, you will likely not stay in business—and therefore in the long run you will not satisfy your customers since you will not be around anymore.

> **You should always strive to satisfy or delight customers—but *at a profit*.**

If you never say no to a customer, as pointed out in Chapters 10 and 11, then you do not have a strategy—no clear target market and no clear positioning. It is also true that if you never say no to a customer, then you may go out of business.

Your decisions regarding what you give to your customers always involve a trade-off between the added perceived value you provide the customer and the added costs you assume. If the additional perceived value you are providing is less than the added cost, then the organization is actually reducing its contribution to society, should go out of business, and eventually will.

Yes, being customer-driven is delighting customers—but do so at a profit.

## How to Increase Customer Satisfaction

Customer-driven organizations can manage customer satisfaction by following my COPS model: *Culture; Organization; Process; Strategy. Culture* consists of the fundamental values of your organization. *Organization* refers to how your organization is structured to support customer satisfying efforts. *Process* is the way you deal with customers. *Strategy* concerns the way you make decisions that have an impact on your customers.

## Culture

Make customer satisfaction everyone's responsibility. If your organization is customer-driven, then *everyone* in your organization is committed to satisfying customers (at a profit). That includes the CEO. When Lou Gerstner took the top job at IBM, he made it clear that he would be the sales representative for five customers and sent a very clear message to all those in the organization regarding the importance of customers to IBM. For many years, ARA-MARK has had what they called the 20/20 rule—that every manager at every level of the company had to know the top 20 customers in their area and the top 20 potential customers in their area. Top executives in some banks and airlines are required each year to spend time in positions that bring them into contact with customers.

If your highest level managers show that they consider customers to be important, then your organization is likely to be customer-driven. However, if your highest level managers do not show attention to customers, then your organization is likely not to be customer-driven.

Once when I was the first person getting on an aircraft, I heard one of the attendants exclaim, "Here come the animals." For that attendant, passengers were a nuisance and it is very likely that that attitude carried over into how the attendant dealt with passengers during the flight. Members of an organization must show *respect* for customers—not thinly disguised contempt (TDC). One study showed that nearly 70 percent of customers quit being customers because of the attitudes of those employees serving customers.

Sanity Music, a chain in Australia, doubled their market share in just two years and earned more than $1.50 more per CD than their competitors due in part to the enthusiasm of their staff. Ticket takers at the Disney theme parks receive hours of instruction about treating park visitors— guests—before they begin work. What type of training do you give your customer servers?

Members of customer-driven organizations need to have what Tom Peters has called a "passion for perfection." *Passion for perfection* is a concern to get things right and get them right the first time. A dry cleaner who will not return clothing with stains or missing buttons or an accountant who reminds the client when to submit his or her tax forms can have a passion for perfection. Buck Rogers, former head of sales at IBM, believed that in customer-driven organizations, employees dealing with customers must have "thoughtfulness, courtesy, and integrity." In short, they must treat customers the same way that they would like to be treated.

## ORGANIZATION

Make it easy to satisfy customers. If you are the person who deals with customers face-to-face or even on the telephone or Internet, you have a hard job. When customers have something to say to you, it often will concern a problem, and, if you are not able to help, the situation may become even more unpleasant. That is why customer-oriented organizations *empower* their employees to solve their customer's problems.

British Air has gone to enormous lengths to provide their customer servers with power to solve customers' problems such as lost baggage or mishandled reservations. They can provide customers with gifts, upgrades, and other favors to help preserve their relationship. United Airlines allows flight attendants to recommend that passengers receive flight certificates or frequent flyer miles in reparation for problems encountered during flights such as videos or headphones that do not work.

Empowerment also raises employee morale. Employee morale in turn affects customers. Marriott has found that a 10 percent reduction in employee turnover reduced customer defections by 1 percent to 3 percent and raised revenues by millions of dollars.

Customers need to be able to *communicate* with customer servers, but some organizations make that communication very difficult. One oxymoronic phrase in customer service is what some organizations have on their automated customer response systems: "Your call is very important to us." That statement is usually followed with: "All customer servers are busy working with other customers." The question is: If the call is so important to them, why don't they have more customer servers working?

Dealing with customers requires skills and that means customer servers need *training*. USAA, a large insurance company highly regarded for their customer service, often leads their industry in the percentage of their budget spent on training.

Certainly the customer servers must understand the organization's products, services, and policies, but there are many other dimensions to dealing with customers—the human dimensions. In particular, customer servers must know how to listen and how to empathize with customers with problems. Customer servers need be trained in how to manage upset people. In some organizations, the newest and least experienced employees answer the complaint line. The employees on the complaint line should be highly trained and experienced in dealing with difficult situations.

Customer-driven organizations reward employees who satisfy customers. The rewards may be recognition such as "Employee of the Month" or bonuses. (Note that Employee of the Month parking spaces may be counterproductive if they displace customer parking places.) Nordstrom's has established a Hall of Fame for acts of great customer service.

For rewards to be effective, you must publicize them. Customer-oriented organizations spotlight those who perform well with customers. They also disseminate information as to how well the organization is serving customers by publishing information on customer ratings and other measures of customer performance.

## PROCESS

Establish systems to support customer satisfaction. To manage customer satisfaction, you need to *stay close* to customers. You may have heard the old story of the organization that did away with its complaint line because too many customers were complaining! Customer-driven organizations talk to their customers and listen to them. Communication may be informal. If you are running a health club, it is easy and natural to talk to your customers and ask them how they like (or don't like) the club. Or focus groups or surveys may be used. Xerox is known for regularly surveying its customers. The main point is that the communication takes place on a regular basis.

When your customers complain, they are telling you that the relationship can still be saved. Most unhappy customers do not complain—they simply take their business elsewhere. When you do not hear from your customers and then do not see them, you know you are in trouble.

Processes need to be designed from the *customers' viewpoint*, not from the viewpoint of the organization. Many years ago, the only way to buy a ticket to a Broadway show in New York City was to go to the theater and purchase the tickets with cash. That process had a lot of advantages to the theater but was relatively difficult for the theatergoer—and consequently probably discouraged some potential customers from ever going to the theater. For many years, retail banks in the United States closed at 3 P.M.—what were known as "bankers' hours." Again the process had been designed to make things easier for the banks but that made it more difficult for the customers.

Organizations should look for *best practices* and benchmark on the best performers for whatever they do, including managing the relationships with their customers. Many organizations have been cited for high performance on customer satisfaction—Southwest Airlines and USAA insurance, for example. Managers should identify those organizations that best satisfy customers and try to learn from them.

*Communications* with customers must be in both directions. Hearing their opinions is very important, but it is also important to talk to them and let them know what is happening. Airlines have often done a poor job of not explaining situations to passengers when flights are delayed. One of the jokes shared among passengers of the New York City subway system is the public address system—when there is a problem on the line, the sound quality of the communications equipment is so bad it is usually impossible to understand what the problem is and when it will be fixed.

There are many ways to communicate with customers—in person, of course, but also through newsletters and e-mails.

## STRATEGY

Focus efforts on customer satisfaction. Jan Carlzon's book, *Moments of Truth*, clearly set forth the idea that if customer satisfaction is not the focus of an organization, then the organization may fail.[1] The "moments of truth" to which he referred were all the *points of contact* that his airline, SAS, had with customers—when reservations were made, when customers checked in, when they retrieved their baggage. He pointed out that if SAS did not win these moments of truth, then their planes would be empty.

A marketing strategy must have the *customer at the center* to be successful. The two strategic components of a marketing plan are the target market and the positioning. These two decisions are closely interlinked. Selecting a target market identifies customers and their needs. Customer needs then determine the positioning (key benefits) required to satisfy them. In customer-oriented organizations, the target market and positioning decisions are made with care and thoughtfulness, not by expediency. Wendy's has a customer focus in their marketing strategy. They were first among U.S. fast-food chains to launch entrée salads and among the first to have extended hours and improved nutritional information—all part of their customer-centered strategy.[2]

---

**A marketing strategy must have the *customer at the center* to be successful.**

---

Over time, all organizations need new customers. However, for many organizations the real problem is *retaining current customers*. Revenue, profitability, and cash flow are all extraordinarily sensitive to customer retention rates. Customer-oriented organizations understand this and focus on doing things to retain customers. At Master Care Auto Service, employees who kept customers loyal received a bonus that could be as much as 10 percent of their salary.

In the Rocks section of Sydney, Australia, is a restaurant called Wolfie's Grill, that I have gone to over many years. The view of the Harbour Bridge is spectacular but that's not why I continue to go there. I go for the service. The first time I went there one of our sons was only a year old and rather finicky. Wolfie's chef produced a meal our boy would eat and the waitstaff didn't seem to mind the clean-up afterward. Since then I have returned often and always found their service delightful—even over many changes in managers. What is that consistency worth? A lot.

A focus on retaining customers brings in new customers as well. The habits you need to keep your customers are exactly the habits that you need to attract new customers. Plus positive word-of-mouth from your current customers is probably more effective than any advertising you could devise to persuade new customers to try your product or service. I have recommended Wolfie's to many friends and relatives when they visit Australia.

Customer satisfaction is linked to revenue, profits, and cash flow through perceived value. Therefore, it is a *leading indicator* for the financial performance of an organization and must be monitored. The monitoring can be done directly with surveys or indirectly with operations measures (e.g., process times, number of complaints), but monitoring must be done to provide the organization with steering control. When Swissair surveyed their passengers, they expected good or excellent ratings to be close to 100 percent. (See Chapter 27 for more on how to survey your customers.)

## CONCLUSIONS

Customers are the source of all your financial returns—your revenue, profits, and cash flow. Therefore, they are also the source of shareholder value. Satisfying customers—at a profit—should be a major objective of any organization if it is to have success over time.

For review questions for this chapter and for a test as to how well your organization satisfies customers, log on to www.trumpuniversity.com/marketing101.

# III

## IMPLEMENTING YOUR STRATEGY

# 16

---

# PRODUCT/SERVICE DESIGN

Good design, from a marketing perspective, means tailoring your product or service so that it successfully meets the needs of your target customers. A sales-oriented organization "sells what they make" while a marketing-oriented organization "makes what will sell." The difference between the two is design.

In this chapter, you learn how to systematically evaluate your design compared to those of your competitors and how you can determine the ways you can make the design of your product or service more attractive to your target customers.

## DESIGN AND CUSTOMERS

In a sales-oriented organization, the product or service is developed with minimal attention paid to the needs of the customer in the target market. Consequently, a lot of sales effort is typically needed to sell the product or service if in fact it can be sold at all.

In a marketing-oriented organization, before the product or service is developed, information on customer needs is gathered *from the customers themselves*. Then the product or service is designed to meet those needs.

## KNOWING WHAT YOUR CUSTOMERS WANT: CASINO VIP

Virginia McDowell, executive vice president of Trump Entertainment Resorts, provides a classic example of the need to understand customers and what is important to them. There was a very high-end table customer who used to visit a Trump casino in Atlantic City on junkets—private flights that are scheduled for customers who usually stay overnight. He would spend as much time in the casino as possible, often taking only a quick break for a meal before he returned to the gaming floor. He was always booked into one of most luxurious suites in the hotel when he came to visit, and no expense was spared to make him feel welcome. So the management of the property was surprised and concerned when he started taking his business to a competitor in Atlantic City. After several meetings between the player development staff, casino and hotel operations, and the food and beverage managers, none of the executives could identify anything that could have caused this valuable customer to defect. So they finally decided to ask him, and they were shocked by the response.

The customer explained that he didn't get to Atlantic City very often, and when he did, he came to play. So while he appreciated the luxuri-

A Trump Casino Suite.
Photo courtesy of the Trump Organization.

ous suite, he felt that it was wasted on him because he really only used the suite to grab a couple of hours of sleep, take a shower, and then return to the casino. And while the suite was wonderful, and the view was incredible, and fresh flowers in the room were a welcoming touch, what he really wanted were just two things—a comfortable bed and fluffy towels. And while he was fine with the quality of the bed, it was his opinion that the quality of the towels was inferior. So he took his considerable business to a competitor smart enough to appreciate the importance of this detail in a suite. The situation was addressed very quickly by the property, and the customer returned. And the management team learned a valuable lesson—never assume. The best way to find out what is important to customers is to ask them.

Some of the most infamous disasters in the history of marketing—Ford's Edsel, RCA's Videodisc, Polaroid's Polavision, Northrup's Tigershark—all shared the same mistake: lack of attention to customer needs in the design process. The Edsel deserves special mention. While customer research was done, it was conducted several years before the automobile was introduced, and by then customer needs had changed. That shows how difficult marketing can be. Customers are moving targets, and product or service design must consider not only the current needs of the current customer, but the future needs of the future customer.

## DETERMINING DESIGN

You need to bring customers into your design deliberations by considering what they expect to obtain from your product or service and comparing those expectations to what you and your competitors are currently providing. You can do that systematically with a Design Analysis (Exhibit 16.1). The steps in the process are:

- Select a target segment.
- Select a target member of the decision-making unit.
- List the main competitors.
- List the benefits associated with the product or service.
- Estimate the relative importance of each benefit to your target customer.

**Downloadable Exhibit 16.1    Design Analysis Chart—Soap Example**
**Target Customers: Women, 35–50 Years Old\***

| | | Offerings | | | | | |
| | | | | Competitors | | | |
| Relative Importance | Benefits Sought | Target Customers | Organization | Q | R | S | T |
| | | Expected | Actual | Actual | Actual | Actual | Actual |
| 9 | Moisturizes | 5 | 3 | 4 | 2 | 5 | 1 |
| 9 | Cleans | 5 | 4 | 2 | 3 | 2 | 5 |
| 6 | Scent | 3 | 4 | 2 | 3 | 4 | 1 |
| 3 | Size | 3 | 3 | 3 | 2 | 4 | 4 |

Possible Design Gap

*Note:* Relative importance 1—Not important, 10—Very important
Performance ratings: 1—Weak, 5—Strong

*Source:* "Arrow Guide—Design Analysis," Copyright © 2004, The Arrow Group, Ltd.®, New York. Used with permission. ***A blank version of this page can be downloaded from www.trumpuniversity.com/marketing101 and customized for your personal use.*** For any other use, contact Don Sexton at Marketing101@thearrowgroup.com.

- Estimate the performance for each benefit expected by the target customer.
- Evaluate the actual performance of your organization and each competitor on each benefit.

> **You need to bring customers into your design deliberations by considering what they expect to obtain from your product or service and comparing those expectations to what you and your competitors are currently providing.**

This analysis builds on the results of an Actual Value Analysis (discussed in Chapter 6) by adding information as to what your target customer expects as regards the performance on each benefit.

## DESIGN ANALYSIS—SOAP EXAMPLE

Suppose you have developed a soap that you would like to market to 35- to 50-year-old women. You have done some research by asking women in that age range what benefits they would like in a soap, how important they are, and, on a 1 to 5 scale, how would their ideal soap score on each benefit. You have also looked at some competing brands of soap to see what they offer.

Compared to the Actual Value Analysis (Chapter 6), the new information in this analysis is what level of performance for each benefit does your target customer want and expect. These would be *ideal values*—what your customers hope to receive from your product or service. You find out these expectations by asking customers—either in person or through surveys.

Again, all information regarding benefits, priorities, perceived values, and expected values, if at all possible, must come from the customers themselves. You can start the analysis with your own opinions but it is very important to check your opinions with those of your customers. When there is a conflict, use your customers' opinions.

Exhibit 16.1 shows that your target customers have high expectations regarding performance of those benefits of most importance to them—moisturizes and cleans. You need to compare your actual performance to these expectations to see if you might be successful with this group of customers. If their expectations are different from the actual value you provide them, then there are *design gaps* that you may want to consider filling. For example,

---

 ## PRODUCT DESIGN: LifeSavers

Product design must be based on what your customers want. That's why LifeSavers candy asked consumers to vote on which flavors should be included in a five-flavor roll. The choices included the traditional flavors, pineapple, cherry, orange, lemon, and lime, and new flavors, raspberry, watermelon, blackberry, tangerine, mango, and melon/tangerine. The winners: Pineapple, cherry, raspberry, watermelon, and blackberry. Andrew Burke of Kraft Foods explained: "We said, 'Let's give [the customers] a chance to voice their opinion and help us pick the new face for a classic.' . . . Tastes change, and everything else changes."

*Source:* "LifeSavers Introduces New Candy Flavors," *National Petroleum News,* vol. 95 (October 2003), p. 11.

---

Exhibit 16.1 shows that your actual performance on both moisturizes and cleans falls short of the expectations of these target customers. You may want to reformulate your soap to better meet their needs. If your performance does not meet your customers' expectations *and* there is a competitor that is more successful in meeting their expectations, if you do nothing, you can expect your customer base to shrink.

---

**If your performance does not meet your customers' expectations and there is a competitor that is more successful in meeting their expectations, if you do nothing, you can expect your customer base to shrink.**

---

## PRODUCT SPACE

You can also detect design gaps by plotting the information in Exhibit 16.1 on a graph of what is known as product or service space (Exhibit 16.2). Each axis refers to a different benefit and shows how each competitor performs on that benefit. Usually you begin by plotting the positions of your organization and those of your competitors on the two most important benefits to your target customers. If there are other benefits you feel you need to examine, simply make a new graphs with those pairs of benefits. There are ways to place more than two benefits on the same graph but they are rather cumbersome. It's usually easier to graph just two benefits at a time and develop as many graphs as needed.

Besides the positions of your organization and those of your competitors, you also locate the expected values for your target customers on the benefits. This point is known as the *ideal point* because it should describe the product or service that these customers would like to purchase. If you have the position closest to the ideal point for customers in a given segment then you should be able to win that segment—*if* that benefit is important to the target customer and *if* the customer accurately perceives your performance on that benefit.

## PRODUCT SPACE—SOAP EXAMPLE

In Exhibits 16.2 and 16.3, you can see how your soap compares to both what 35- to 50-year-old women want and what your competitors provide.

**Exhibit 16.2  Product or Service Space—Soap: Benefits 1 and 2**

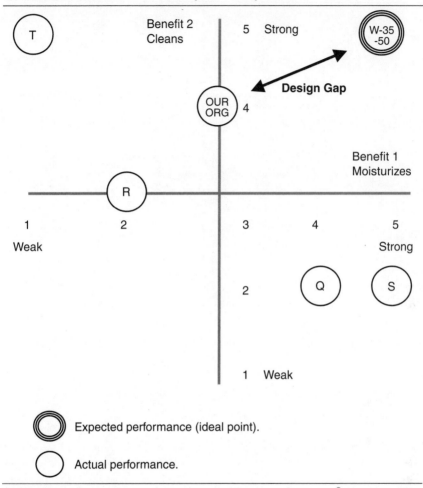

Expected performance (ideal point).

Actual performance.

*Source:* "Arrow Guide—Product Space Analysis," The Arrow Group, Ltd.®, New York, 2004. Used with permission.

In Exhibit 16.2, overall your soap is closer to your target market's ideal point than any other competitor. There are two competitors, Q and S, that do better than you do on the "moisturizes" benefit but are not as good on the "cleans" benefit. You may want to consider filling your design gaps on both the "moisturizes" and "cleans" gap if it is possible—especially because competitors Q and S might be trying to improve their performance in regard to cleaning.

**Exhibit 16.3   Product or Service Space—Soap: Benefits 3 and 4**

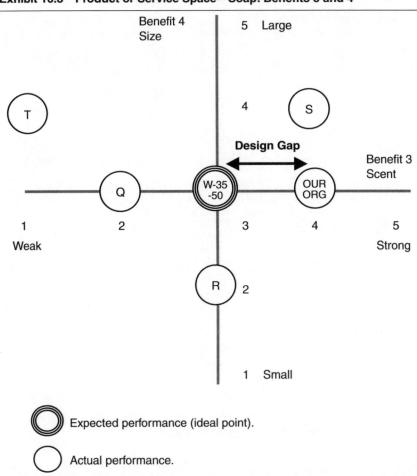

*Source:* "Arrow Guide—Product Space Analysis," The Arrow Group, Ltd.®, New York, 2004. Used with permission.

The less important benefits are shown in Exhibit 16.3. You do reasonably well but could improve your position by cutting back on the scent in your soap.

## PRODUCT SPACE—OTHER SEGMENTS

The product space analysis can be expanded to help you evaluate whether you would like to try to design your product or service to appeal to other market segments. To do that you would add to your graph the ideal points for the customers in the other segments.

For example, Exhibit 16.4 includes the ideal point for 20- to 34-year-old men who might have higher expectations for the cleaning power of a soap and not care much about moisturizing. Competitor T seems targeted toward them.

You can do one more thing with the product space graph that will help you decide the positioning for your organization. You can make the areas of

**Exhibit 16.4   Product or Service Space—Soap: Other Market Segment**

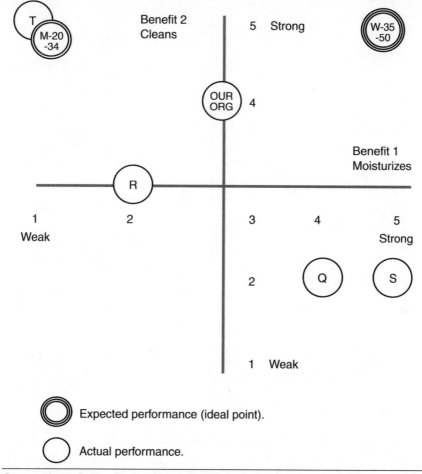

*Source:* "Arrow Guide—Product Space Analysis," The Arrow Group, Ltd.®, New York, 2004. Used with permission.

the circles showing the segment ideal points larger or smaller depending on the size of that market segment.

In Exhibit 16.5, the market consisting of 35- to 50-year-old women is shown as larger than the market consisting of 20- to 34-year-old men. While size is not the only characteristic that makes a market attractive, the difference in sizes of the segments might persuade you to continue to target your

**Exhibit 16.5   Product or Service Space—Soap: Size of Market Segments**

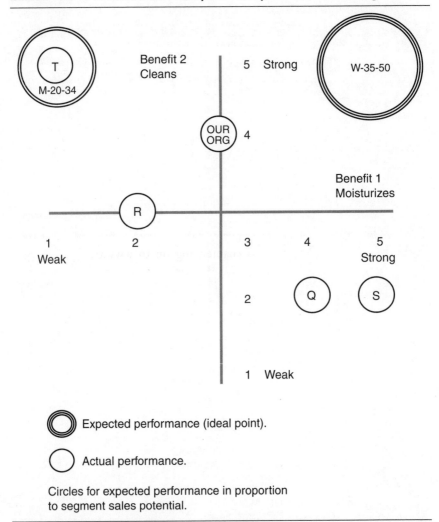

Expected performance (ideal point).

Actual performance.

Circles for expected performance in proportion to segment sales potential.

*Source:* "Arrow Guide—Product Space Analysis," The Arrow Group, Ltd.®, New York, 2004. Used with permission.

soap to women although you might consider developing another soap for men at some other time.

## DESIGN DECISIONS

The Design Analysis and Product Space Analysis described in this chapter can provide you with ideas as to how you might tailor your product or service to various target markets. Whether you should do so or not depends on both the cost of making the design changes and how much you will change customers' perceived value and consequently demand for your product or service by doing so. You can estimate those effects with the techniques discussed in Chapter 5 on "Perceived Value," and/or with statistical techniques such as conjoint analysis.

## CONCLUSIONS

Design focuses on how well your product or service meets customer needs. To make design decisions effectively requires an understanding of customer needs and customer response and also an understanding of the costs of making changes in your product or service.

For review questions for this chapter, log on to www.trumpuniversity .com/marketing101.

# 17

## INTEGRATING CUSTOMER COMMUNICATIONS

You can communicate with members of your target markets in a variety of ways: advertising, brand identifiers, sales promotion, personal selling, and public relations.

All the communications aimed at a member of your target market should be consistent and deliver the same message. If they are uncoordinated, the messages from different communications approaches will be less effective and might even cancel each other. That is why you need an integrated communications strategy, one that looks at all your contacts with your target customers.

> **All the communications aimed at a member of your target market should be consistent and deliver the same message.**

Coordinating communications requires you to look horizontally—at all your communications programs. In later chapters, you look at specific forms of communications. In this chapter, you look at them all at once.

## ESTABLISHING AN INTEGRATED COMMUNICATIONS STRATEGY

The idea of an integrated communications strategy is really straightforward. It requires some work to put one together, but it is not that difficult in concept. It is easier to construct an integrated communications strategy in a small organization than in a large organization, but it still requires work and attention to detail.

In large organizations, often the primary barrier to developing an integrated communications strategy is the structure of the organization. Branding efforts may be managed separately from product or service advertising and sales promotion. Managers who manage product or service advertising and promotion may not work closely with managers who manage the sales force. And often the public relations managers may not even report to or talk much with anyone in the marketing area.

To build an integrated communications strategy requires someone to look horizontally—across the organization—at all the ways the organization communicates with the target customer. Those are known as the *touch points*. That individual must coordinate these touch points and have the power or influence to ensure that any needed coordination takes place. In a small organization, that individual may be the owner, the business manager, or the marketing manager.

## RELATIONSHIP BETWEEN MARKETING STRATEGY AND COMMUNICATIONS STRATEGIES

Strategies for most communications typically consist of:

- *Target market:* The intended audience for the communications.
- *Communications objectives:* What a member of the intended audience should think, feel, or do as a result of the communications.
- *Tactics:* The specifics of that communications approach which usually includes message, media, and effort (or expenditure).

Communications strategies are integrated—directly or indirectly—by three major components of the product/market strategy (Exhibit 17.1): target market, business objectives, and positioning. Note that as the strategy for a

**Exhibit 17.1 Linkages between Product/Market and Communications Strategies**

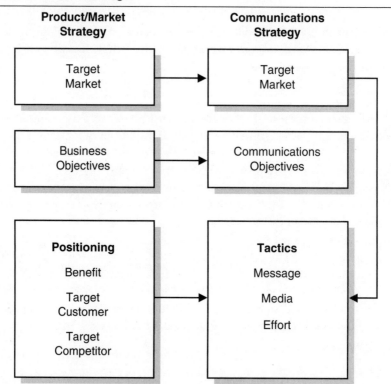

Source: "Arrow Guide—Advertising Decisions," The Arrow Group, Ltd.®, New York, 2004. Used with permission.

specific market may need to change over time, the business objectives and positioning will change and therefore you will need to change your communications strategies for that market as well.

## Target Market

Before you communicate anything, you need to know to whom you want to talk. That would be the members of your target market. The target market will influence the choice of communications media used—whether it be print, broadcast, outdoor, the Internet, or nontraditional advertising such as events. Similarly, promotions and public relations need to be directed at the members of your target market.

The target market also affects selling efforts. Sales representatives need to be directed or given incentives to call on customers in the target markets. Such guidance may be especially important for new salespeople who do not have a clear idea of the target customers.

If possible, communications should be directed not only at a target market but at a specific member of the decision-making unit within the target market. That is what salespeople do, for example, communicating with purchasing agents or design engineers differently. Some advertisers do direct their advertising to individual members of the decision-making unit, such as men, women, or children, rather than broadly to market segments.

## Business Objectives

Objectives of the product/market strategy will typically include revenue, market share, profit, and cash flow. All of these objectives are achieved only if the target customers take action—purchase for the first time, purchase again, or purchase more (Exhibit 17.2).

You must state your communications objectives in terms of actions by the target customers. For example, if you want to increase your market share, then you must persuade customers to try your product or brand. If you want to increase your cash flow, you might try to persuade your customers to use more of your product or service.

---

**You must state your communications objectives in terms of actions by the target customers.**

---

**Exhibit 17.2   Business Objectives and Possible Communications Objectives**

| Business Objectives | Market share | Profitability | Cash flow |
|---|---|---|---|
| Communications Objectives | Product trial<br>Brand trial<br>Brand shift | Brand shift<br>Repurchase<br>Increase usage<br>Model shift | Repurchase<br>Increase usage<br>Model shift |

*Source:* "Arrow Guide—Advertising Decisions," The Arrow Group, Ltd.®, New York, 2004. Used with permission.

However, before the customers take action, they may go through *intermediate objectives* such as awareness of your product or service, knowledge, liking, preference, and conviction to buy (Exhibit 17.3).

While the order of these intermediate objectives varies by product or service, they should also be included in your communications objectives. You must decide which communications approaches will be used to achieve which objectives with the target customer. For example, some years ago Northwest Mutual Life Insurance used their magazine advertising to make target customers aware of the benefits of their product, then used their agents to make the actual sale of the policy.

For products such as frequently purchased consumer products, advertising may be called on to accomplish all of the communications objectives. However, for many products and services, especially consumer durables and business-to-business products, advertising may be focused on intermediate objectives such as awareness or knowledge, while the sales force may be responsible for persuading the customer to make the purchase.

Using more than one communications approach to move the target customer to make a purchase is like "passing the baton" in a relay race. At one

**Exhibit 17.3  Communications Objectives**

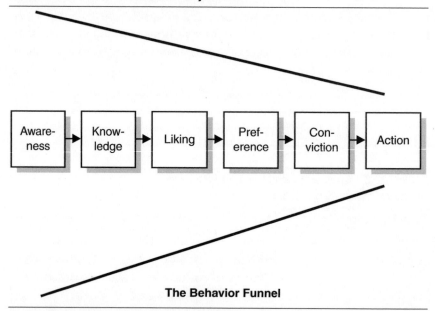

**The Behavior Funnel**

Source: "Arrow Guide—Advertising Decisions," The Arrow Group, Ltd.®, New York, 2004. Used with permission.

point Northwest Mutual Life Insurance decided to spend a considerable amount of money as a major sponsor of the Summer Olympic Games. As a consequence, they had little money left for a print advertising campaign. Right after the Olympics, they had created a huge amount of awareness for their insurance policies. The problem was that they did not have enough agents to follow up immediately on all the leads that had been generated. Because there was little budget for print ads to maintain that awareness, many of those leads could not be pursued immediately. They learned from that experience and are now very effective in managing their communications mix.

You need to coordinate all the objectives *across* all the communications approaches being used to influence the customer to buy. If there is no coordination, then there can be too much effort on one communications approach or not enough on another.

## Positioning

All the contact points with the customer must have the same message. If not, the customer can become confused. The message comes from your positioning choice.

One telecommunications company launched a corporate advertising campaign without any input from the sales force. The result was a campaign that was beautiful (it featured close-up photography of flowers and spider webs) but had—in the words of one sales manager—"no hook my people can use to make the sale." The hook to which the manager was referring was some benefit that the salespeople could mention during the sales call so that the corporate advertising would help prepare the target customer for the sale.

Your positioning must be repeatedly reinforced by a message that is consistent across all your means of communications with your target customer.

## Determining Communications Message

You can determine what should be your main communications message by comparing the actual performance on benefits with what your target customers perceive to be your performance on those benefits.

If your target customer does not perceive all the value you are actually providing on a given benefit, that is a *communications gap* that you must fill—especially if the benefit is very important to that target customer. Experienced salespeople discover communications gaps by asking customers probing questions during their sales call. Then they provide their customers with information to close those gaps.

You can find those communications gaps by systematically comparing your actual performance on benefits with the performance as perceived by your target customers by utilizing a Communications Analysis. The steps include:

- Select a target segment.
- Select a target member of the decision-making unit.
- List the main competitors.
- List the benefits associated with the product or service.
- Estimate the relative importance of each benefit to your target customer.
- Estimate the performance on each benefit expected by the target customer.
- Estimate the performance of your organization and each competitor on each benefit as *perceived* by the target customer.
- Evaluate the actual performance of your organization and each competitor on each benefit.

Besides being used to identify the key messages to be included in an overall communications campaign, the Communications Analysis can also be employed by sales managers to help sales representatives—especially those with less experience—develop their initial benefit statement (their opening statement to a customer).

## COMMUNICATIONS ANALYSIS—SOAP EXAMPLE

To complete Exhibit 17.4, you must estimate not only your actual performance and those of your competitors on each benefit, but also what your target customers perceive to be your performance on each benefit. You need to talk to your customers or survey them to obtain this information. However, if you do not have much time and money for customer research, you can begin by making your own subjective estimates. But you should try to validate as much information as you can by contacting customers.

In Exhibit 17.4, you can see that you do not have any communication gaps on scent and size benefits. However, there are important communications gaps on the two most important benefits. Your soap scores a 3 on its actual performance on cleans but the customer gives it only a 2. Worse, your

**Downloadable Exhibit 17.4  Communication Chart**
**Target Customers: Women, 35–50 Years Old***

| Relative Importance | Benefits Sought | Target Customers | Organization | | Offerings Competitors | | | | | | | |
|---|---|---|---|---|---|---|---|---|---|---|---|---|
| | | | | | Q | | R | | S | | T | |
| | | Expected | A | P | A | P | A | P | A | P | A | P |
| 9 | Moisturizes | 5 | 3 | 2 | 4 | 4 | 2 | 2 | 5 | 5 | 1 | 1 |
| 9 | Cleans | 5 | 4 | 1 | 2 | 2 | 3 | 2 | 2 | 3 | 5 | 5 |
| 6 | Scent | 3 | 4 | 4 | 2 | 2 | 3 | 4 | 4 | 5 | 1 | 1 |
| 3 | Size | 3 | 3 | 3 | 3 | 3 | 2 | 2 | 4 | 4 | 4 | 4 |

Possible Communication Gaps

*Note*: A—Actual value of benefit, P—Perceived value of benefit
Relative importance: 1—Not important, 10—Very important
Performance ratings: 1—Weak, 5—Strong

*Source:* "Arrow Guide—Communication Analysis," Copyright © 2004, The Arrow Group, Ltd.®, New York. Used with permission. ***A blank version of this page can be downloaded from www.trumpuniversity.com/marketing101 and customized for your personal use.*** For any other use, contact Don Sexton at Marketing101@thearrowgroup.com.

soap scores a 4 on its actual performance on moisturizes but the customer gives it only a 1.

Even though your design is somewhat close to what your target consumer wants on cleans and on moisturizes, she perceives your performance as inferior to what it actually is. You must make sure that your message focuses on your performance regarding cleans and moisturizes if you expect to win this target market.

Exhibits 17.5 and 17.6 show this same information in product space. When perceived measures are graphed on product space, it is called a *perceptual map*.

Despite your design being the closest to your target segment's ideal point for cleans and moisturizes, from the point of view of their perceptions, it is the furthest away from the ideal point. *Customers behave according to their perceptions, not according to the actual values.* A first priority would be to improve your communications campaign so that customers will realize the value you are providing them and will purchase your product.

## ASSEMBLING THE INTEGRATED
## COMMUNICATIONS STRATEGY

Given your target market, your business objectives, and your desired message, you can now put together your overall communications strategy. At the

**Exhibit 17.5 Product or Service Space—Soap: Benefits 1 and 2**

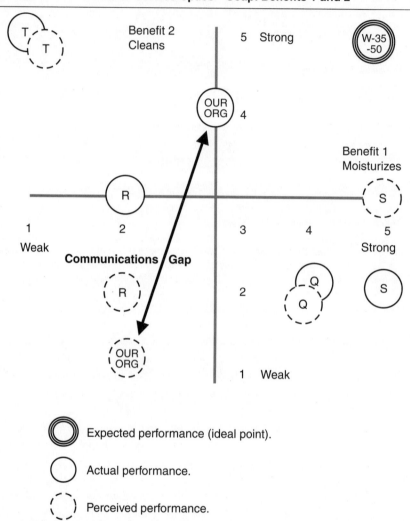

*Source:* "Arrow Guide—Product Space Analysis," The Arrow Group, Ltd.®, New York, 2004. Used with permission.

top of the worksheet shown in Exhibit 17.7 is the summary of the objectives and message for your communications.

The remainder of the worksheet shows the major forms of communication. You would need to decide which communications methods you would use for each of your communications objectives. The message would likely be

**Exhibit 17.6   Product or Service Space—Soap: Benefits 3 and 4**

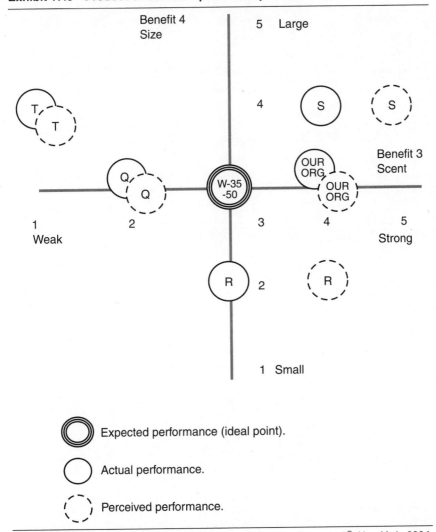

*Source:* "Arrow Guide—Product Space Analysis," The Arrow Group, Ltd.®, New York, 2004. Used with permission.

the same for each method. The media choices would be made as you develop the strategies for each of the communications methods. The effort or budget would also be determined at that time.

Finally, the budgets you set for each communication method in each time period would be totaled to give the overall communications budget for each time period.

**Downloadable Exhibit 17.7   Integrated Communications Strategy\***

Target Segment: _____ Target Decision-Making Unit Member: _____

| Communications | Tactics | Time Period | | | |
|---|---|---|---|---|---|
| | | 1 | 2 | 3 | 4 |
| Overall communications | Objectives | | | | |
| | Message | | | | |
| | Effort | | | | |
| Advertising | Objectives | | | | |
| | Message | | | | |
| | Media | | | | |
| | Effort | | | | |
| Identifiers | Objectives | | | | |
| | Message | | | | |
| | Media | | | | |
| | Effort | | | | |
| Promotion | Objectives | | | | |
| | Message | | | | |
| | Method | | | | |
| | Effort | | | | |
| Personal selling | Objectives | | | | |
| | Message | | | | |
| | Contact | | | | |
| | Effort | | | | |
| Public relations | Objectives | | | | |
| | Message | | | | |
| | Method | | | | |
| | Effort | | | | |

*Source:* "Arrow Guide—Advertising Decisions," Copyright © 2004, The Arrow Group, Ltd.®, New York. Used with permission. *A blank version of this page can be downloaded from www.trumpuniversity.com/marketing101 and customized for your personal use.* For any other use, contact Don Sexton at Marketing101@thearrowgroup.com.

## CONCLUSIONS

Your organization needs to speak with one voice. That is what an integrated communications strategy does for you. It ensures that the message is the same across all contact points with the customer. It also makes sure that the communications objectives support the business objectives over time.

For review questions for this chapter, log on to www.trumpuniversity.com/marketing101.

# 18

---

## ADVERTISING

There are many ways to communicate with the customers in your target market. Advertising is the most visible and pervasive.

Many people seem to feel that advertising has the power to make people buy something and that this power is rather easy to exert. While advertising can persuade, you need an advertising strategy that is well thought-out and one that has sufficient financial support if you are going to move people to buy or take some other action. In this chapter, you learn how to develop an effective advertising strategy for your product or service. The key word—as usual—will be *focus*, focus on target customers and focus on positioning.

### ROLE OF COMMUNICATIONS

Communications of any type—advertising, personal selling, public relations—play a similar *role* in the marketing strategy.

Communicate the benefit advantage to target members of the decision-making unit in the target market so that they will act. A product or service may have the most attractive positioning you can imagine, but if the customer does not know that positioning or does not agree with that positioning then the positioning will have no impact on that customer's behavior.

---

**Communicate the benefit advantage to target
members of the decision-making unit in the
target market so that they will act.**

---

Ralph Waldo Emerson said, "Build a better mousetrap, and the world will beat a path to your door."

The marketing version of that quotation is: If you build a better mousetrap, then customers will buy it only if:

They know they have mice.

They want to get rid of the mice.

They believe a mousetrap is the best way to get rid of the mice.

 ADVERTISING: THE DONALD J. TRUMP
SIGNATURE COLLECTION

There are many approaches to developing advertising copy. Two distinct copy approaches were used for the Trump Signature Collection. A magazine ad showed a man handsomely dressed in one of the suits (see exhibit)—that would be called a *product as focus* ad. Another ad—a newspaper ad—featured Mr. Trump and was what might be called a *brand-building ad*. Its purpose was to associate Mr. Trump and his business success and personality with the Trump Signature Collection.

Suit from the Donald J. Trump
Signature Collection.
Photo courtesy of the Trump Organization.

They believe your mousetrap is better.

They believe your price is reasonable given the competitors' mousetraps and prices.

They know where to buy your mousetrap.

For some products or services—known as *impulse products*, action may occur immediately. For other products or services, the communication process may need to take place over a long period of time. But in any of these situations, your target customer must be provided with a reason to purchase the product or service—that would be the benefit advantage.

## COMPONENTS OF THE ADVERTISING STRATEGY

Advertising is part of the marketing mix and needs to support the product/market strategy especially regarding the choices of target market and positioning. However, there needs to be a strategy for advertising just as there needs to be strategies for personal selling, promotion, pricing, and all the other decision areas in the marketing mix.

An advertising strategy for a specific target market consists of four major components as shown in Exhibit 18.1:

1. *Advertising objectives:* Your hoped-for result of the advertising.
2. *Message:* What you will say to your target customer and how you will say it.
3. *Media:* The type of advertising you use to contact the target customer.
4. *Effort:* The amount spent on advertising and how it is allocated.

## ADVERTISING OBJECTIVES

The objectives of an advertising strategy are what you would like the customer to do, think, or feel as a result of the advertising. Advertising objectives include both action objectives for your target customers, such as trying the product or repurchasing the product, and intermediate objectives, such as awareness or preference (Exhibit 18.2). Advertising objectives are not the same as the business objectives in your product/market strategy (e.g., market share, profitability), but they need to be supportive of and consistent with the business objectives.

**Exhibit 18.1 Advertising Strategy Components**

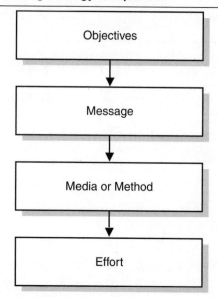

*Source:* "Arrow Guide—Advertising Decisions," The Arrow Group, Ltd.®, New York, 2004. Used with permission.

## *Action Objectives*

Action objectives describe actions you would like to see the target customer take as a result of your advertising. This might include product trial, brand trial, brand shift, repurchase, increase usage, or model shift. Action objectives for an advertising campaign are important because they are directly related to your business objectives. Each action objective has an impact on one of the components of profit (Exhibit 18.3).

In developing any advertising strategy, you first should determine your action objectives. For example, if your primary business objective is to increase market share for your tax advising business, then your advertising action objective might be to persuade your target customers to try your services—what is known as a *brand trial.* If your main business objective for your restaurant is to persuade your target customers to visit your restaurant more often, then your communications action objective would be to persuade your target customers to eat out at *your* restaurant more often what is known as an *increase usage objective.*

Each action objective typically requires a different kind of message or argument to persuade the customer to take action. For example, if you are at-

**Exhibit 18.2   Communications Objectives—Intermediate and Action**

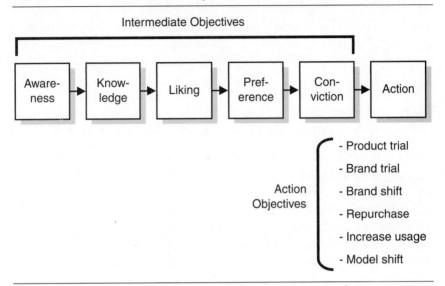

*Source:* "Arrow Guide—Advertising Decisions," The Arrow Group, Ltd.®, New York, 2004. Used with permission.

tempting to persuade a physician to consider an entirely new medication for his or her patients, then you would likely use a brochure that would compare the efficacy of that product to that of other types of medication that the physician is currently using to treat a particular ailment. However, if you are attempting to persuade a physician to consider your brand of a medication, which is similar to ones already on the market, then you would likely want a brochure that would compare the specific benefits of your own version of that medication—such as easier dosage or fewer side effects—to those of the comparable products.

**Exhibit 18.3   Profit Components and Communication Action Objectives**

| Profit = | Number of customers | × Share | × Unit usage | × (Price – Variable cost per unit) | – Fixed costs |
|---|---|---|---|---|---|
| Communication action objective | Product trial<br>Brand trial | Brand shift<br>Repurchase | Increase usage | Model shift | |

*Source:* "Arrow Guide—Advertising Decisions," The Arrow Group, Ltd.®, New York, 2004. Used with permission.

Generally, your action objectives need to be reviewed regularly because they may need to be changed over time. When you are introducing a new product, then you would likely want your target customers to try the product. However, for mature products, the advertising action objective might be to persuade your target customers to increase their usage rate of the product. For example, an insurance agent, new to an area, will be trying to persuade target customers to try or shift to a specific brand of insurance. However, later she might suggest to her long-time customers that they need to increase the insurance coverage on their home—an increased usage objective.

## Intermediate Objectives

Usually, people do not change their behavior immediately. To persuade them to change, you need time and patience. The model in Exhibit 18.4 is well-known in marketing and is called the *hierarchy of effects* model. The idea is that customers travel through different stages before they take action.

**Exhibit 18.4   Communications Objectives**

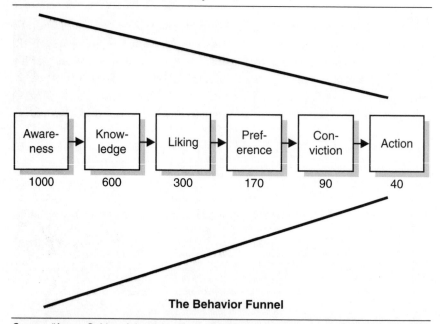

**The Behavior Funnel**

*Source:* "Arrow Guide—Advertising Decisions," The Arrow Group, Ltd.®, New York, 2004. Used with permission.

Intermediate communications objectives focus on those stages and typically include:

- *Awareness:* Recognizing your brand name.
- *Knowledge:* Having some knowledge of what your product or service does.
- *Liking:* Believing that your product or service will meet their needs.
- *Preference:* Believing that your product or service will meet their needs best.
- *Conviction:* Believing that they will take action.

The hierarchy of effects model works best for those situations when customers think about their purchase. The model works less well for products or services that are often purchased on impulse, such as soft drinks or fast food. For impulse purchases, the model really starts with the actions.

Nonetheless, the hierarchy of effects model can be a useful way to think through your advertising strategy. The stages together form what is called the *behavior funnel* or the *sales funnel*. Not every customer moves from one stage to the next. All those aware of a brand do not move on to acquire knowledge about it. You lose customers as you try to move them from stage to stage. To obtain a few purchases, it may be necessary to have hundreds of target customers become aware of your product or service. For example, the numbers in Exhibit 18.4 (which are for example only) suggest that you would need to make 1,000 people aware of your brand to get 40 people to make a purchase.

## MESSAGE

The message is what the target customer will see or hear. In designing a message, you need to think about content, approach, and style.

### Message Content

The message should provide your target customers with the *reason* they should take whatever action you want them to take. In advertising, that is often known as the *Unique Selling Proposition*, a phrase made famous by advertising pioneer Rosser Reeves. "Unique" because yours is the only product or service with that benefit. "Selling" because it appeals to the target customer. "Proposition" because it is an offer to the customer.

The Unique Selling Proposition is the same thing as the benefit advantage and should be the heart of your message. For example, if you want the target customers to try your restaurant for the first time, your advertising should give them an idea of the type of food or service they can expect. If you want your target customers to shop at your store, your advertising needs to let them know what they can find there—either the shopping experience or the merchandise. If you want your target customers to continue to use your car service, you need to show them the benefits of being one of your steady customers.

> **The Unique Selling Proposition is the same thing as the benefit advantage and should be the heart of your message.**

You should be able to look at the positioning for your product or service to find the core message for your advertising strategy.

## Message Approach and Style

Message is not just about what you want to say in your advertising, but how you want to say it. For example, here are a few of the approaches you might consider in developing your message:

- *Assertion:* Simply state your message without proof.
- *Product as focus:* Show the product attractively—works especially well for products where appearance is important.
- *Facts:* Provide factual support for the superiority of your product or service.
- *Brand-building:* Inform or remind the customer of the attributes associated with your brand.
- *Demonstration:* Show how your product or service works.
- *Comparison:* Provide evidence that your product is better than other products or services.
- *Testimonial:* Have someone express their satisfaction with your product or service.
- *Celebrity:* Have someone well-known endorse your product or service.
- *Slice of life:* Show your product or service in a use situation.
- *Command:* Order someone to take action.
- *Reminder:* Remind someone to use your product or service.
- *Bribe:* Use discounts or gifts.

What approach is appropriate depends on the target market and target customer, the positioning, and the approaches followed by your competitors.

The style of your message is where you add your creative input. What signals might you use to get your target customer's attention and interest? There is no recipe approach to style. You must experiment until you find what seems to work best for your product or service with your target customers.

## Message Criteria

Here are five questions to raise about any advertising message. Use them whenever you are evaluating advertising creative work:

1. What are the intermediate and action objectives of the message and are they clear?
2. What reason are we providing customers to change their behavior or attitudes? What is the benefit advantage?
3. Is the approach of the message effective given the situation?
4. Is the style of the message attention getting, understandable, and memorable?
5. Is the brand name mentioned?

Look at ads in magazines, on television, or wherever you might find them and try to answer these questions. You might be surprised how many ads have unclear objectives or provide no reason to the customer or use an ineffective approach or are confusing and difficult to remember. You might be even more surprised how many ads do not seem to mention the brand name or, if they do, make it very difficult to find. If the target customer doesn't know who paid for the ad, it is unlikely that the ad will be effective for that product or service.

## MEDIA

The media is how the message reaches the customer (Exhibit 18.5). Traditional advertising media include television, radio, magazines, newspapers, outdoor advertising, and the Internet. Nontraditional advertising includes a variety of diverse choices such as trade shows, events, sponsorships, and product placements.

Within a given type of traditional media, a specific television show or a specific magazine is known as a *vehicle*.

**Exhibit 18.5   Types of Media**

| Advertising | Identifiers | Sales Promotion | Personal Selling | Public Relations |
|---|---|---|---|---|
| Television | Packaging | Couponing | Qualifying customers | Press relations |
| Radio | Brochures/ manuals | Rebates | Presentations | Product publicity |
| Print | | Premiums | Consultative selling | Company communications |
| Cinema | Décor (Atmospherics) | Samples | | |
| Outdoor | | Contests | Entertainment | Donations/ sponsorships |
| Point of purchase | Spokesperson | Sweepstakes | Trade shows | Special events |
| | Stationery | Trade shows | Telemarketing | Community relations |
| Direct mail | Signs | | | |
| Internet | Uniforms | | | Lobbying |
| Nontraditional advertising | Vehicles | | | Crisis management |
| | Web site | | | |

*Source:* "Arrow Guide—Advertising Decisions," The Arrow Group, Ltd.®, New York, 2004. Used with permission.

## Media Criteria

Advertising media and vehicle decisions are typically made by considering the following dimensions:

- *Coverage:* Often known as "reach"—the number of customers potentially exposed to the advertising—and "frequency"—the average number of times a customer is exposed to the advertisement.
- *Cost per customer:* The cost to reach one customer, often expressed as cost per thousand (CPM) customers reached.
- *Selectivity:* The ability to focus primarily on the customers in your target market (which means less waste).
- *Timing:* The ability to manage the time of the advertising to maximize coverage and minimize costs.
- *Presentation:* The appearance of the advertisement, including the effects of the media.
- *Flexibility:* The ability to change the media plans if necessary.

For a small organization, the key issues in your media choice will probably be coverage of the customers in your target market and cost. There is no simple answer to what will be the best media for you. You need to examine the choices available and compare the coverage to your communications objectives and the cost to your budget.

Always be on the lookout for new ways to reach your customers. For example, in Beijing, Ikea is using the interiors of *elevators* in low-income apartment buildings as advertising media by placing floor-to-ceiling posters in each elevator along with chairs, cabinets, tea pots, and mugs to give a home-like feel.[1] Bombay Sapphire, Virgin Atlantic, and Jack Daniel's, among others, are at work to use mobile phones to provide consumers with a brand experience.[2]

## BUDGET

Three common ways to determine the amount of money to be spent on advertising are:

1. Percentage of sales.
2. Competitive parity.
3. Objective and task.

### Percentage of Sales

With this method, you apply a percentage to your expected sales to calculate the advertising budget. Such a process is widely used but is way too simplistic. It is backward as it seems to make sales determine advertising rather than advertising lead to sales. One situation where it might make sense is a mature market where all the competitors are accepting the status quo. Then you might try to find what typical percentage of sales is being spent on advertising.

### Competitive Parity

Here you try to spend or outspend the competition. There is actually some rationale for this approach in that often sales can be expected to be correlated with your share of overall advertising expenditures ("share of voice") rather than the absolute level of your spending. This approach can be dangerous because it can lead to a war of advertising spending that may be just as destructive as a price war.

### Objective and Task

With this method, you set a sales objective, then use the behavior funnel to determine how many customers are required at each stage to end up with your sales objective. The *objective* is the sales (or action) objective; the *tasks* are

**Exhibit 18.6   Estimating Advertising Results—Soap Example**

| Specific Advertising Campaign | Number Who Hear Advertising | Percentage Who Purchase | Number Who Purchase | Percentage Who Become Long-Term Customers | Number Who Become Long-Term Customers |
|---|---|---|---|---|---|
| Moisturizer advertisement | 8,000 | 0.5% | 40 | 50% | 20 |

*Source:* "Arrow Guide—Advertising Decisions," The Arrow Group, Ltd.®, New York, 2004. Used with permission.

the intermediate objectives (e.g., 170 customers prefer our product or service). For example, according to the numbers in Exhibit 18.4, you will need to make 1,000 customers aware of your product or service in order for you to have 40 customers actually make purchases.

To use the objective and task method, you need to estimate how many people will purchase your product or service as the result of a specific advertising campaign (Exhibit 18.6). It is not easy to make those estimates but you can make a subjective estimate as to what you think might be the percentage who saw or heard your ad and would purchase your product or service.

Next you would need to make an estimate of what you think a new customer might be worth to you. That would be based on how much you think they might purchase over time and your profits on those purchases. Then you can estimate the extra profit that you think you might obtain from an advertising campaign. By comparing it to the cost of the campaign, you can decide if you wish to go ahead with the advertising.

The objective and task approach can be very helpful in giving you an overall idea of what type of advertising effort you will need to meet your business objectives. It requires you to think through the process of how you acquire customers and that is often a very useful exercise.

## EVALUATING BUDGET—SOAP EXAMPLE

Suppose you were launching a soap and felt you could advertise its moisturizing abilities to your target market, women 35 to 50 years old. You are considering a local radio spot. The radio station claims it will be heard by 8,000 35- to 50-year-old women. You believe that 12.5 percent of those who hear the ad

**Exhibit 18.7   Evaluating Advertising—Soap Example**

| Specific Advertising Campaign | Number Who Become Long-Term Customers | Value of Long-Term Customer[a] | Value of New Long-Term Customers | Cost of Advertising | Profit (Loss) of Advertising |
|---|---|---|---|---|---|
| Moisturizer advertisement | 20 | $200 | $4,000 | $800 | $3,200 |

[a] Estimated discounted net profit over time.

*Source:* "Arrow Guide—Advertising Decisions," The Arrow Group, Ltd.®, New York, 2004. Used with permission.

(or 1,000) will become aware of your brand and 0.5 percent of those who hear the ad (or 40) will eventually make a purchase. Of those making a purchase, you estimate that 50 percent will like the soap and become long-term customers.

According to the calculations in Exhibit 18.6, your local radio spot will bring you 20 new long-term customers.

You estimate that each long-term customer is worth $200 over time in discounted profits. The spot costs you $800 so your net profit increases by $3,200 if you run the radio advertisement (Exhibit 18.7). You may want to go ahead with the advertising although you might also evaluate other possible advertisements the same way and select the best alternative.

## ASSEMBLING THE ADVERTISING STRATEGY

You assemble an advertising strategy the same way you assemble an integrated communications strategy (Chapter 17), by setting the advertising objectives and message content, then building it up by selecting different media and vehicles.

First you would fill out the objectives row for your overall advertising strategy in Exhibit 18.8, paying attention to both the intermediate objectives and the action objectives and how they must be coordinated. If you use the objective and task approach, you would also know how many customers you would want in each stage and when. You would also determine the message you would want your advertising to deliver to your target customer.

**Downloadable Exhibit 18.8   Advertising Strategy***

Target Segment: _____   Target Decision-Making Unit Member: _____

| Communications | Components | Time Period | | | |
|---|---|---|---|---|---|
| | | 1 | 2 | 3 | 4 |
| Overall advertising strategy | Objectives | | | | |
| | Message | | | | |
| | Effort | | | | |
| Newspapers | Objectives | | | | |
| | Message | | | | |
| | Vehicles | | | | |
| | Effort | | | | |
| Magazines | Objectives | | | | |
| | Message | | | | |
| | Vehicles | | | | |
| | Effort | | | | |
| Radio | Objectives | | | | |
| | Message | | | | |
| | Vehicles | | | | |
| | Effort | | | | |
| Television | Objectives | | | | |
| | Message | | | | |
| | Vehicles | | | | |
| | Effort | | | | |
| Other media | Objectives | | | | |
| | Message | | | | |
| | Vehicles | | | | |
| | Effort | | | | |

*Source:* "Arrow Guide—Advertising Decisions," Copyright © 2004, The Arrow Group, Ltd.®, New York. Used with permission. ***A blank version of this page can be downloaded from www.trumpuniversity.com/marketing101 and customized for your personal use.** For any other use, contact Don Sexton at Marketing101@thearrowgroup.com.

Next, you would need to select which media *and* which specific vehicles you would employ to carry the message to your target customers to achieve your intermediate and action objectives. You would also decide how much to spend for each of those media and vehicles. Finally, the spending on the individual media and vehicles would be totaled to show you the overall budget needed for that particular advertising strategy. If the budget was too high or if it did not seem possible to achieve the objectives because the budget was too low, you would repeat the process until you obtained an acceptable advertising strategy.

## CONCLUSIONS

Your target customers must know why they should purchase from you. Advertising is potentially one of your more important ways to communicate with customers. However, advertising can be expensive. It is important to be clear about advertising objectives and message for your target market so you can be efficient in developing your advertising budget and allocating it among advertising media and vehicles.

For review questions for this chapter, log on to www.trumpuniversity .com/marketing101.

# 19

IDENTIFIERS

Identifiers stimulate a customer to think of all the attributes of your brand. Identifiers include your name, logo, tag line, color scheme, type font, shape, and sound. Identifiers can even be a distinctive aroma—like that of KFC or Mrs. Fields's cookies—or a distinctive taste—such as that of Listerine mouthwash.

Brands are symbols and you must manage them carefully.

When you make any changes in your brand identifiers, you are changing your brand—one of your most valuable business assets. You can change your identifiers but, if you do, you need to be sure you are changing them in ways that support your brand and marketing strategies.

> **When you make any changes in your brand identifiers, you are changing your brand.**

You need a strategy for your brand identifiers to make sure that they communicate what you want your target customers to know about your brand. That is what this chapter is about.

## PACKAGING: DONALD TRUMP, THE FRAGRANCE

Donald Trump, The Fragrance, is positioned to express the confidence, success, and character of Mr. Trump. The packaging reinforces this message. The bottle is a "tall, sleek, architectural sculpture," evoking a New York City skyscraper—symbol of the Trump Empire. "A clear, ridged geometric glass bottle and strong, angular gold cap generate a powerful synergy that communicates the energy and pace of the Trump lifestyle."

Photo courtesy of the Trump Organization.

## COMPONENTS OF YOUR IDENTIFIER STRATEGY

There are four main steps in your identifier strategy. (These are the same steps in your communications strategy, shown in Exhibit 18.1):

1. *Identifier objectives:* The role of your identifiers in your marketing and branding strategies.
2. *Message:* The attributes of your product or service with which your identifiers are associated.
3. *Media:* The contact points with your customer—when your identifiers are visible.
4. *Effort:* The amount of expenditure for your identifiers.

### Identifier Objectives

Generally, your identifiers help you in the first few stages of the communications process (see Exhibit 18.2). They establish awareness and knowledge in the mind of your target customer. Other communications methods can be used to move your target customer to action.

However, with impulse products or services especially, identifiers can also prompt purchasing. Packaging may be so appealing that it persuades your customer to take action immediately. Examples of using identifiers to generate impulse can be seen in the packaging of many prepared foods in supermarkets.

## Message

*Brand image* consists of the attributes associated with the brand. Your desired brand image is specified by your brand position, at most a few of the qualities that you want associated with your brand (Chapter 12) by customers in a given target market. These qualities should be benefit advantages—reasons that persuade your target customer to buy from you.

The message of your identifiers should consistently convey your brand position. For example, if your organization is an insurance company and you wish to be known for "caring," then your logo should convey caring and not consist, for example, of hard-edged block letters. If the name of your restaurant chain includes the word "fried," but you wish to move from that attribute association then you may change your name to initials, as did KFC.

## Determining Identifier Message—Dry-Cleaning Example

Suppose DES Cleaners (Chapters 4 and 6) wanted to build a strong brand.

They have decided that one of their target markets is households with two wage earners and no one free during the day. The benefits that they provide relatively well include cleaning clothes, removing stains, quick turnaround, and convenient hours. Suppose that their superior performance levels on cleaning clothes, stain removal, and quick turnaround are already strongly associated with DES Cleaners (Exhibit 19.1). For customers in this particular target segment, convenient hours may have special appeal. If the customers in the target market do not associate DES Cleaners with convenient hours (Exhibit 19.1), then that benefit might be featured in the identifiers seen by these target customers.

## Media

All the contact points where your identifiers are visible to your target customers comprise the media for identifiers (see Exhibit 18.5). Such contact points include:

**Exhibit 19.1 Associations and Attributes**

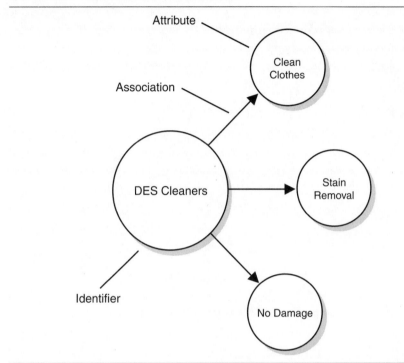

*Source:* "Arrow Guide—Brand Attribute Analysis," The Arrow Group, Ltd.®, New York, 2004. Used with permission.

- *Advertising:* Any representation of your product or service should clearly display the brand identifier.
- *Packaging:* Packages are like small billboards. They should be designed and evaluated the same way you would view an advertisement.
- *In use:* Some identifiers can be visible when the product or service is in use. DuPont's construction material, Tyvek, displays its name in large letters easily visible by anyone driving by a construction site where Tyvek is being used.
- *Brochures/manuals:* Any material that accompanies the product or service should show the identifiers.
- *Stationery:* All documents should clearly display identifiers. Notice that if the identifiers are changed, the stationery should be changed immediately.
- *Signs:* Any sign showing your brand should be consistent with your identifiers in color and type font.

- *Web site:* The look and feel of any web site must support the brand strategy.
- *Motor vehicles:* Vehicles are roaming billboards—an excellent opportunity to show identifiers.
- *Uniforms:* Employees represent the organization. DHL, FedEx, and UPS, for example, use very distinctive color schemes for the uniforms of their employees—the same color schemes that are used in their delivery trucks.
- *Décor:* The ambience of offices and service areas should reflect the organization's brand. Sometimes the décor and general ambience is known as *atmospherics*. For airlines and banks, for example, the environment may have a major impact on the service experience.
- *Spokesperson:* Anyone serving as a spokesperson for your product or service becomes an identifier.

## DEVELOPING IDENTIFIERS

Developing identifiers is both science and art. The science part is making sure that the attributes you want attached to the brand are associated with the identifier. The art part is graphic design—making sure that the appearance of the identifier is clear, balanced, and appealing.

---

**Developing identifiers is both science and art.**

---

When Burger King revised their logo, they considered a number of possible logos that showed flames—an association with their longstanding "flame-broiled burger" benefit. However, none of the logos with flames they tested looked graphically sound (and possibly some people did not want to eat a hamburger that was in flames) so they decided not to include flames in their new logo, even though it was an attribute often linked to their brand. The logo they chose consisted of the old logo tilted and the color blue added. They likely made the right choice as their new logo is quite effective—preserving the meaning of the old logo while making a more powerful graphic statement.

For any product or service that is being sold internationally, it may be especially difficult to find effective identifiers as colors, shapes, and animals have different meanings around the world. In addition, words that make sense in one language may be nonsense or unpronounceable in another language.

To systematically develop identifiers such as names or logos, you must:

- Generate alternatives.
- Screen and evaluate alternatives.
- Market test final candidates.

## NAMING

Suppose you were trying to find a name for a new product or service. You first need to generate some possible names. At the outset, you should simply list all possibilities that occur to you. They may involve your name, the name of your product or service, your location, customer needs, initials, objects—whatever you think might work. Just write down all the names that you would like to consider. The more the better. You can edit them during the next phase in the process.

Once a list of possible names has been generated, you must evaluate them on several criteria such as:

| | |
|---|---|
| Easy to pronounce | Associations with desired brand attributes |
| Easy to spell | Clear |
| Sounds good | Memorable |
| Looks good | Free of potential "new meanings" |
| Unique | Free of legal threats |
| Appealing | |

After passing criteria such as these, you should test the remaining names with members of the relevant audience for the product or service. The target markets are certainly one of your relevant audiences. However, you may want to test the name with other groups such as employees and members of the financial community. Again, if the name will be used internationally, it is important that you repeat the testing in all the countries where the product or service will be sold—certainly in the largest country markets.

The process of generating/evaluating/market testing can and should be used for any identifiers, names and logos, tag lines, colors, shapes—all possible identifiers.

## TRUMP IDENTIFIERS: BUILDINGS AND PRODUCTS

Your brand name should always appear in the same type font and, if possible, the same color. Notice in the photos below that "Trump" appears in the same font both in the lobby of the Trump Building at 40 Wall Street in New York City and in the label for the Donald J. Trump Signature Collection.

Wall Lobby.
Photo courtesy of the Trump Organization.

## *Coordinating Identifiers*

Just as any other method of communicating with your target customer, identifiers need to be coordinated.

Many organizations accomplish this coordination with what is known as a style guide or brand book (discussed in Chapter 12—See Exhibit 12.3). A style guide describes in detail the name, logo, and all other identifiers by

**Downloadable Exhibit 19.2   Identifier Strategy***

Target Segment: _____ Target Decision-Making Unit Member: _____

| Communications | Components | Time Period | | | |
|---|---|---|---|---|---|
| | | 1 | 2 | 3 | 4 |
| Overall identifier strategy | Objectives | | | | |
| | Message | | | | |
| | Effort | | | | |
| Packaging | Objectives | | | | |
| | Message | | | | |
| | Sizes/Types | | | | |
| | Effort | | | | |
| Signs | Objectives | | | | |
| | Message | | | | |
| | Locations | | | | |
| | Effort | | | | |
| Vehicles | Objectives | | | | |
| | Message | | | | |
| | Types | | | | |
| | Effort | | | | |
| Uniforms | Objectives | | | | |
| | Message | | | | |
| | Staff | | | | |
| | Effort | | | | |
| Other identifiers | Objectives | | | | |
| | Message | | | | |
| | Opportunities | | | | |
| | Effort | | | | |

*Source:* "Arrow Guide—Brand Identity," Copyright © 2004, The Arrow Group, Ltd.®, New York. Used with permission. ***A blank version of this page can be downloaded from www.trumpuniversity.com/marketing101 and customized for your personal use.** For any other use, contact Don Sexton at Marketing101@thearrowgroup.com.

specifying font, type size, colors, even types of actors used in ads. Sometimes the managers who administer the style guide are known as "logo cops," but that is rather unfair because keeping the logo uniform is important to the value of the brand.

## ASSEMBLING THE IDENTIFIER STRATEGY

The main purpose of the identifier strategy is coordination—coordination of the identifiers experienced by your target customer at all contact points. The identifier strategy shown in Exhibit 19.2 is really an inventory of all the ways you are in contact with your customer and what message you are conveying at all those points. If one or more media are not on strategy—that is, they are not supporting your brand position—then expenditures on them may be wasted and, worse, may be blunting the effects of your other identifiers.

## CONCLUSIONS

All of your identifiers—name, logo, tag line, and so on—constantly communicate to your customers what your organization, products, and services stand for. That communication should be consistent with your positioning. That communication is more powerful if all your identifiers are coordinated to give the same message.

For review questions for this chapter, log on to www.trumpuniversity .com/marketing101.

# 20

---

## SALES PROMOTION

Sales promotion concerns the management of a number of quite diverse marketing tools, such as contests, special discounts, trade allowances, coupons, and premiums. Sales promotion methods support the efforts of other communications such as advertising and personal selling and typically are not recurring but developed for a specific communications task.

In a world where customers swim in an ocean of advertising, promotion tools can be very effective in prompting customers to purchase. Usually, sales promotion can get you short-term results. The challenge of using sales promotion often is to convert those customers you convince to buy now into long-term customers.

You need to be familiar with and consider using the various sales promotion methods because they can be an important way to influence your target customers.

### GROWTH OF SALES PROMOTION

Over the past several years, sales promotion has gained in importance relative to advertising as a communications approach. There are several reasons:

- *Advertising clutter:* Traditional advertising has become pervasive and crowded with products and services. Frequently, you find many different brands in the same product category advertised on the same advertising vehicle, for example, automobiles on televised professional football games. Sales promotion can help break through that clutter to capture the customer's attention.
- *Reduced media effectiveness:* Because of advertising clutter and because of the wide variety of media and vehicles available, a specific advertising vehicle, such as a magazine or television show, may not be as effective as it once was.
- *Brand proliferation:* In many product categories, there is truly a plethora of brands—sometimes more than a potential customer can comprehend. Sales promotion can help give a brand character and distinctiveness.
- *Mature markets:* In a mature market, most customers may be well aware of most brands and, in addition, may not perceive all these brands to be very different. Sales promotion is an additional way to differentiate a specific brand of a product or service in a mature market.
- *Customer knowledge and behavior:* Once a customer or reseller has developed habits of purchasing a specific brand of product or service, those habits may persist. Sales promotion can sometimes break those habits and persuade the customer or reseller to try a new brand.
- *Power of the trade:* The trade consists of all the resellers involved in getting a product or service into the hands of the end-user. In many industries, the trade has substantial power. Sales promotion techniques are a way to gain the attention of resellers and obtain their cooperation.
- *Shorter-term focus:* Many managers are under pressure to deliver favorable financial returns in a short time. Sales promotions often have strong short-term effects on sales. (These short-term effects can later be a problem if sales increases today are borrowed from sales tomorrow.)
- *Need for accountability:* Marketing managers are being asked to justify their expenditures by evaluating the return on their marketing investment. Because customers or resellers participating in a promotion usually need to identify themselves, you can often track the impact of a promotion more easily than the impact of advertising.

## COMPONENTS OF THE
## SALES PROMOTION STRATEGY

The sales promotion strategy has components similar to that of the advertising strategy (see Exhibit 18.1, page 168):

- *Promotion objectives:* What you would like your target customer to do, feel, or think, as a result of the promotion.
- *Message:* What the promotion conveys to your target customer.
- *Media or method:* The specific type of promotion you employ.
- *Effort:* The expenditure on promotion.

## PROMOTION OBJECTIVES

Sales promotion objectives often concern actions—by the customer in the target market or by a reseller somewhere in the distribution chain between producer and end-user. Such action objectives may be trial, repurchase, or increased usage (see Exhibit 18.2, page 169). When promotions are focused on action objectives, they often consist of an added inducement to stimulate the customer to purchase a product or service or a reseller to stock it. For example, a clothing manufacturer may offer two-for-one deals to consumers and advertising support to retailers. H&R Block has offered customers the chance of receiving double their tax refund if they have the firm do their income taxes.

Promotions can also be used to achieve intermediate communications objectives such as awareness, knowledge, liking, preference, and conviction in much the same way brand identifiers do. For example, Pillsbury has conducted their Bake-Off® Contest for many years and Marlboro offers a line of Western clothing, both activities help reinforce their brand positions.

## MESSAGE

The message of your sales promotion should be consistent with your positioning. A company selling power tools should offer premiums of interest to do-it-yourselfers, such as a tool box just as a cosmetic company might offer a makeup bag. Promotions can be used to reinforce your brand positioning. For example, shoe companies may sponsor basketball tournaments to showcase the attributes of their products. Health-care companies may sponsor marathons to publicize the benefits they can provide.

**The message of your sales promotion should be consistent with your positioning.**

In developing your sales promotion, you should consider not only message content but message tone. If you are selling fine automobiles, any contests or premiums you might offer should be top-of-the-line as well. In fact, if you are selling top-of-the-line products or services, you may choose not to use sales promotion at all because it may seem out of character.

## MEDIA OR METHOD

There is an extraordinary variety of types of sales promotion methods (see Exhibit 18.5). Usually, they are first classified by their target audience—the trade or consumers. Within those broad categories, the methods include incentives, allowances, discounts, selling aids, contests, premiums, samples, giveaways, and loyalty programs. (For more promotion suggestions, see Chapter 25.)

### Consumer-Oriented Promotions

Methods of consumer-oriented promotion include price deals, coupons, contests and sweepstakes, refunds and rebates, premiums, bonus packs, sampling, specialty advertising, licensing, and loyalty/continuity programs.

#### Objectives of Consumer-Oriented Promotions

Consumer-oriented promotions often focus on managing the transaction with the consumer or customer, but sometimes are intended to have longer-term effects. Objectives include:

- *Gain trial:* Promotions such as coupons, deals, refunds or rebates, premiums, and contests can be effective in persuading the target customer to try your product or service.
- *Accelerate purchase process:* Promotions such as contests, premiums, and rebates can influence the consumer to buy now rather than postpone the purchase.
- *Increase repurchase:* The customer retention rate can be increased with coupons or with loyalty programs. Airlines have pioneered here with their frequent flyer programs.
- *Increase usage:* Customers can be persuaded to buy more of a product or service by offering volume discounts or bonuses.
- *Build the brand:* If promotions are chosen carefully, they can enhance the brand. Land Rover dealers sell a wide range of clothing, luggage, and other items that are identified as Land Rover and use the Land Rover brown and green color scheme. The items are chosen to reinforce the Land Rover brand image of ruggedness and adventure.

## *Trade-Oriented Promotions*

Methods of trade-oriented promotions include: contests and sweepstakes, dealer incentives, trade allowances, point of purchase displays, merchandising kits, cooperative advertising, training programs, selling aids, trade shows and exhibits.

### Objectives of Trade-Oriented Promotions

Generally, the objectives of trade-oriented promotions are to build support by your resellers. Specific objectives include:

- *Stimulate trade merchandising and sales support:* By providing trade allowances (discounts) or cooperative advertising, for example, one can try to influence the reseller to expend sales efforts on your products or services.
- *Expand into new markets or attract new customers:* Sales promotion can provide incentives for resellers to handle new products or services. In Latin America, 3M packaged some of their medical tape in a first-aid kit—an attractive product for many of their retailers to sell to new customers and one that also generated excitement for a somewhat dull product category.
- *Create excitement:* Creative promotions can kindle interest in resellers. For example, when BMW launched their Z-3 sports car in conjunction with *Golden Eye*, a new James Bond movie, dealers were given copies of the film to show in special screenings to their best customers. In addition, the car itself was presented at various dealerships and created much "buzz" among prospective customers and local media.

---

**Generally, the objectives of trade-oriented promotions are to build support by your resellers.**

---

## EFFORT

The amount to spend on promotions depends on the estimated effects over time—especially regarding acquiring new customers and increasing usage and loyalty of current customers.

Probably the most useful approach to employ in budgeting for sales promotion is the "objective and task approach" discussed and applied in Chapter 18 (Advertising). In that approach, you begin by deciding on the number of new purchases or new customers you wish to obtain. Then you make assumptions regarding what percentage of those seeing your promotion will take advantage of it (see Exhibit 18.6). You also need to estimate the value of a new customer. That would be the revenue you might expect from them over the next few years less the cost of serving them. Then you can compare the value of the new customers brought in by the promotion versus its cost to determine whether or not you wish to go ahead with the promotion (see Exhibit 18.7). You can also use the objective and task approach to compare different promotions you might be considering.

## Evaluating Promotion Budget—Health Club Example

For example, suppose you are running a small health club for people whom you provide personal trainers. A typical membership includes 20 workouts. To enroll more members, you are thinking of running an ad in the local newspaper offering a free workout with a trainer. Just as you did with the soap example in the advertising chapter (Chapter 18), you estimate that of the people who see the ad, maybe 1 percent will follow up on the offer. Of those who have the free workout, you believe maybe 25 percent will buy a 20-workout membership in your club. The newspaper tells you that their circulation consists of 10,000 adults. Based on your assumptions, the ad would lead to 25 new members for your health club (Exhibit 20.1). You do have capacity to handle that number of new members. Whether you go ahead or not depends on whether you feel the extra 25 new members would justify the cost of the ad *and* the cost of the 100 free workouts. (There is a cost to the workouts because you must pay the trainers.) You estimate the net profit of 20-workout customers to be $600. That would be based on their $1,200 membership fee

**Exhibit 20.1   Estimating Promotion Results—Health Club Example**

| Specific Promotion Method | Number Who See Promotion | Percentage Who Participate in Promotion | Number Who Participate in Promotion | Percentage Who Become 20-Workout Customers | Number Who Become 20-Workout Customers |
|---|---|---|---|---|---|
| Free workout | 10,000 | 1% | 100 | 25% | 25 |
| Towel premium | 10,000 | 2% | 200 | 5% | 10 |

*Source:* "Arrow Guide—Sales Promotion Decisions," The Arrow Group, Ltd.®, New York, 2004. Used with permission.

**Exhibit 20.2   Evaluating Promotion—Health Club Example**

| Specific Promotion Method | Number Who Become New 20-Workout Members | Value of Each 20-Workout Member | Value of New 20-Workout Members | Cost of Promotion | Profit (Loss) of Promotion |
|---|---|---|---|---|---|
| Free workout | 25 | $600[a] | $15,000 | $3,100[b] | $11,900 |
| Towel premium | 10 | $600[a] | $6,000 | $600[c] | $5,400 |

[a] Net profit for 20-workout member.
[b] $100 for ad plus 100 lessons @ $30 for trainers.
[c] $100 for ad plus 100 towels @ $5.
*Source:* "Arrow Guide—Sales Promotion Decisions," The Arrow Group, Ltd.®, New York, 2004. Used with permission.

less your costs, including paying your trainers. According to the calculations in Exhibit 20.2, the free workout promotion would bring in more profit than it costs so you may want to go ahead with it.

In Exhibits 20.1 and 20.2, there are also calculations for a second promotion—running an ad in the same newspaper and offering a free towel for anyone who stops by your club. While you estimate that promotion will bring you more prospective clients, you believe a lower percentage will enroll since they may be coming by just for a free towel. However, that promotion is also profitable, so you might considering doing that one too, providing you had capacity to accommodate the new members from the promotion.

## ASSEMBLING THE SALES PROMOTION STRATEGY

Overall, you want to be sure that whatever promotions you employ, they support the positioning of your product/market strategy and the message of your communications. Sales promotion is especially helpful when you would like to stimulate purchases. For example, perhaps you operate a motel and want to increase occupancy during the off-season. You might use promotion methods to attract more customers. You need to look at your overall communications objectives and decide where your purchases might require a boost. You might then consider if the promotion should be directed to the consumers or customers or to the trade for maximum effect. The worksheet in Exhibit 20.3 allows you to include several promotion methods at different times. Finally, you would estimate the cost of each of the promotions you are planning and enter that in the budget lines.

**Downloadable Exhibit 20.3   Sales Promotion Strategy***

Target Segment: _____ Target Decision-Making Unit Member: _____

| Communications | Components | Time Period | | | |
|---|---|---|---|---|---|
| | | 1 | 2 | 3 | 4 |
| Overall promotion strategy | Objectives | | | | |
| | Message | | | | |
| | Effort | | | | |
| Consumer-oriented promotion | Objectives | | | | |
| | Message | | | | |
| | Method | | | | |
| | Effort | | | | |
| Consumer-oriented promotion | Objectives | | | | |
| | Message | | | | |
| | Method | | | | |
| | Effort | | | | |
| Consumer-oriented promotion | Objectives | | | | |
| | Message | | | | |
| | Method | | | | |
| | Effort | | | | |
| Trade-oriented promotion | Objectives | | | | |
| | Message | | | | |
| | Method | | | | |
| | Effort | | | | |
| Trade-oriented promotion | Objectives | | | | |
| | Message | | | | |
| | Method | | | | |
| | Effort | | | | |

*Source:* "Arrow Guide—Sales Promotion Decisions," Copyright © 2004, The Arrow Group, Ltd.®, New York. Used with permission. *A blank version of this page can be downloaded from www.trumpuniversity.com/marketing101 and customized for your personal use.* For any other use, contact Don Sexton at Marketing101@thearrowgroup.com.

## CONCLUSIONS

Sales promotion methods can be very effective in changing the behavior of consumers, customers, or the trade in the short-term. Once you change behavior, however, you need to follow up to make sure that you keep the attention of the consumers or customers so that they continue to buy from you and the attention of the trade so that they continue to support you. Although promotion methods can be very helpful to stimulate sales, keep in mind that they cannot rescue a failing product or service.

For review questions for this chapter, log on to www.trumpuniversity .com/marketing101.

# 21

---

# PERSONAL SELLING

Personal selling embraces all those transactions where there is human interaction between the seller and buyer. Personal selling is used in most business-to-business transactions and a great number of consumer transactions.

The key resource in personal selling is *time*. Time spent with the customer is known as *face time* and it is very precious. Successful salespeople understand the value of face time and always try to make the most of it. The overall time of all the sales representatives, including face time, is sales force time and in many organizations it is often a bottleneck resource. Everyone wants sales force time but there may not be sufficient time to meet everyone's business objectives. Often marketing is organized by product and sales is organized by geography. Product managers may request more sales force time than is available in the sales territories.

---

### The key resource in personal selling is *time*.

---

You need a sales strategy to resolve these possible conflicts and focus your organization's selling efforts. This chapter shows you how to make the best use of your salespeople's time.

## SALES STRATEGY—THE STRATEGY OF THE SALES MANAGER

The strategy for personal selling is known as the *sales strategy*. An effective sales strategy provides a plan for where and how members of a sales force will spend their time, especially their time interacting with customers. The sales strategy described here is the strategy that the manager of a team of sales representatives develops and uses.

Note that there are similar sales strategies for national or regional sales managers and for the sales representatives themselves. Each of those strategies would have the same components but at a different level of aggregation. For example, the sales strategy for the national sales manager would show the allocation of the selling time of the entire sales force across all products and services. The sales strategy for the individual sales representative would show the allocation of their selling time across the products and services that they are responsible to sell.

## COMPONENTS OF THE SALES STRATEGY

The main components of a sales strategy are (Exhibit 21.1):

- *Sales objectives:* These objectives derive from those for the marketing strategy. Usually they are expressed in unit or monetary sales. Some organizations also provide their sales managers with profit objectives.
- *Effort allocation:* These are guidelines for where the sales representatives should spend their time—on which products and services and on which customers. Sometimes these decisions are known as *time and territory management.*
- *Selling strategy:* Included here are guidelines—sometimes very specific—as to how the sales representative should approach the customer, including what benefits should be stressed during the sales call and what should be the result of the call.
- *Support:* Salespeople require ongoing support in the field, ranging from materials to be used during sales calls to lists of prospects. Also included in this part of the sales strategy would be the policy for compensation and other rewards.

**Exhibit 21.1   Components of Sales Strategy**

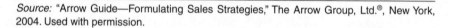

*Source:* "Arrow Guide—Formulating Sales Strategies," The Arrow Group, Ltd.®, New York, 2004. Used with permission.

## SALES OBJECTIVES

Objectives in the sales strategy are usually expressed as unit or monetary sales and are based on objectives stated in the marketing strategies for the products or services being sold. You should state these objectives quantitatively and break them out by product or service and by market. These objectives are the overall sales objectives for the sales manager who then allocates these objectives among the sales representatives who they direct.

For example, the annual sales objectives for the sales manager associated with Exhibit 21.2 total $88 million. In turn, the sales manager has allocated those objectives among the four sales representatives whom they manage.

If you add up all the sales objectives for a specific product or service for all an organization's sales representatives, then you should obtain the overall sales objective for that product or service. One exception is that, in some or-

**Exhibit 21.2  Sales Objectives (in Millions)**

| Representative | Product | | | |
| --- | --- | --- | --- | --- |
| | A | B | C | Total |
| 1 | $7 | $5 | $2 | $14 |
| 2 | 12 | 14 | 3 | 29 |
| 3 | 10 | 9 | 2 | 21 |
| 4 | 9 | 11 | 4 | 24 |
| Total | $38 | $39 | $11 | $88 |

*Source:* "Arrow Guide—Formulating Sales Strategies," The Arrow Group, Ltd., New York, 2004. Used with permission.

ganizations, sales objectives for particular products or services may be set high to motivate salespeople.

You may set sales objectives in terms of both profits and sales. However, in some organizations, sales managers prefer not to provide their salespeople with information as to the profitability of their various products and services as they do not want to encourage salespeople to give discounts. However, if salespeople do not know which products or services are the most profitable, then it is especially important for you to sort out sales objectives by product and by market, as discussed next.

## Sales Objectives by Product and Market

Sales objectives should be made clear for specific products or services and for specific markets. Without that focus, sales representatives may spend their selling effort on the products they prefer and on the customers they prefer rather than on those where the company would like selling effort. For example, Exhibit 21.3 shows a growth matrix (similar to what was discussed in Chapter 13).

> **Sales objectives should be made clear for specific products or services and for specific markets.**

Suppose you are a salesperson, who would you rather call on—a customer you know really well or someone you've never met? Many people prefer to talk to people they already know. Similarly, would you rather try to sell a product that you know very well because you have been selling it for a long time or a product that you have just heard about? It is true that salespeople want new products but the comfort level for selling current products is often higher.

**Exhibit 21.3   Allocating Sales Effort**

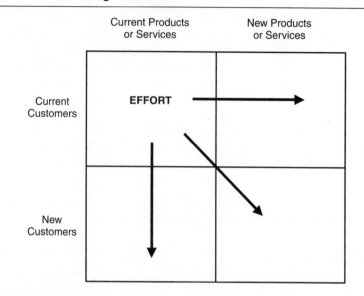

| | Current Products or Services | New Products or Services |
|---|---|---|
| Current Customers | EFFORT → | |
| New Customers | ↓ | |

*Source:* "Arrow Guide—Formulating Sales Strategies," The Arrow Group, Ltd.®, New York, 2004. Used with permission.

If sales representatives are spending their time on current customers and on current products, then what happens to the organization? It may die—strangled by its sales force—because new customers or new products are not receiving sufficient sales effort.

You can solve this effort problem a variety of ways. The most direct way is for you to assign objectives to specific products or services and to specific markets and then pay for attainment of each of those objectives. For example, some companies do not pay any sales bonus unless the objectives for every product or service and for every market are achieved. Another way for you to encourage attaining sales objectives for new customers and new markets is to improve training of salespeople through joint calls or product seminars. Such training can increase the comfort level of selling in new areas. Finally, you can establish two sales forces. Members of one sales force—the *farmers*—maintain relationships for current customers and current products. Members of the other sales force—the *hunters*—focus their efforts on new sales, new products or new customers. Of course, to have two sales forces, there must be sufficient sales opportunities to support both of them.

## EFFORT ALLOCATION

Given sales objectives, how should members of the sales force allocate their efforts among products or services and among customers? The allocation of sales force time is summarized in the time allocation table (Exhibit 21.4) that has the same dimensions as the sales objective table (Exhibit 21.2). The difference is that the sales objective table shows all the sales objectives, while the time allocation table shows the time needed to achieve those objectives for each product or service and each customer or market.

The time allocation table is developed by considering how much selling time is available and how much time is required to sell a specific product to a specific customer. For example, generally, you would expect more time to be required to sell a new product or service (such as product C in the exhibits) or to sell to a new customer.

Experienced salespeople usually have a fairly accurate idea as to how much time and how many calls will be needed to make a sale. That information is used to estimate the time allocations for each product and customer. For example, if you estimate that 10 hours of face time with a certain type of customer is needed to make a $500,000 sale, then you might estimate that a total of 500 hours or 62.5 days might be needed to make total sales of $25 million. While these estimates may not be accurate for each customer, they provide an overall forecast for the time that might be needed to achieve your sales objectives.

The total selling time available to the sales manager can be found by doing an analysis of how the sales representatives currently spend their time. Suppose, for example, the sales manager associated with Exhibit 21.4 shows that there is a total of 434 selling days available from the four sales representatives. The sales manager will allocate that time among products (and also markets) to maximize the chances that the sales

**Exhibit 21.4   Selling Time Allocation (Person-Days)**

| | Product | | | |
|---|---|---|---|---|
| Representative | A | B | C | Total |
| 1 | 52 | 37 | 24 | 113 |
| 2 | 46 | 41 | 28 | 115 |
| 3 | 44 | 38 | 25 | 107 |
| 4 | 40 | 33 | 26 | 99 |
| Total | 182 | 149 | 103 | 434 |

*Source:* "Arrow Guide—Formulating Sales Strategies," The Arrow Group, Ltd., New York, 2004. Used with permission.

objectives in Exhibit 21.2 will be met. In practice, the salespeople will likely not spend exactly the amounts of time shown in Exhibit 21.4 on the three products. You will expect that unforeseen events, emergencies, and targets of opportunity will occur and change the plan somewhat. The purpose of these time allocations is *not* to be rigid but to provide guidelines for the salespeople. Without such guidelines, sales time may be misallocated or wasted.

## SELLING STRATEGY

A sales call must be managed. The sales representative should have a plan for how the discussion will flow, what will be discussed, and what should happen as a result of the call. That is the purpose of a selling strategy.

There are a variety of models used to develop a selling strategy. One of the most well-known is the AIDA model—attention/interest/desire /action:

- *Attention:* Engaging the potential customer so that they will want to talk. Often this can be accomplished by identifying a problem the customer has.
- *Interest:* Continuing the discussion with the potential customer so that they will come to understand that you may have a viable solution for their problem.
- *Desire:* Persuading the potential customer that your solution to their problem is the best available.
- *Action:* Asking for the order—going for the "close."

Throughout this process, *listening* and, if the call is face-to-face, *observing* can be crucial to managing the sales call. You need to listen to the customer to learn what they want and to identify any possible objections they might have. Observing is important because there is much communication in body language—ranging from boredom to high interest.

A salesperson should always prepare an *Initial Benefit Statement*—a clear statement of the key benefits of your product or service that you present, formally or informally, to your target customer. The Initial Benefit Statement often starts your discussion with the customer, but how you continue the discussion is crucial. Effective salespeople are those who can manage the call as it proceeds, probing and following the customer's concerns but still controlling the conversation.

## Support

Support falls into three areas: materials, information, and compensation:

1. *Materials* include sales presentations, brochures, demonstrations—everything that might help the salesperson make his or her case to the potential customer.
2. *Information* on customers and on products or services (yours and those of your competitors) help the salesperson make more efficient use of his or her time. Prospect lists are a starting point for developing sales. Criteria for qualifying customers are valuable, particularly for new salespeople.
3. *Compensation* issues include straight salary versus commission or some combination. Generally, commissions are more effective and appropriate in those situations where the salesperson has significant ability to make the sale during the sales call. For example, if a prospective customer were interested in a tailored information system, then the salesperson may need to "design" the product during the sales call—this would be a situation where a commission or bonus might be effective.

Your salespeople should know exactly what they need to do and how they will be rewarded when they do it if compensation is to be effective.

## Assembling the Sales Strategy

The selling strategy begins with the sales objectives. (See Exhibit 21.5.) You must consider how those objectives will be attained and consequently what will be the necessary objectives for each of the sales representatives.

Next, you make an allocation of selling time. These time allocations are based on the sales objectives and on the selling time each sales representative has available and his or her abilities and selling efficiency (time required to get a sale).

The contents of the selling strategy, especially the Initial Benefit Statement, come from the positioning of the product or service as you described it in your product/market strategy. The selling strategy will typically include the Initial Benefit Statement and guidelines or suggestions for managing the sales call.

Summing the sales objectives and selling time allocations of all of your sales representatives gives your overall sales objectives and the overall selling time available to you (the sales manager).

**Downloadable Exhibit 21.5   Sales Strategy***

Target Segment: _____ Product or Service: _____

| Personal selling | Components | Time Period | | | |
|---|---|---|---|---|---|
| | | 1 | 2 | 3 | 4 |
| Sales manager | Objectives | | | | |
| | Selling strategy | | | | |
| | Effort allocation | | | | |
| Sales representative 1 | Objectives | | | | |
| | Selling strategy | | | | |
| | Effort allocation | | | | |
| Sales representative 2 | Objectives | | | | |
| | Selling strategy | | | | |
| | Effort allocation | | | | |
| Sales representative 3 | Objectives | | | | |
| | Selling strategy | | | | |
| | Effort allocation | | | | |
| Sales representative 4 | Objectives | | | | |
| | Selling strategy | | | | |
| | Effort allocation | | | | |

*Source:* "Arrow Guide—Formulating Sales Strategies," Copyright © 2004, The Arrow Group, Ltd.®, New York. Used with permission. ***A blank version of this page can be downloaded from www.trumpuniversity.com/marketing101 and customized for your personal use.*** For any other use, contact Don Sexton at Marketing101@thearrowgroup.com.

## CONCLUSIONS

Many products or services may require personal interaction for a sale to take place. Selling time and in particular face time is precious time and must be managed and allocated carefully to achieve the maximum objectives possible. Selling strategy is the plan for what happens during selling time. Such plans must also be developed carefully so that sales contacts are effective and are consistent with the product/market strategy.

For review questions for this chapter, log on to www.trumpuniversity .com/marketing101.

# 22

---

# PUBLIC RELATIONS

How do you manage your relationships with all the people who have an interest in what you do? That is what public relations does. You need a public relations strategy just as you need a strategy for advertising or for personal selling—your public relations efforts should be proactive, not reactive. And your public relations efforts need to be integrated with all your other communications activities.

Small organizations especially can benefit from public relations. Public relations can be a very cost-effective substitute for advertising. Managing your public relations requires you to be patient, prepared, and creative in finding ways to publicize your business.

---

**Managing your public relations requires you to be patient, prepared, and creative in finding ways to publicize your business.**

---

## ADVANTAGES OF PUBLIC RELATIONS

While you may find it difficult to measure the effects of public relations, many managers consider it a cost-effective means of communication. Having positive news about your product or service featured on a news show is extraordinarily valuable exposure. Not only did BMW launch their Z-3 sports car with the James Bond movie, *Golden Eye*, they placed other BMW models such as the Z-8 sports car in later James Bond movies, then kept the buzz going by commissioning short movies by famous directors such as Ang Lee, John Frankenheimer, and Guy Ritchie. All of these efforts brought them priceless coverage from the news media. A local auto repair shop or beauty salon can get similar exposure in their market by sponsoring local teams, supporting local not-for-profit organizations, or other activities.

Contrary to the opinion of many, public relations does allow you to target particular groups and in a credible way. Public relations methods such as trade shows and sponsorships speak to members of particular audiences. For example, sponsoring a NASCAR car can build strong loyalty among NASCAR fans. Sponsoring a Little League team may create loyalty among Little League parents.

When information about your product or service appears in the media, it usually has more *credibility* than if the same information appeared in a paid advertisement. Think about it. When you see a product or service evaluated by the press, don't you give those statements a bit more weight than if you saw them in an ad?

Just as sales promotion methods, public relations can help you *break through the clutter* of paid advertising. Events, sponsorships, and product placements, for example, can gain attention that would be difficult to achieve with traditional media.

---

**Just as sales promotion methods, public relations can help you *break through the clutter* of paid advertising.**

---

## DISADVANTAGES OF PUBLIC RELATIONS

Public relations is more difficult to manage than most other communications programs since you do not have the same degree of control overall. For example, when you pay for an advertisement in a newspaper, you feel reasonably confident that the ad will appear when scheduled and the message will be what you planned. However, when you send a press release to a newspaper, you do not know whether the information will appear in the newspaper and, if it does, when, where, and in what form.

Public relations is also more difficult to manage because of the diversity in the audiences with which you need to deal. Audiences for your public relations efforts certainly include current and potential customers, but they also include investors, community members, politicians, regulators, and—a very important constituency—your employees. Each of these audiences likely has different needs and interests and must be approached in different ways.

Determining the return on investment of public relations is also particularly difficult because it is not easy to link changes in customer attitudes or behavior to public relations efforts.

## TARGET AUDIENCES

The target audience for your advertising, promotion, and personal selling is typically the members of your target markets. Public relations efforts may be focused on a variety of audiences, including target customers, suppliers, community members/general public, opinion leaders, media representatives, educators, civic and business organizations, government, current investors and shareholders, potential investors and shareholders, employees. For each of these audiences, you need a public relations strategy—plus an overall strategy that pulls all those efforts together.

## PUBLIC RELATIONS STRATEGY

A public relations strategy includes the same major components as other types of communications strategies (see Exhibit 18.1):

- *Public relations objectives:* As with any type of communications, you should have in mind what effects you hope will occur due to the communications. Such effects may include building excitement for a product or service, managing a crisis, or increasing the price of your stock.
- *Message:* The message is the information about your organization, products, or services that you want the target audiences to know.
- *Method:* Public relations methods consist of all the ways you can convey information to your target audience.
- *Effort:* The amount of effort—time and money—invested in public relations.

## OBJECTIVES

Public relations may be used to achieve several quite different kinds of objectives that affect the attitudes or behavior of target customers and members of other target audiences (see communications objectives in Exhibit 18.2):

- *Build marketplace excitement:* If you can create "buzz"—intense and positive word-of-mouth—about your product or service, then you are creating awareness and moving your target customer toward a purchase.
- *Create news:* You would like positive information about your product, services, or your organization itself to be newsworthy—such coverage is essentially free advertising and provides your customer with knowledge about the product or service.
- *Provide value:* If you send information to your customers on an ongoing basis, such as newsletters with advice, you are giving them extra value that may persuade them to try your product or service or continue to purchase it. For example, a company that makes bath products for babies may provide advice on the Internet regarding how to care for babies. A store selling scuba equipment may send their customers a newsletter filled with diving tips and suggested dive locations.
- *Sell products or generate leads:* You should target information about your products or services to persuade the target customer to like, prefer, and decide to purchase the product or service. If you sponsor a local soccer team, that may make people receptive and interested in buying your product or service.
- *Develop relationships with customer or client:* You can use some public relations tools, such as e-mailed newsletters, to maintain a relationship with your customers so that you will remain in their minds. Consulting firms often update their clients with concepts presented in their newsletters.
- *Build brand:* Every contact point you have with your customer is an opportunity to build your brand. The message in all your public relations activities should be consistent with and reinforce your brand position.
- *Encourage investors:* Favorable press, annual reports, or charitable contributions can increase the attractiveness of publicly owned organizations to investors.
- *Influence opinions:* You may seek to influence the opinions of members of the general public, politicians, and bureaucrats.
- *Crisis management:* A crisis—for example a problem with your product—can destroy your organization if you do not handle it properly. Crisis management is a very special use of public relations but a very important one. You need to be prepared should an unfortunate incident occur that puts your organization at risk.

## MEDIA OR METHODS

Methods used by public relations are classified into the uncontrolled media and the controlled media. The news media is the most obvious example of uncontrolled media. Controlled media includes newsletters, trade shows, and public service advertising (see Exhibit 18.5).

*Uncontrolled media* represent situations where you provide information but whether or not the information will be used and, if so, in what form, when, and where are beyond your control. Such methods include: news releases, press conferences, media tours and materials (e.g., press kits), interviews, speakers, public service announcements, events, community relations, sponsorships and donations, lobbying, crisis management.

With *controlled media*, the organization has more direct influence on the content and timing of the information being disseminated. Such methods include house (aimed at employees) advertisements, house communications (print and video); customer or client communications (e.g., newsletters, e-mails); annual reports and similar communications, displays, exhibits (e.g., trade shows); events, sponsorships, product placements, online communications, public service advertising, corporate or advocacy advertising. If your company or organization is small, you may not be able to use all of these public relations methods but you can certainly use some of them. (See Chapter 25 for more public relations suggestions.)

## *Dealing with the Press*

Working with local media is especially helpful for small organizations. If you provide them with newsworthy items, they will appreciate it and you will benefit from the publicity.

To utilize your local media, follow these suggestions:

- Take an inventory of the newspapers, magazines, radio programs, and television programs in your area that might carry information about your product or service or organization.
- Learn the deadlines for the print media and for the broadcast media.
- Find out how they prefer to receive information. For example, if a newspaper prefers 4 × 6 color photos with a glossy finish, that's what you need to provide.
- Prepare a short (one page if possible) press release that you can send to all the media. The contents should make clear why the information will be of interest to their audience. Be sure to include your contact information on the release.

## PRESS RELEASE: DONALD J. TRUMP SIGNATURE COLLECTION EYEWEAR

Here's an example of a press release for one of the Trump licenses, eyewear. It provides the journalists with the essential facts as well as quotes from all those involved. A press release might also include contact information so the reporters can pursue the story if they wish.

### EYEWEAR DESIGNS LAUNCHES DONALD TRUMP SIGNATURE COLLECTION

Syosset, NY (7/1/05)—Eyewear Designs Ltd. has announced the arrival of The Donald Trump Signature Collection. The company has long enjoyed an impressive cadre of licenses. With its newest addition of Trump eyewear, there promises to be a buzz from the industry about this hot new signature brand. The new collection includes both men's and women's optical styles and is aimed at the sophisticated eyewear consumer.

"We are extremely excited to partner with The Trump Organization," says Andrea Gluck, Co-President of Eyewear Designs. "The timing is perfect. With Donald Trump's long standing success as a prominent businessman and his recent accolades with his top ranked reality TV show, it's clear that his popularity has reached enormous heights. He is the very definition of the American success story."

Mr. Trump stated, "Eyewear Designs Ltd. has all of the qualities I look for in a business partner . . . drive, integrity, vision and an entrepreneurial spirit. Eyewear Designs' commitment to excellence is the reason we have forged this relationship."

Cathy Hoffman Glosser, Vice President of Licensing for The Trump Organization, expressed equal enthusiasm regarding the launch of The Donald J. Trump Signature Collection. "Through our licensee partnership with Eyewear Designs Ltd., we are taking our accessory line to the next level. This trendy luxury eyewear collection will appeal to professional men and women who understand the importance of image. The styles are fabulous, with rich design elements and classic colors, and will be a stunning addition to the already successful Trump brand."

Wait to see what happens. Don't expect all the media to use your information but you may be pleasantly surprised by the publicity you will get.

## Exhibits

You may find it helpful to participate in conferences or fairs or similar events that associations or others have established. Here is a checklist to help you prepare for an exhibit:

- Try to find out the type of audience that attends the event where you might exhibit.
- Plan your exhibit so it looks neat and attractive.
- Position your products or services as the central focus of your exhibit.
- Keep track of those who drop by—try to obtain their contact information for follow up.
- Have materials for potential customers to look at during their visit or later. Be sure your contact information is included in the materials.
- Hand out give-away items if appropriate.
- Have your order book ready.

## Events

Events that you host include receptions, parties, contests—anything that might draw a crowd of potential customers. You need to plan events carefully. Here are some things to keep in mind:

- Check to make sure that no competitive event is occurring on the day and time when you schedule your event.
- Make up your guest list or, if you plan to use mass communications for your invitations, choose media so that the attendees will be potential customers.
- Try to have some kind of "draw"—a celebrity, a contest, a curiosity, a celebration—that will attract the interest of potential customers.
- Make sure you have a way to capture the contact information for those who attend so you can follow up later if necessary.
- If possible, have give-away items with your contact information on them.
- Have your order book available.

## Newsletters

For some businesses—especially personal services like health clubs or consulting firms—a newsletter can be a cost-effective way to maintain contact with your customers or potential customers. Some authors use newsletters to stay in touch with people who buy their books.

You can either mail or e-mail your newsletter—depending on what you think your customers or potential customers would prefer. An e-mailed newsletter is easier to manage but may not allow you to reach any customers who are not regularly online. Here's a checklist to use when planning a newsletter:

- Assemble a list of your customers and others who might be potential customers. Try to obtain both their physical address and e-mail address.
- Plan your newsletter so the name of your organization or your brand is clearly visible.
- Include content of value for the reader. For example, a health club might include information on healthy eating and a consulting firm might provide business tips.
- Provide a way for your reader to contact you easily.

## Crisis Management

Crises deserve special mention. A crisis is any situation that may cause your organization harm. Often they escalate in intensity and disrupt all your operations. They can destroy your organization.

Living through a true crisis is described as being in a firestorm. There is information overload, anxiety, stress, and a compulsion to take action without knowing what action to take.

If some tragic event occurs and you do face a crisis, you should keep the following in mind:

- Take charge and make sure you understand what the situation is.
- Get others' opinions because your judgment may be affected by the crisis atmosphere.
- Think through the consequences and develop a strategy for rectifying the situation.
- Communicate to the public and communicate consistently across audiences and over time.

Even better, prepare your plans before a crisis occurs. Know who will be in charge and who will communicate your positions.

### EFFORT

The public relations budget is difficult to evaluate since it may be difficult to link public relations efforts to customer behavior—especially for activities such as publicity and sponsorships.

**Exhibit 22.1   Estimating Public Relations Results—Beauty Salon Example**

| Specific Public Relations Activity | Number Reached by Public Relations Activity | Percentage Who Become Long-Term Customers due to Public Relations Activity | Number Who Become Long-Term Customers | Value of Long-Term Customer | Value of New Long-Term Customers | Cost of Public Relations Activity | Profit (Loss) of Public Relations Activity |
|---|---|---|---|---|---|---|---|
| "Get Acquainted" open house | 90 | 20% | 18 | $800 | $14,400 | $2,900 | $11,500 |

*Source:* "Arrow Guide—Public Relations Decisions," The Arrow Group, Ltd.®, New York, 2004. Used with permission.

There often may be volatility in the effects of public relations and that also makes it difficult to evaluate the public relations budget. If an organization undergoes a crisis dealing with product safety and the situation is mishandled, the organization itself may be at risk. How do you evaluate the return on those public relations efforts?

However, for some public relations activities you can evaluate your spending the same way you can evaluate the impact of sales promotions (Chapter 20). Such activities would include newsletters, exhibits, and events. In each of those situations, you would know your expenditures on public relations and, if you kept accurate records of the contacts you made through those activities, you would know how many customers you obtained due to the public relations effort (Exhibit 22.1).

## Evaluating Public Relations Budget—Beauty Salon Example

Assume that you were opening a new beauty salon and thought you might introduce yourself to the community with an open house. You advertise the event in the local newspaper. You purchase decorations and some snacks. You also pay a few of your staff to do free manicures during the day of the open house. The total cost of your open house, including advertising, comes to $2,900.

You estimate that you make an average profit (discounted net profit) of about $800 from each new customer over the period they stay with you.

Suppose that 90 women come to your open house and, because you kept track of their names, you know that 20 percent or 18 became new customers. If you assume that these women became customers only because of your open house, then the net profit you obtained directly from the open house is $11,500 (Exhibit 22.1). Notice that you actually may have received a higher profit from the event because some women may become your customers later because your open house raised their awareness of you now.

**Downloadable Exhibit 22.2   Public Relations Strategy***

Target Audience: _____ Target Decision-Making Unit Member: _____

| Communications | Components | Time Period | | | |
|---|---|---|---|---|---|
| | | 1 | 2 | 3 | 4 |
| Overall public relations strategy | Objectives | | | | |
| | Message | | | | |
| | Effort | | | | |
| Press relations | Objectives | | | | |
| | Message | | | | |
| | Method | | | | |
| | Effort | | | | |
| Product publicity | Objectives | | | | |
| | Message | | | | |
| | Method | | | | |
| | Effort | | | | |
| Company communications | Objectives | | | | |
| | Message | | | | |
| | Method | | | | |
| | Effort | | | | |
| Donations/ sponsorships | Objectives | | | | |
| | Message | | | | |
| | Method | | | | |
| | Effort | | | | |
| Special events | Objectives | | | | |
| | Message | | | | |
| | Method | | | | |
| | Effort | | | | |

*Source:* "Arrow Guide—Public Relations Decisions," Copyright © 2004, The Arrow Group, Ltd.®, New York. Used with permission. * *A blank version of this page can be downloaded from www.trumpuniversity.com/marketing101 and customized for your personal use.* For any other use, contact Don Sexton at Marketing101@thearrowgroup.com.

## ASSEMBLING THE PUBLIC RELATIONS STRATEGY

The starting point for your public relations strategy is your message (Exhibit 22.2). What message do you want to convey to all your various constituencies? Often that will be your brand position or will be related to your brand position. Then you must make sure that message is consistent across all your public relations approaches. Exhibit 22.2 shows a few of those approaches but does not include all the possible programs that may fall under public relations. For each approach, such as product publicity or donations, the message must reinforce your positioning. Your specific objective may vary by target audience but, in general, your objectives will focus on persuading members of each audience to think and act favorably toward your product, service, and organization. For each approach, there may be several specific methods. For example, product publicity includes product placements and trade shows while company communications includes videos, house advertising, newsletters, and contests. Together the strategies of each public relations method form your overall public relations strategy.

## CONCLUSIONS

Public relations is an important way for you to communicate with customers and potential customers, but also with members of the many other audiences that can affect your marketing performance. As is true for all other forms of communications, public relations must be integrated into the organization's overall communications strategy and provide a message consistent with your position.

For review questions for this chapter, log on to www.trumpuniversity .com/marketing101.

# 23

---

# INTERNET MARKETING

These days you need a presence on the Internet, and you should be actively marketing on the Internet. Whether you want to use the Internet simply to provide information to your customers or go far beyond that to provide customer service and take orders, you need to understand what it can do for your business.

> **These days you need a presence on the Internet and you should be actively marketing on the Internet.**

The Internet is a deceptively simple medium. You need to know its tone and its capabilities. Direct approaches that work in other media may not work on the Internet. Generally, you cannot simply take the content of your brochures or sales pitches and put them on the Internet.

> **Direct approaches that work in other media may not work on the Internet.**

You need to tailor, and think about not only what you want to say, but how you want to say it. In addition, the Internet has rapid interaction capabilities that no other medium possesses—you need to consider whether you want to use them. Marketing on the Internet can involve advertising, identifiers, sales promotion, selling, and public relations—all the communications approaches covered in the preceding chapters. But because the Internet is special, it deserves its own chapter.

## INTERNET MARKETING STRATEGY

Your Internet marketing strategy should consist of four major components (see Exhibit 18.1, page 168):

1. *Internet objectives:* The impact you hope to make on your target customer.
2. *Message:* The opportunities you provide your target customer, for example, to obtain information, provide comments, or order product.
3. *Method:* The Internet capabilities you plan to use such as maintaining a web site or sending e-mail.
4. *Effort:* Your expenditures on your Internet marketing activities.

## WEB SITE

A web site can help you accomplish many different types of marketing and communications objectives, including:

- Outbound activities that:
  — Build awareness of your brand.
  — Convey knowledge by providing information on your products or services.
  — Increase liking or preference for your products or services.
  — Encourage conviction to purchase by promoting your products or services.
- Inbound activities that:
  — Enable transactions.
  — Manage transactions.
  — Gather information.

While traditional advertising can accomplish most of the outbound objectives, a web site is special because you can use it to *develop a relationship* with your customers, especially through the inbound activities.

You can develop relationships with personal selling but usually at a much greater cost and one that is probably not justified for many products or services. Internet marketing is a relatively low-cost way of accomplishing what the corner store used to do—understanding and satisfying customer needs and building a long-term relationship with the customer.

Keep in mind that while the Internet can be effective with many of your customers, customers in some market segments may not be online and you will not reach them with your Internet efforts.

Remember also that others besides customers will be looking at your site—suppliers, members of the press, potential employees, investors, and banks, even competitors. You may want to have specific sections on your web site addressing the needs of each group (with the notable exception of your competitors).

## Building a Web Site

You first need to consider what you hope your web site will accomplish. Usually, it is a good idea to start simply—perhaps just providing information to your customers. Later you can add more capabilities.

You can rough out the contents of your web site by developing draft pages. For example, suppose you have a small business where you give presentations on selling techniques to sales representatives. The four sample pages in Exhibit 23.1 include: a home page, a page with your credentials, then two pages that each describe one of your presentations. As you add more presentations to your portfolio, you can simply add more descriptive pages to your web site. At some point, you might also add video clips of you presenting to each of the pages that describe your presentations. You need to think about how the pages should link to each other and how your visitors will navigate the site. For example, you probably want to make it possible for a visitor to reach any page on the site from any other, as shown in Exhibit 23.1.

Unless you are very comfortable and capable with web site software, you should hire someone to build the site for you. As you would with any supplier, you should consider at least three possible site builders. Look at their work on the Internet—they should be proud of it—and of course contact their references. You should also be sure that you own the web site that they construct for you as a "work for hire."

**Exhibit 23.1   Web Site Construction—Speaker Example**

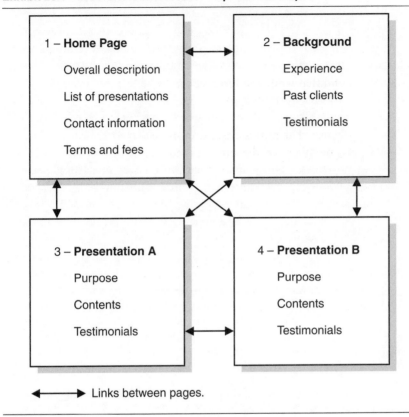

Links between pages.

## *What Makes an Effective Web Site*

Your web site should:

- *Be easy to find:* Choose a domain name that most people would think of if they were trying to find you and one that is easy to remember. Manage your positioning on search engines.
- *Download quickly:* Most Internet users are impatient and if a site does not download in a matter of seconds they may move on.
- *Be inviting:* The home page needs to be attention getting. Look at other web sites—inviting and not inviting—to stimulate your ideas.
- *Provide comprehensive content:* Information on the site should cover all the areas of interest to the target customer.

- *Have the right tone:* Information should be presented without the spin or hard sell present in advertisements.
- *Be engaging (be "sticky"):* The contents should be kept fresh and in depth. If possible, the information provided should be tailored to the visitor's needs and interests and interactive. If appropriate, activities that appeal to your visitors (e.g., contests, games, surveys) should be built into the site.
- *Create buzz (be "viral"):* If you can get your visitors to recommend your site to others and send them your link, then your web site takes on a life of its own.
- *Be easy to navigate:* Information the customers need most should be easy to find and access. Moving from one part of the web site to another should not require much time. Waiting time on the Internet is magnified in your customers' perceptions and can seem interminable to them.
- *Be personal:* The visitor to your web site should feel like a member of a community. If feasible, there should be opportunity for interaction and communication. Be sure to make your privacy policy clear.
- *Support your product or service market strategies:* The messages on your web site should be consistent with your positioning and the objectives for your customers should fit in with your overall marketing objectives.

## Web Site Effort

To evaluate your web site, you can set up a counter to determine the number of visitors and you can also obtain other measures of their visits to your site. You can even include a survey focusing on your customers' attitudes and behavior.

However, the real measure of the impact of your site is how it helps you find and obtain long-term customers (Exhibit 23.2). You might include a code

**Exhibit 23.2    Estimating Web Site Results—Speaker Example**

| Web Site | Number of Potential Customer Contacts due to Web Site | Percentage of Contacts Who Become Long-Term Customers | Number Who Become Long-Term Customers | Value of Long-Term Customer | Value of New Long-Term Customers | Cost of Web Site | Profit (Loss) of Web Site |
|---|---|---|---|---|---|---|---|
| Inquiries from Web Site | 40 | 5% | 2 | $20,000 | $40,000 | $2,000 | $38,000 |

*Source:* "Arrow Guide—Internet Marketing Decisions," The Arrow Group, Ltd.®, New York, 2004. Used with permission.

word or number and provide a discount or small premium to those who mention the code word or number when they contact you or order from you to allow you to credit certain orders or customers to your web site efforts. Then you can develop a measure of the return you receive much like the way returns were estimated for promotions (Chapter 20) and public relations (Chapter 22).

For example, suppose a speaker obtained 40 leads from their web site, of whom 5 percent or two eventually became clients (Exhibit 23.2). If an average client was worth $20,000 and the web site cost $2,000 then the speaker received a net return of $38,000 on the web site.

# E-MAIL

E-mail can have objectives similar to those for advertising. E-mail marketing has some of the properties of direct-mail advertising, such as immediacy. However, e-mails have special characteristics, such as the ability to tailor a message and the ability to facilitate a response from the target customer.

E-mails can be announcements or calls to action for your customers. You can also use e-mail to provide your customers with a newsletter like the one described in Chapter 22 on public relations.

## What Makes a Successful E-Mail

Your e-mails should:

- *Be targeted:* Don't be seen as a spammer.
- *Be engaging:* The subject line and the opening line of the message should intrigue your recipients.
- *Have the appropriate tone:* No outrageous claims. No smiley faces. No all-caps text or screaming.
- *Provide value to the recipient:* All customers need reasons for actions including why they should read your e-mail message.
- *Be consistent with your positioning:* Provide the recipient a reason to take action.
- *Allow replies:* To which you respond in a timely way.
- *Make clear your privacy policy to encourage replies.*

Finally, write your e-mails as if everyone in the world might see their contents—it's possible that they will.

## E-Mail Effort

You should keep track of what happens as a result of your e-mail messages. In particular, you would like to know how many leads came from which messages and how many of those leads you were able to convert to long-term customers. The calculations would be similar to those in Exhibit 23.2.

## INTERNET ADVERTISING

Banner ads are not viewed with much favor these days. People can delete them very quickly and they do. If you are going to place ads on the Internet, they need to be *sticky* and *viral*.

*Sticky* means that people will want to read them and pursue their links. That means you need to include value in your ads, such as customer advice or time-limited discounts. *Viral* means they will want to send them to others. That means whatever value you put in your ads must be seen by the recipient of your ad as worthwhile to pass along to others—perhaps an interesting news item or contest or a special short-term offer.

## BLOGS

*Blogs* are informal communications among you, your customers, your employees, and anyone else who might be interested. They are opportunities to encourage word-of-mouth for your products, services, and brands and develop relationships with your customers on a personal level.

Blogs can:

- Develop a community related to your products or services.
- Make information available on your products or services, including advice on using them.
- Provide an opportunity for customer feedback about your products or services.
- Allow you to interact with your customers.
- Create buzz.

## What Makes a Successful Blog

Because blogs are relatively uncontrolled, you may be apprehensive about using them. However, it is exactly that lack of control that makes blogs credible, leads to their impact on your customers and potential customers, and helps create buzz.

Your blog needs to be:

- *Easy to find:* You would like a name that is descriptive and stimulating. Just as with a web site, it should be easy to remember.
- *Engaging:* Your graphic design should involve your visitors but should not be a distraction.
- *Uninhibited (within reason):* Resist the urge to overmanage the contents. If all postings are edited for content, you run the risk of losing the freshness and spontaneity that is expected of blogs. However, it is okay to have rules such as being truthful and accurate and not being insulting.
- *Updated often:* Post new material regularly, otherwise visitors will stop coming around.
- *Content rich:* Advice, issues, information—anything that will involve your visitors and make their visit worthwhile.

## Blog Effort

Blogs represent an enormous opportunity to get close to your customers. Be careful that you do not get too greedy and try to sell too aggressively. As the relationships with your customers develop, sales will follow. Calculations such as those in Exhibit 23.2 can also be performed for your blog efforts. Remember that you can ask your blog visitors for their thoughts on your products and services. You may find their comments invaluable as guidance to how to design your product or service. In addition, the trust you show them may be reflected in the trust they show you.

## INTERNET MARKETING STRATEGY

Assembling your Internet marketing strategy follows the same process used in the earlier chapters for other communications approaches (Exhibit 23.3). Your objectives for your target customers who are Internet users are stated over time and support the objectives for your overall product or service marketing strategy. Next, you would consider how your different Internet activities might help you achieve those objectives. It might be easiest to start that

**Downloadable Exhibit 23.3   Internet Marketing Strategy***

Target Segment: _____ Target Decision-Making Unit Member: _____

| Communications | Components | Time Period | | | |
|---|---|---|---|---|---|
| | | 1 | 2 | 3 | 4 |
| Overall Internet marketing strategy | Objectives | | | | |
| | Message | | | | |
| | Effort | | | | |
| Web site | Objectives | | | | |
| | Message | | | | |
| | Type | | | | |
| | Effort | | | | |
| E-mail | Objectives | | | | |
| | Message | | | | |
| | Type | | | | |
| | Effort | | | | |
| Advertisements | Objectives | | | | |
| | Message | | | | |
| | Type | | | | |
| | Effort | | | | |
| Blog | Objectives | | | | |
| | Message | | | | |
| | Type | | | | |
| | Effort | | | | |
| Other | Objectives | | | | |
| | Message | | | | |
| | Type | | | | |
| | Effort | | | | |

*Source:* "Arrow Guide—Internet Market Decisions," Copyright © 2004, The Arrow Group, Ltd.®, New York. Used with permission. *A blank version of this page can be downloaded from www.trumpuniversity.com/marketing101 and customized for your personal use.* For any other use, contact Don Sexton at Marketing101@thearrowgroup.com.

thinking with your web site and what it might do for you. In particular, will your web site be passive or will it be interactive? Will customers be able to place orders on your web site? The answers to these questions will lead to a statement of your web site objectives. Then you might consider other Internet activities such as e-mails and blogs and consider how they will help you attain your objectives. Your message should be consistent throughout. Your efforts or expenditures should be sufficient for you to develop your Internet presence. Big budgets are *not* necessary to get big effects.

## CONCLUSIONS

The targeting and interaction possible with Internet marketing have created enormous opportunities for marketers to develop relationships with their customers. As with any relationship, Internet relationships must be managed and should not be abused. While the monetary cost of an e-mail contact is low, the time costs for the recipients are often perceived to be high. Respect for the customer must guide your Internet contacts.

For review questions for this chapter, log on to www.trumpuniversity .com/marketing101.

# 24

---

# PRICING

Surveys have shown that marketing managers typically consider pricing to be the most difficult of the marketing mix to manage. When setting prices, managers often have the feeling that they have priced too low and "left something on the table." But they also often feel that they have priced too high and lost business because they did not price correctly. Making matters worse, many of the common ways prices are set almost ensure that pricing mistakes will be made.

You can price well. But to price well, you need to consider pricing systematically and you need to understand how pricing works. That is what you learn in this chapter.

## ROLES OF PRICING

Pricing is difficult because of the many roles prices play:

- *Captures value:* Price generates return for the organization either through margin or demand or both.
- *Covers costs:* If price is not sufficient to provide a contribution that covers costs, eventually the organization is out of business.

- *Affects top and bottom lines:* The price level determines the top line through price and unit demand and affects the bottom line through contribution per unit and through total contribution.
- *Pressures competitors:* Pricing can be used to cut into competitors' cash flow although you must be careful not to cut severely into your own cash flow.
- *Allocates:* In free-market economic systems, prices serve as signals for which activities should receive more resources. The same is true within organizations.
- *Communicates:* For some customers, higher prices signify higher performance on benefits and lower prices signify lower performance.
- *Attracts regulatory attention:* Pricing probably receives the most regulatory attention of any program in the marketing mix. When making a pricing decision, if you are in any doubt regarding the legal issues, you should always talk to an attorney.

## COMMON APPROACHES TO PRICING

The common approaches to pricing are comparatively simple and usually lead to prices that are too high or too low and do not secure the optimal financial return.

### Competitive Parity Pricing

In this approach, you simply match the prices of your competitors. The first problem is that you may ignite a price war, which no one will win except perhaps the customers. The second problem is that if you price at the same level as a competitor, what are you suggesting to the customer? Often the customer will assume the two offerings are the same and there is no need to compare them. If you have a strong position for your product or service, you want your customers to think and compare when they are making the purchase.

### Target Return on Investment Pricing

This approach can make sense in situations that are not open market. The process starts by defining a specific return desired for the investment being made. Given that target return on investment (ROI), financial calculations are made to determine the price that would need to be charged. The main problem with this method is that the volume needs to be known before the price is set. In an open-market situation, price influences demand and you cannot estimate demand without first knowing price. This same problem occurs with cost-plus pricing. The one area where target ROI pricing might be appropriate consists of contracts—such as certain government contracts—where agreement as to the volume purchased is made before the price is set, typically on the condition that a specific ROI be allowed.

## Cost-Plus Pricing

This approach to pricing is quite common because it is very simple and does not require much thinking. Unfortunately, it can easily result in prices that are wrong.

Cost-plus pricing begins with a demand estimate. Based on that demand estimate, average cost per unit is calculated. A markup is added to the average cost per unit and that is the price.

The first problem is the same problem as with target ROI pricing, namely that demand is being estimated without knowing price which means that the impact of price on demand is assumed to be nil. The second problem is that average cost is often computed with allocated overhead costs (also known as indirect costs), which means that how a company allocates its overhead is determining its pricing. Often the person doing that allocation is the most removed from the customer. The third problem is that some people seem to believe that the mark-up percentage is guaranteed profit per unit. Unfortunately, that is true only if the organization sells exactly the number of units assumed when the price was set. If fewer units are sold, the profit per unit may be lower than the mark-up profit and could easily be negative. Of course, if more units are sold, the profit would be higher than the mark-up profit. The difficulty is not knowing which events will occur.

## HOW PRICE WORKS

The ceiling on your price is perceived value—the maximum the target customer will pay for your product or service. The floor on your price is the incremental cost per unit. Between those two values is the range of possible prices you can charge (Exhibit 24.1).

Where you price determines two quantities: your margin per unit and the incentive for the customer to buy. Your variable margin per unit is the difference between your price and your incremental cost per unit. That is how much incremental profit you make for each unit of your product or service sold. The incentive for your customer to buy is the difference between the perceived value and your price. The larger the incentive, the more likely the customer is to buy. To show how all these elements work, consider two different pricing strategies: penetration and skimming (Exhibit 24.2).

In a *penetration strategy*, you set price low. That yields a low unit margin but creates a high incentive for the customer to purchase and allows you to penetrate a market quickly.

In a *skimming strategy*, you set price high. Your unit margin is now high but you have left the customer with very little incentive to buy so your sales growth will be slow—coming only from those customers willing to pay the high price.

**Exhibit 24.1   Determinants of Price**

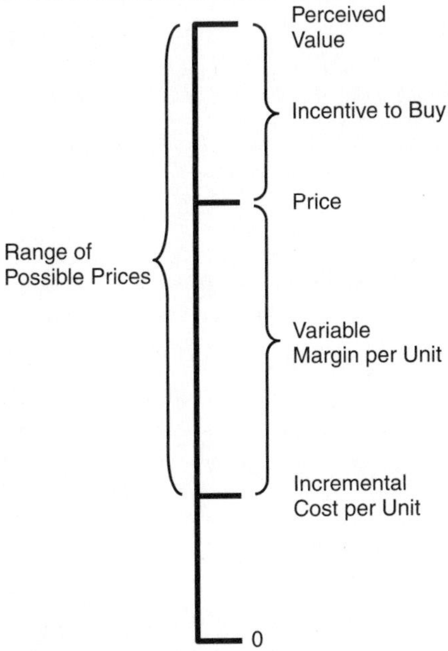

*Source:* "Arrow Guide—Pricing Analysis," The Arrow Group, Ltd.®, New York, 2004. Used with permission.

**Exhibit 24.2 Pricing Strategies**

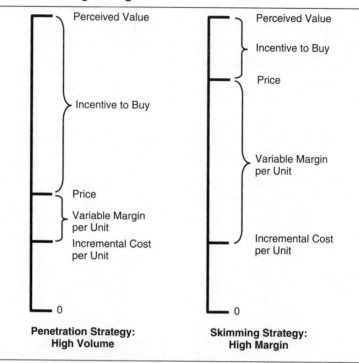

*Source:* Don Sexton, "Pricing, Perceived Value, and Communications," *The Advertiser* April 2006, pp. 56–58. Used with permission.

Pricing is a trade-off between how much of the difference between perceived value and cost per unit you will keep for yourself in the form of margin and how much will you give to your customer in the form of the incentive to buy.

## VALUE/COST™ PRICING

Value/Cost™ Pricing is an approach to pricing I developed that maximizes contribution by managing the trade-off between unit margin and incentive to the customer. It is not simpler to apply than the common approaches to pricing described earlier but it does not have their weaknesses. Value/Cost™ Pricing makes sense conceptually and can give you financial returns superior to those from the common approaches such as cost-plus pricing.

> **Value/Cost™ Pricing is an approach to pricing I developed that maximizes contribution by managing the trade off between unit margin and incentive to the customer.**

Value/Cost™ Pricing consists of six steps:

1. Estimate perceived value.
2. Determine incremental cost per unit.
3. Set objectives for overall contribution.
4. Forecast likely actions of competitors.
5. Develop tentative product/market strategy, including tentative price.
6. Evaluate financial consequences of price.

## Estimate Perceived Value

*Perceived value* is the ceiling on your price and should be the starting point for setting your price. Perceived value should be well above your unit costs. If it is not, then your product or service is what is known as a *commodity* and you may have very little latitude as to the price you can charge (Exhibit 24.3).

There are many ways to estimate perceived value such as the value-in-use, direct customer response, and indirect customer response methods discussed in Chapter 5. If you cannot use some of the Chapter 5 methods because of budget issues or because of a lack of time, you will still find it very useful to estimate perceived value. One inexpensive way is to discuss perceived value with some trusted customers. Another is to examine current prices in the marketplace for products and services similar to your own—or even prices for products and services either inferior or superior to your own—then make subjective estimates of what perceived value might be. Such ad hoc methods will not have the statistical rigor the Chapter 5 methods provide but will still allow you to bring thinking about perceived value into the pricing process. One final suggestion: When in doubt about perceived value, choose a higher value. It is always easier to lower price than to raise it.

## Determine Incremental Cost per Unit

Incremental cost per unit is the floor on your price. You cannot price below your unit costs for any length of time and expect to stay in business. Surprisingly, managers in many organizations do not seem to know the incremental

**Exhibit 24.3   Types of Products**

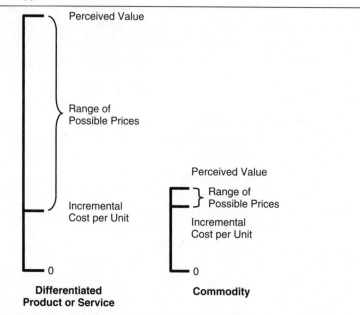

Differentiated
Product or Service

Commodity

*Source:* Don Sexton, "Pricing, Perceived Value, and Communications," *The Advertiser* April 2006, pp. 56–58. Used with permission.

cost per unit of their product or service, If that cost is known, organizations do not seem to do an effective job of communicating it to their managers. I frequently conduct programs on measuring and managing marketing ROI, with hundreds of managers in many countries and few of them say that they know the incremental cost per unit of their product or service.

If incremental cost per unit is not known, then you might use average cost per unit in developing pricing, but keep in mind that average cost per unit will be higher than incremental cost per unit and in some industries, such as service industries, the disparity between average and incremental costs per unit may be extremely large.

## Set Objectives for Overall Contribution

Typical financial objectives are unit sales and margin per unit (return on sales). Unit sales objectives are most likely achieved with low prices and re-turn on sales objectives are most likely achieved with high prices. In fact, if you use contribution as your objective, you are considering both the unit sales objective and the margin objective:

Contribution = Unit sales × Variable margin per unit

A demand curve shows the relationship between your price and the units that would be sold at that price (Exhibit 24.4). Most managers do not know the demand curve for their product or service so it may be necessary to sketch out your demand curve by trying out different possible prices and, for each, estimating the unit sales. In turn, that allows you to make estimates of the contribution from that price. In this step of the pricing process, it is necessary to make at least a rough determination of the contribution you hope to receive from the product or service.

## Forecast Likely Actions of Competitors

Obviously, you must price with regard to what competitors might do. That does not mean you need to price at the same level as competitors. It does mean that your price should be set with some consideration given to what you expect your competitors to do.

**Exhibit 24.4   Demand Curve**

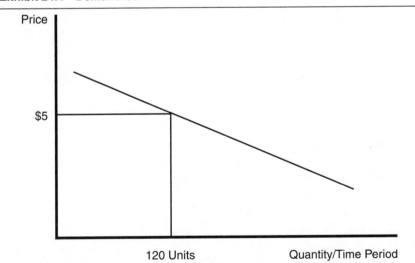

Source: "Arrow Guide—Value/Cost™ Pricing," The Arrow Group, Ltd.®, New York, 2004. Used with permission.

---

**Obviously, you must price with regard to
what competitors might do.**

---

If competitors seem likely to price low, you must be concerned about a price war and, if you do not plan to follow with a low price, then you must develop a strategy that focuses on target markets or customers who will accept higher prices or includes a product or service with added qualities for which members of the target market would be willing to pay higher prices.

## Develop Tentative Product/Market Strategy, Including Tentative Price

The tentative product/market strategy should include all the components of a product/market strategy: target market, positioning, programs (such as advertising and distribution).

A tentative price is part of the tentative product/market strategy. Given a tentative product/market strategy, it is now possible to forecast unit sales. If you will recall, inability to make a reasonable unit sales forecast was a major weakness of both target ROI pricing and cost-plus pricing.

## Evaluate Financial Consequences of Price

When you have a unit sales forecast, you can evaluate the *financial impact* of your tentative price. (See Chapter 26 for more on financial analysis and Chapter 28 for more on forecasting.) Your price must pass the following four tests:

1. Is price greater than the variable cost per unit? If not, we lose money on every sale!
2. Is estimated contribution greater than direct fixed costs? Direct fixed costs are those costs that would disappear if this product or service were not produced. If the contribution of the product or service is not greater than its direct fixed costs, the business is below what is called the *shutdown level*.
3. Is estimated contribution greater than direct fixed costs plus indirect fixed costs? Indirect fixed costs are also known as *overhead*. Typically, they are general to the organization and are allocated to specific prod-

ucts or services. If the contribution of the product or service is not sufficient to cover all fixed costs. Then the business is below the *break-even level*.

4. Is estimated contribution greater than direct fixed costs plus indirect fixed costs plus target profit? *Target profit* is what you hope to obtain from the sales of this product or service. If the contribution of the product or service does not provide sufficient profit after all costs have been deducted then you should challenge the use of this particular price.

## DETERMINING PRICE—SOAP EXAMPLE

Suppose you are selling a soap to 35- to 50-year-old women on the basis of its cleaning and moisturizing capabilities. You need to price it.

First you need to get some idea of the perceived value for your soap. Where you can start is examining the prices of products you think are similar to yours. You will find the prices of high-end soaps most relevant since the low-end soaps will likely be well below their perceived values. If you think your soap is superior to the other soaps on the market, you may want to add a premium to the prices of those soaps to estimate the perceived value for your soap. If you have the budget and the time, you can also conduct some marketing research regarding perceived value as discussed in Chapter 5.

Once you have an idea of the ceiling for your price, you need to know the floor. You should know your incremental cost per bar of soap. Most likely it will consist of materials and labor. Your contribution objective is how much you hope to make from this venture. It should be enough to cover all your costs and leave enough profit so this business is an attractive use of your time.

To forecast competitors' actions, you start by making a list of those brands of soap you think might be closest to yours in the minds of your target customers. You decide which of them will be the most dangerous competitors to you. Then you forecast what you think they will do in the future—especially when they see you entering the market. They may ignore you or perhaps they might do a special promotion to try to make it difficult for you to come in to the market. You have to think through how their actions might cause you to change your pricing.

Now you are ready to put together a tentative product/market strategy, including price. It need not be as detailed as a final marketing plan. However, you do want to think about how much you might spend on communications to support your price—for two reasons. You want to decide how much you will spend to ensure the target customer values your product and you need to know the amount of communications expenditures that have to be covered by the contribution of your product. Based on your tentative marketing strategy, you predict your unit sales. You may want to consider three sales forecasts: pessimistic, optimistic, and most likely. Then perform the four financial tests to see if your tentative price makes sense. If it doesn't, then repeat the process.

## ASSEMBLING THE PRICING STRATEGY

As competitive conditions change, you may need to change your pricing strategy. For example, over time customers typically become shrewder and competitors become more aggressive. The worksheet in Exhibit 24.5 allows

**Downloadable Exhibit 24.5   Pricing Strategy***

Target Market: _____

|  | Time Period | | | |
|---|---|---|---|---|
|  | 1 | 2 | 3 | 4 |
| Pricing strategy |  |  |  |  |
| Objectives |  |  |  |  |
| Perceived value |  |  |  |  |
| Incremental cost per unit |  |  |  |  |
| Competitors |  |  |  |  |
| Capacity |  |  |  |  |

*Source:* "Arrow Guide—Value/Cost™ Pricing," Copyright © 2004, The Arrow Group, Ltd.®, New York. Used with permission. ***A blank version of this page can be downloaded from www.trumpuniversity.com/marketing101 and customized for your personal use.** For any other use, contact Don Sexton at Marketing101@thearrowgroup.com.

you to display your estimates as to how you think perceived value, incremental cost per unit, and competitor actions might change over time. You also need to keep in mind your capacity over time, because that will limit your sales at lower price levels. By examining some of the key drivers of price, you can consider your objectives over time and whether you wish to change them. In turn, that will provide a foundation for determining your general price level over time.

## CONCLUSIONS

You price to be rewarded for the value you are providing your customers. Sound pricing starts with perceived value. The role of costs in pricing is to veto prices that do not allow you to cover costs and make the profit you deserve and want. Costs alone should never be used to set prices. Perceived value and costs must be considered *together* when setting price.

For review questions for this chapter, log on to: www.trumpuniversity.com/marketing101.

# 25

---

# GUERRILLA MARKETING

You probably do not have the marketing budgets of Toyota or Procter & Gamble or Nokia. In fact, when you think of all the companies in the world, very few organizations command those amounts of resources. Guerrilla marketing is about marketing without a large budget.

When you do not have a huge budget, do the principles of marketing still apply? Of course they do. Maybe even more so because smaller organizations with limited resources cannot afford to squander their resources without a strategy. And they cannot afford to make foolish mistakes. The marketing principles still work—you just need to be more creative and perhaps more careful about how you put them into practice.

---

**When you do not have a huge budget, do the principles of marketing still apply? Of course they do.**

---

Many small businesses fail because they do not understand the power of the basic principles of a marketing strategy: *target* your market and *position* your product or service to be superior to the products or services of your competitors.

## *Concentrating the Guerrilla Marketing Strategy*

Your guerrilla marketing strategy *must* concentrate your efforts on a specific target market. Without a clear target market, smaller businesses do not concentrate their efforts on specific markets. They may end up spreading their resources too thin. Instead of focusing on target customers and building loyalty among them, they obtain occasional purchases from customers who know them only slightly and have no reason to return.

## *Coordinating the Guerrilla Marketing Strategy*

Your guerrilla marketing strategy must coordinate all of your efforts to support the positioning of your product or service. Without clear positioning, it is difficult to communicate with your customers and build your brand position. The temptation is to tell customers every good thing possible about your product or service. The consequence is that your customers may remember very little about what is good about your product or service that is important to them.

## *Communicating the Guerrilla Marketing Strategy*

Guerrilla marketing starts with a clear statement of your target market and a clear statement of the positioning of your product or service. Your staff must have a clear understanding of your target market so their actions will support your strategy. For concentration and coordination to occur, the marketing strategy must be communicated to all those in your organization who will be involved in implementing your marketing strategy. The guerrilla marketing strategy can be communicated very simply—with *just one page* consisting of the answers to the questions in the worksheet in Exhibit 25.1.

---

**Guerrilla marketing starts with a clear statement of your target market and a clear statement of the positioning of your product or service.**

---

**Exhibit 25.1   Guerrilla Marketing Strategy Summary**

| | |
|---|---|
| What Customers Do We Want? (Target Market) | People 30 and older interested in significant fiction and nonfiction |
| To Whom Specifically Do We Need to Communicate? (Target Decision-Making Unit Member) | The individual reader |
| What Competitor Do We Want to Beat? (Target Competitor) | Outlets of large chain bookstores |
| Why Should Customers Buy from Us? (Benefit Advantage) | Personal attention and advice |
| Why Will We Win? (Competitive Advantage) | Personal interest in our customers |

*Source:* "Arrow Guide—Formulating the Product/Market Strategy," The Arrow Group, Ltd.®, New York, 2004. Used with permission.

## Guerrilla Marketing Strategy—Bookstore

Suppose you run a small bookstore on the main street of your town.

You have a long and abiding interest in books and you enjoy sharing your passion with your customers. Your target market consists of people with similar views on reading and books. You try to focus your communications on the individual reader.

Your competitors are large bookstores that are part of national chains. You feel that you can differentiate yourself from your competitors through your personal knowledge of your customers and your ability to advise them about books that you believe will be of high interest to them. That level of personal attention will be difficult for a large store to match.

## GUERRILLA TARGET MARKET

Your target market consists of those customers with whom you wish to do business. Ideally, you need to describe them with demographics or some other basis that allows you to find them, talk to them, and persuade them to do business with your store.

For example, a family restaurant should focus their efforts on families. That sounds reasonable and also simple. However, that assumption has tremendous implications. A focus on families will affect the menu, the chef, the waitstaff, the décor, and that's just the start. A family focus will also guide how you price, where you advertise, and whether you might sponsor a youth soccer team.

## GUERRILLA POSITIONING

Positioning is crucial. Positioning is how you distinguish yourself from your competitors. It is how you might distinguish your family restaurant from other family restaurants. The difference might be what's on the menu, what's on the walls, and how the waitstaff sing "Happy Birthday." One family restaurant in my neighborhood distinguishes their establishment by serving large colorful fruit drinks specially for children while another has chocolate cereal as an entrée on their children's menu.

You should be able to defend your positioning. It should be difficult for another restaurant to copy. Perhaps your fruit drinks have a secret recipe or your waitstaff sing a special version of "Happy Birthday."

Positioning includes specifying your target competitors. If you have a small organization, do not go head-to-head with large competitors. Instead, try to find out what you can do better than they can. Generally, large organizations use "fixed cost" weapons because they can spread those costs over more customers. For example, a restaurant chain may use a promotion featuring a round-the-world trip as a prize. Smaller restaurants are typically better off using "variable cost" weapons such as personalized service—tailoring dishes for finicky children.

If you can, tailor your guerrilla marketing position at the level of individuals. For many years, McDonald's and Burger King positioned themselves for children while Wendy's positioned themselves for adults. Those different choices affected their menus, their promotions, and their advertising and made their strategies more precise and more effective.

## GUERRILLA BRANDING

What is the secret of building a strong brand? Consistency—over time and over everything that you do. That is true for large and for small organizations.

Once you have decided on the positioning of your product or service, then you define the brand position—for what should the product or service be known? It should be something the target customer wants—a benefit or a need—and something that you do well. Then every contact you have with the target customer should repeat that brand position. The name, the logo, the tagline—all should reinforce that brand position.

## Suggestions

- Select a name that communicates what you offer to your customers. Your name need not be fancy but should be distinctive. For example, instead of Dr. J. J. Jones, a children's dentist might be known as The Painless Dentist or The Smile Doctor.
- Develop a tagline. "Where teeth are happy."
- Keep the typeface the same in all your communications.
- Choose colors that you keep the same in all your communications.
- Develop a logo. It need not be fancy but it should be easy to recognize (like a tooth or a smile).

## GUERRILLA SERVICE

Much of the satisfaction of your customers depends on the interactions between them and your people.

## Suggestions

- Be sure that your employees who are in touch with your customers are polite, courteous, and friendly—and have sufficient training, especially regarding listening to customers' problems.
- Keep your business space clean and neat—your employees also should appear clean and neat.
- Be open for business when your customers are available to do business with you.
- Add small touches that people appreciate and remember—like cookies or doughnuts in your waiting area. And fresh coffee, including decaffeinated.

## GUERRILLA·COMMUNICATIONS

Guerrilla communications are precisely targeted. If they are not targeted, money is being wasted on eyeballs or ears that are not connected to the target customers. Guerrilla communications do not overwhelm with volume—they achieve their goals through selectivity.

Guerrilla communications clearly state your position—your key benefits—and how to contact you. Find out where your customers get information—bulletin boards, radio stations, mailers, wherever. Then try to utilize those communications channels.

## GUERRILLA ADVERTISING

Keep in mind that there are a great variety of ways to advertise—many that can be much more precisely targeted than the mass media.

### Suggestions

- Make your signs work for you—they should be easy to see, make clear what you do, and show your contact information. "Reliable Plumbing—no water worries. Telephone: (area code)—your number."
- Print one-page advertisements that you can use as mailers, circulars, signs, mini-posters, inserts, and handouts.
- Place circulars on local bulletin boards.
- Your business cards are small billboards—they should look good—perhaps multiple colors or photos. They can also do much more than providing your name and contact information. They can provide reasons why customers should buy from you and they can show how to find your establishment. Use both sides of the card if necessary.
- Your stationery should also be well designed, include your logo and tagline, and communicate what you do that your customers should want.
- Use unusual media. Consider banners, sidewalk displays, searchlights, skywriting, or tethered balloons or blimps.
- Send customers or clients personal messages—on holidays, their birthdays or anniversaries, or on other occasions (such as when they need a medical checkup or when their furnace needs to be cleaned). Send them thank-you notes for their business.
- Contact your customers or clients with newsletters. They should have the same look as all your other communications and contain information of value. For example, a hardware store might provide do-it-yourself advice and a bookstore might give previews of new releases.
- Send videos. Many service businesses, for example summer camps and bands, send these out to give customers a feel for the experiences they provide.

- Use Yellow Page ads—consider what your competitors' ads look like, then decide on the size of your ad and the use of color or photos to make it stand out. Provide as much information in the ad as possible, including why a customer should buy from you and how to contact you or find your business.
- If you would like to use mass media such as print or broadcast advertising, keep in mind that some print and broadcast advertising can be purchased as *remnants,* which are advertising spaces or times that are unsold and can be purchased at the last minute at relatively low rates.
- Be sure that if you run ads, you run them on days you are open.

## GUERRILLA SELLING

Selling is like hand-to-hand combat. You need to give your salespeople all the help they can get.

### Suggestions

- Provide training for your people in basic selling skills and also in knowledge of your products or services.
- Develop circulars, brochures, or other material for your salespeople to hand out—be sure your contact information and an order blank are included.
- Inform your salespeople on which products or services you want them to focus, either because they are more profitable or for some other strategic reason.
- Use a commission compensation system for maximum effort.

## GUERRILLA PROMOTIONS

All promotions should have themes that amplify your brand positioning.

### Suggestions

- Use contests. Perhaps develop relationships with other local businesses and trade products or services to use as prizes. An optician might give away eyeglass frames, a garage an oil change, or a bookstore a new mystery novel.
- Organize contests where the winner is someone who says something nice about you, "Why I like . . ." You can use these testimonials in ads

(with permission) and, if you do, use the names of the people providing the endorsements as many people believe that makes testimonials more effective. Try to arrange the contest so that people come to your store to enter and provide their contact information. Have several winners. Remember that winners tend to become steady customers.

- Hand out inexpensive items that will remind customers and potential customers of your products or services. Examples include T-shirts, caps, or paperweights, but perhaps you can be more creative. A therapist gave out rubber balls to squeeze to "relieve stress." Lexus dealers in Germany give their customers surprise gifts such as bottles of wine or elegant clocks.
- Develop customer groups. Shisheido has a club in Japan for millions of their customers who receive custom magazines and various offers. Huggies has sent personalized letters and magazines on baby care to women who are pregnant. In France, Nestlé has provided parents 24-hour access to nutritionists specializing in child care. You can develop the same relationships with your customers. One local store selling children's clothing uses mailing lists of their customers and potential customers to support a group interested in parenting issues.

## GUERRILLA PUBLIC RELATIONS

Public relations is the quintessential guerrilla communications—low cost, high impact.

### Suggestions

- Develop a conversational relationship with your local newspaper and radio station reporters so that they will consider your ideas for news items.
- Write short, content-rich press releases and direct them to reporters *before* their deadlines. Include photos if they are accepted.
- Print reprints of articles about your business and use them as mailers or circulars.
- Be part of the community. Show the work of local artists. Contribute to auctions of local not-for-profit organizations.
- Join local associations—but do not appear to have joined only for sales contacts.
- Give talks for local associations.

## GUERRILLA INTERNET

Remember that all communications with customers should have the same look and feel, including your web site and e-mail messages. When you have a small budget, it is especially important that all communications reinforce each other.

### Suggestions

- Set up a web site that communicates your positioning *and* includes your contact information, including an easy to use e-mail service.
- Put (limited use) coupons and other offers on your web site.
- E-mail a newsletter to your customers and prospective customers.
- Use chat rooms.
- Set up a blog.
- Get listed on free directories.
- Manage your search engine placement.

## GUERRILLA PRICING

Small organizations are generally more flexible than larger ones. They can more easily tailor product or services to their customers, including price. That does not mean small organizations should necessarily compete on price with large organizations. In a price war between a large organization and a small organization, it should not be difficult to guess the winner. What is true, however, is price discounts are more expensive for a large organization to maintain because they may have to offer the same discount to all their customers. A discount offered to thousands of customers can add up to a rather large expense. The small organization may be able to tailor prices because they are tailoring their offering to different customers.

### Suggestions

- *Know your competitors' prices:* Do not price exactly the same as your competitors do. You want your customers or prospective customers to think of both your value and your price and not focus only on price.
- *Use coupons:* Often coupons can build trial or traffic for you. For example, restaurants often provide two-for-one meal coupons and health clubs might give a first session for free. *Note:* Coupons should have a triangle shape so they can be cut easily from a page. Your contact infor-

mation should be both on the coupon and the page so what remains after the coupon is gone still functions as your ad.

- *Use gift certificates:* They can also build trial and traffic.
- *Target your pricing,* if feasible, with discounts for your customers who buy more.
- *Consider simplifying your pricing:* For example, use the approach of a salad bar where the customers make their own salad, then pay for it by weight regardless of the ingredients.
- *Be careful* that you don't use low price to offset poor product or service performance.

## GUERRILLA MARKETING RESEARCH

Guerrilla organizations are usually close to their customers. Talk to them, get to know their concerns and needs.

### Suggestions

- Collect the contact information of customers and prospective customers wherever and whenever you can. For example, ask people to leave their business cards in a bowl and each month select cards for winners of some product or service.
- Trade leads with other businesses with which your customers are likely to do business. For example, a caterer might trade wedding contacts with a florist.
- Try to get leads from your own customers by offering them discounts or premiums for the names of potential customers.
- Keep track of where your leads come from—so you can target your future efforts.
- During transactions, try to find out how satisfied your customers are with your products or services and see if they have any suggestions.
- Ask friends how they are treated when they visit your place of business. On occasion, call your business to see how you are treated on the telephone.
- Organize informal focus groups—where you invite 5 or 6 of your customers or potential customers to discuss your products or services over coffee or snacks.
- Conduct a mail survey or use students as interviewers.
- Determine the value of your customers. Estimate the average sales per customers per year and your profit on those sales. Be sure your employees know the value of each of your customers.

## CONCLUSIONS

Marketing does not have to be expensive to be effective. It does need to be targeted to be effective. Guerrilla marketers know the customers they want and know the reasons those customers should be buying from them. All their marketing efforts are guided by those principles.

For review questions for this chapter, log on to www.trumpuniversity .com/marketing101.

# IV

## UNDERSTANDING THE NUMBERS

# 26

---

# FINANCIAL ANALYSIS

## FOR SMART

## MARKETING DECISIONS

To make the right marketing decisions, you need to know their financial consequences.

Understanding the financial impact of your marketing decisions is not difficult if your cost and revenue information is organized properly. Unfortunately, the revenue and cost information you need as a marketer is not always available in the financial records kept by most organizations.

There is one piece of financial information in particular that you need to evaluate most marketing decisions. That is the *variable margin rate*—the incremental profit rate. If you know it, you can evaluate pricing decisions, product or service decisions, advertising decisions, selling decisions, and customer decisions. If you don't know your variable margin rate, you may be guessing at the profit you think you might make. In this chapter, you learn what financial information you need to find your variable margin rate and how to use it to make marketing decisions that are sound financially. Of course, you can never predict for sure the financial impact of any action, but you can analyze the likely financial consequences and improve your marketing decisions.

## TYPES OF ACCOUNTING SYSTEMS

Most accounting documents, like the income statement in Exhibit 26.1, are designed to tell you your financial results *after* you have made your marketing decisions and seen their consequences. For example, Exhibit 26.1 shows you what happened to a small business last year as regards revenue, costs, and profits (before taxes).

The income statement in Exhibit 26.1 is in *custodial* format. The upper part of the typical custodial income statement describes the Costs of Goods Sold (or the Costs of Services Provided). These are all the costs involved with producing your product or service, such as materials, compensation for your production employees, and manufacturing overhead including rent and utilities for your production facility. The lower part of the custodial income statement describes expenses. These include advertising, compensation for managers, and general and administrative expenses such as payments for legal and tax advice.

The typical custodial income statement shows only what happened in the past because it is constructed for people—outsiders—who are interested primarily in your past performance—tax authorities and lenders for example.

Custodial income statements are not constructed for the marketing manager. They do not make it easy for you to evaluate the financial effects of marketing decisions. For example, suppose the sales in Exhibit 26.1 increased by 10 percent, can you tell from the numbers presented what would be the impact on your operating profit? The answer is no because the numbers are not provided in a form that allows you to answer any type of what if question about your sales.

**Exhibit 26.1   Custodial Income Statement**

| Net Sales | | $200,000 |
|---|---|---|
| Less:  Material | $80,000 | |
| Direct labor | 35,000 | |
| Manufacturing overhead | 20,000 | |
| Cost of Goods Sold | | 135,000 |
| Gross Margin | | 65,000 |
| Less:  Advertising | $5,000 | |
| Management | 30,000 | |
| General and administrative | 10,000 | |
| Expenses | | 45,000 |
| Operating Profit | | $20,000 |

---

**Custodial income statements are not constructed
for the marketing manager.**

---

The information you need to make marketing decisions requires you to reorganize the information in the custodial income statement and make a new income statement, the *contribution* income statement. With your income statement in contribution format, you can answer what if questions such as what would be the impact of a 10 percent increase in sales on profits? In turn, you can then make marketing decisions *a priori* rather than *ex post*. That is, you can perform a financial evaluation of your marketing decisions *before* you make them.

## Reorganizing the Income Statement into Contribution Format

You can classify costs broadly into fixed costs and variable costs. Fixed costs do not change over a given range of output for your product or service (Exhibit 26.2). Typical fixed costs include salaries, rent, and depreciation. For a restaurant, for example, fixed costs would include wages, advertising on a local radio station, depreciation on the equipment and fixtures, and property taxes. Variable costs change as output change. While variable costs are often assumed to follow a straight line, in fact any cost that changes with volume in any way is a variable cost. Typical variable costs include materials, electric power, and commissions. For the restaurant illustration, a major variable cost would be the meat, vegetables, beverages, and other supplies needed to make a meal. Labor costs may be a variable cost but also may be a fixed cost, depending on how easy it is to change the number of employees.

In Exhibit 26.1, the costs are organized into "Costs of Goods Sold" and "Expenses." Both those categories include fixed and variable costs. If you reorganize the costs in Exhibit 26.1 as "Variable Costs" or "Fixed Costs," you have an income statement in Contribution format, Exhibit 26.3.

## Contribution Format—Frame Store Example

Assume that you own a small framing store. You have a store manager and a few part-time employees who do the actual framing. As shown in Exhibit 26.1, last year your sales were $200,000.

**Exhibit 26.2 Types of Costs**

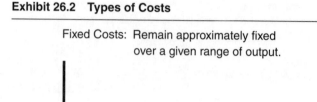

Fixed Costs: Remain approximately fixed
over a given range of output.

Costs

Output

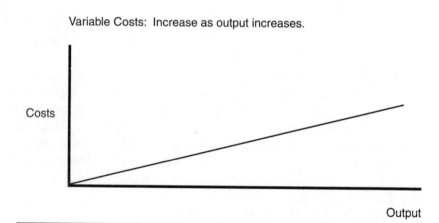

Variable Costs: Increase as output increases.

Costs

Output

You share a small sales area in a mall. The actual framing is done in another location, where the rent is cheaper. Overall, last year your costs of producing the frames included $80,000 for materials such as wood and metal frames, glass, mats, and backing. Your part-time employees received $35,000. Your manufacturing overhead included the rent and utilities on the space where the framing is done as well as depreciation for equipment you use for framing. Total costs of goods sold were $135,000.

Your largest single expense was compensation to your store manager—$25,000 in salary plus a bonus which is 2.5 percent of the total revenue generated by the store—last year the bonus was $5,000. General and administrative

**Exhibit 26.3  Contribution Income Statement**

| | | |
|---|---:|---:|
| Net Sales | | $200,000 |
| Less:  Material | $80,000 | |
| Direct labor | 35,000 | |
| Manager bonus (2.5%) | 5,000 | |
| Variable Costs | | 120,000 |
| Contribution or Variable Margin | | 80,000 |
| Less:  Advertising | $5,000 | |
| Management | 25,000 | |
| Manufacturing overhead | 20,000 | |
| General and Administrative | 10,000 | |
| Fixed Costs | | 60,000 |
| Operating Profit | | $20,000 |

includes the rent on the selling space and other expenses such as legal and tax advice. You spent $5,000 on advertising last year, mainly on advertisements in the local newspaper.

Looking at the information in Exhibit 26.1, you need to consider which costs are variable and which are fixed. Material and direct labor will be assumed to be variable costs. The part-time employees who do the framing are paid based on the value of the frames they produce. The manager's bonus is also a variable cost. All the other costs and expenses are assumed to be fixed costs. In general, some of the manufacturing overhead might be a variable cost—for example, utilities. However, in this example, such costs would likely not be variable because the framing space is kept lighted and heated (or cooled) most of the time whether framing is being done or not. Note that in general some costs or expenses such as telephone may have both a variable and a fixed component. The fixed component would be your telephone usage with no sales; the variable component would consist of the calls you make related to your sales. In the frame store example, all costs are assumed to be either variable or fixed. Given these assumptions, the contribution format income statement is shown in Exhibit 26.3.

## CONTRIBUTION OR VARIABLE MARGIN

From a marketer's viewpoint, the most important number in Exhibit 26.3 is the contribution or variable margin. That is the amount of money you have

**Exhibit 26.4    Variable Cost Rate and Variable Margin Rate**

$$\text{Variable cost rate} = \frac{\text{Variable costs}}{\text{Sales}}$$

$$\text{Variable margin rate} = \frac{\text{Variable margin}}{\text{Sales}}$$

*Note:* Variable cost rate + Variable margin rate = 100%

before you pay for your fixed costs. After you pay your fixed costs what is left over is your operating profit.

The contribution is important because most of the decisions you make in marketing directly affect the amount of contribution you achieve. Usually it is easiest to employ the contribution or variable margin as a *rate*—as a percentage of your sales dollar. To calculate the variable margin rate, you simply divide the contribution or variable margin by the sales (Exhibit 26.4). If you know your variable margin rate, you can evaluate the likely financial impact of many marketing decisions.

## Calculating the Variable Margin Rate— Frame Store Example

In the frame store example, the contribution or variable margin was $80,000 on sales of $200,000. Then you can calculate:

$$\text{Variable margin rate} = \frac{\$80,000}{\$200,000} = 40\% \text{ or } 0.40$$

The variable margin rate is the percentage of each additional sales dollar that represents incremental profit to you. For example, if you sell $1,000 worth of frames to a customer, then 40 percent of that or $400 is contribution or incremental profit that will show on your bottom line. Now you can answer the question asked earlier. If sales for the frame shop increase by 10 percent, what will be the impact on profit?

A 10 percent increase in sales of $200,000 would be $20,000. Because you know the variable margin rate is 40 percent, then 40 percent of that $20,000 would be your increase in operating profit. If sales go up $20,000, then your profits would go up $8,000—from $20,000 to $28,000.

**Exhibit 26.5    Useful Formulas**

$$\text{Breakeven sales level} = \frac{\text{Fixed costs}}{\text{Variable margin rate}}$$

$$\text{Target profit sales level} = \frac{\text{Fixed costs} + \text{Target profit}}{\text{Variable margin rate}}$$

$$\text{Target ROS sales level} = \frac{\text{Fixed costs}}{\text{Variable margin rate} - \text{Target ROS}}$$

$$\text{Shutdown sales level} = \frac{\text{Direct fixed costs}}{\text{Variable margin rate}}$$

Notice that a sales increase of 10 percent leads to a profit increase of 40 percent! If your income statement was in custodial form, you would not know that. Only by having your income statement in contribution form are you able to figure out correctly the profit increase due to your sales increase.

## IMPORTANT SALES LEVELS

*Once you know your variable margin rate, you can easily calculate some benchmark sales levels* (Exhibit 26.5):

- *Breakeven sales level:* The sales level such that sales exactly cover your fixed costs but nothing is left over for profit. (See Exhibit 26.6)
- *Target profit sales level:* The sales level that covers your fixed costs and what remains is the profit you want.
- *Target ROS sales level:* The sales level that covers your fixed costs and what remains is profit such that profit divided by sales gives you the Return on Sales percentage you wish to obtain.
- *Shutdown sales level:* The sales level such that sales exactly cover your direct fixed costs but nothing is left over for overhead or for profit. (See Exhibit 26.7.)

## DIRECT AND INDIRECT FIXED COSTS AND SHUTDOWN LEVEL

It can be very useful to classify your fixed costs into what are known as *direct fixed costs* and *indirect fixed costs*. Direct fixed costs are all the costs that are required for a business—if the business disappears, then so do the direct fixed costs. Indirect fixed costs are all the other fixed costs.

For example, suppose you do other things besides framing services. If you close down your framing operation, then you will no longer advertise ($5,000), pay a salary to your frame store manager ($25,000), or pay your manufacturing overhead ($20,000). You will continue to keep your mall store and pay the other General and Administrative expenses such as attorney and accountant fees and store rent. That means if you close your framing operation, your fixed costs will decrease by $50,000—those are the direct fixed costs of your framing services.

Why you want to know your direct fixed costs is that they determine your shutdown level. Even if you are not making a profit, you may want to keep an operation going if you have no better use of the resources you are using (including your time). As long as you are more than covering your direct fixed costs, you are at least helping pay for your overhead and that may be worthwhile.

The level of sales when you are just covering your direct fixed costs is known as the shutdown level. If your sales are above the shutdown level, you may or may not be making a profit but at the least you are contributing to covering your overhead (Exhibit 26.7). Below the shutdown level, your business is a cash drain.

---

**The level of sales when you are just covering your direct fixed costs is known as the shutdown level.**

---

## Important Sales Levels—Frame Store Example

The calculations for key sales levels for the frame store are shown in Exhibit 26.8. The breakeven sales level is $150,000. Below that sales level, the frame store does not make a profit (Exhibit 26.8). If you want a target profit of $40,000, then your sales level must be $250,000. In other words, to double your current profit, you need to increase your current sales level by 25 percent or $50,000. If you set your objectives in terms of Return on Sales (profit as a percentage of sales) and you want to achieve an ROS of 20 percent, then you must have sales of $300,000. Your shutdown sales level is $125,000. If your sales fall below $125,000, then you are not even covering the costs di-

**Exhibit 26.6    Breakeven Level**

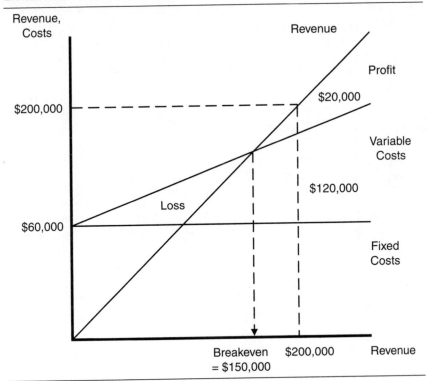

rectly associated with the framing operation. You are losing money and should consider closing down the operation unless you can figure out how to turn it around.

## EVALUATING THE FINANCIAL IMPACT OF MARKETING DECISIONS

The variable margin rate allows you to convert changes in sales into changes in profit so you can evaluate many types of marketing decisions. The calculation is straightforward:

Change in profit = Change in sales × Variable margin rate

**Exhibit 26.7   Shut-Down Level**

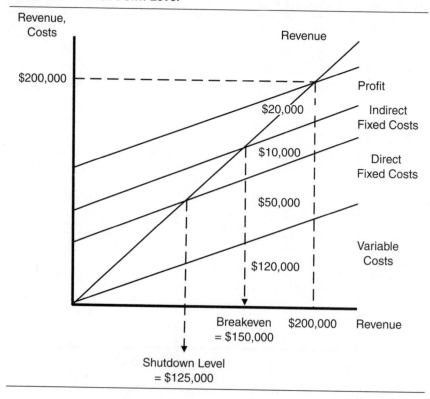

So, for example, if you think a promotion will increase sales of your product or service by $100,000 and your variable margin rate is 32 percent, then you would expect your contribution to increase by $32,000. If the fixed cost of the proposed promotion is $10,000, then you may want to go ahead as your net profit will increase $22,000.

You can use this approach to evaluate many marketing decisions such as advertising, sales promotion, and personal selling.

## Evaluating the Financial Impact of Marketing Decisions —Frame Store Example

Suppose that you are considering the following options:

- Increase newspaper advertising by $7,000.
- Remodel the interior of your mall shop at a cost of $9,000.

**Exhibit 26.8   Important Sales Levels—Frame Shop Example**

$$\text{Variable magin rate} = \frac{\$80,000}{\$200,000} = 0.40$$

$$\text{Breakeven sales level} = \frac{\$60,000}{0.40} = \$150,000$$

Check: $(\$150,000) \times (0.40) = \$60,000 = \text{Fixed costs}$

$$\$40,000 \text{ Target profit sales level} = \frac{\$60,000 + \$40,000}{0.40} = \$250,000$$

Check: $(\$250,000) \times (0.40) = \$100,000 \rightarrow \text{FC of } \$60,000 \text{ and profit of } \$40,000$

$$20\% \text{ Target ROS sales level} = \frac{\$60,000}{(0.40 - 0.20)} = \$300,000$$

Check: $(\$300,000) \times (0.40) = \$120,000 \rightarrow \text{FC of } \$60,000 \text{ and profit of } \$60,000 = 20\% \text{ sales}$

$$\text{Shutdown sales level} = \frac{\$50,000}{0.40} = \$125,000$$

Check: $(\$125,000) \times (0.40) = \$50,000 = \text{Direct fixed costs}$

- Add an assistant store manager at a cost of $10,000. (*Note:* The store manager and assistant manager would each get the 2.5 percent bonus on sales made while they were at the store. Only one would be at the store at any time.)

To evaluate each of these alternatives, you would need to estimate what you think might be the resulting change in your sales. For example, perhaps you feel that the increased newspaper advertising might generate another $40,000 in sales while remodeling your shop will lead to a sales increase of only $20,000. Hiring an assistant store manager would allow you to keep the store open longer and suppose you feel that will increase your sales by $50,000.

Applying the variable margin rate (Exhibit 26.9), you find that remodeling the shop will have a net negative effect on your profit in the short run. However, both the newspaper advertising and assistant store manager options would increase your contribution and operating profit.

**Exhibit 26.9   Marketing Decisions—Frame Store Example**

*Increase in Newspaper Advertising*
$$\text{Estimated change in sales} = \$40,000$$
$$\text{Estimated change in contribution} = (\$40,000) \times (0.40)$$
$$= \$16,000$$
$$\text{Estimated net change in contribution} = \$16,000 - \$7,000$$
$$= \$9,000$$

*Remodel Interior of Shop*
$$\text{Estimated change in sales} = \$20,000$$
$$\text{Estimated change in contribution} = (\$20,000) \times (0.40)$$
$$= \$8,000$$
$$\text{Estimated net change in contribution} = \$8,000 - \$9,000$$
$$= -\$1,000$$

*Add an Assistant Store Manager*
$$\text{Estimated change in sales} = \$50,000$$
$$\text{Estimated change in contribution} = (\$50,000) \times (0.40)$$
$$= \$20,000$$
$$\text{Estimated net change in contribution} = \$20,000 - \$10,000$$
$$= \$10,000$$

## Minimum Sales Change Needed

Knowing your variable margin rate also allows you to determine the *minimum* level of sales change you would need to justify a marketing decision. To make that kind of calculation, you simply divide the cost change associated with your proposed marketing decision by the variable margin rate:

$$\text{Minimum sales change needed} = \frac{\text{Change in cost}}{\text{Variable margin rate}}$$

In the frame shop example, suppose you were thinking of spending $4,000 on local radio advertising. By how much would your sales need to increase to justify that expenditure?

$$\text{Minimum sales change needed} = \frac{\$4,000}{0.40} = \$10,000$$

If you think that the radio advertising will increase your sales by $10,000 or more, then you may want to purchase the advertising, since your net contribution will increase as a result. For example, if sales were to increase $12,000 as a result of your radio advertising, then your contribution would increase by $12,000 × 0.40 or $4,800, less the $4,000 cost of the advertising, for a net change of $800.

This simple approach can be used for any change of a fixed marketing expenditure which you think will lead to a change in sales.

Calculating the minimum sales change can be especially useful for evaluating decisions involving activities where making an exact estimate of sales change is difficult. For example, you may be considering sending a newsletter to potential clients or hosting an open house or setting up an exhibit at a show. You can evaluate whether you want to spend money on those activities by determining the minimum amount of sales they would need to generate to justify their expense. However, to do this you do need to know your variable margin rate.

## CONCLUSIONS

You can evaluate the financial impact of marketing actions if you have the appropriate information. Unfortunately, often traditional accounting documents do not provide the information that marketing managers require. However, you can reorganize traditional accounting information into a contribution format that permits you to determine the variable margin rate. You can then apply the variable margin rate to evaluate the financial consequences of many marketing decisions.

For review questions for this chapter, log on to www.trumpuniversity .com/marketing101.

# 27

---

## CONDUCTING

## MARKETING RESEARCH

Marketing research is the eyes and ears of marketing. Many marketing failures can be traced to not understanding customers, not understanding competitors, or not understanding trends in the competitive environment. Marketing research can be highly sophisticated and cost a lot of money. However, you can also learn a lot from much more modest techniques. Simply talking to your customers can provide a very high payoff in terms of knowledge about their needs, about what competitors might be doing, and about what trends in the environment might cause the customers to change their behavior.

When you are conducting marketing research or even just looking at the results of a study, you need to understand the strengths and weaknesses of how the information is collected and how it is analyzed and presented. Those strengths and weaknesses may affect your interpretation of the results and how useful they may be to you. This chapter is a short course in understanding different kinds of marketing research and the possible reservations to any study.

## KEEPING CUSTOMERS SATISFIED: MARKETING RESEARCH IN THE TRUMP CASINOS

Management of the Trump casinos in Atlantic City survey their patrons regularly. They ask the customers to rank several attributes of service—first by importance and then again based on their delivery (in a manner very similar to the Perceived Value Analysis described in Chapter 4). The difference, or gap, between the importance rating and the satisfaction rating provides them with a blueprint for how to improve their operations.

Many customer needs in a casino relate to operations, and do not require a tremendous amount of capital. An example would be security—something as simple as increasing the visibility of security patrols in the parking garage by putting a flashing light on top of the security vehicles can positively impact the perception of security, and help close a gap. Another would be the buffet—displaying food in smaller decorative bowls and containers (instead of institutional sheet pans) not only makes the display of the food more attractive, it also increases the perception of freshness.

The higher the ranking, the more important the attribute; the larger gaps tell what they need to work on. Large gaps for more important attributes are particularly troubling as they indicate that there may be a

Photo courtesy of the Trump Organization.

significant problem with an issue that is very important to their guests. They pay particular attention to addressing these issues. By focusing on closing the gaps, particularly at the high end of the scale, they increase customer satisfaction. The surveys are an iterative process; as improvements are made, the customers expect more. The casino managers constantly measure themselves against this raised bar.

## Focus of Marketing Research

The purpose of marketing research is to help you make better marketing decisions. Marketing research can be focused on all the players and drivers that affect the marketing performance of the organization (see Exhibit 8.1, page 67). These include end-users, resellers, competitors, suppliers, and trends. Much of marketing research focuses on customers—their needs, their attitudes, and their behavior. End-user studies include:

*Segmentation:* Characteristics that can be used to identify and distinguish segments.

*Buying behavior:* How they learn about products and services and make their choices.

*Needs:* Benefits sought by customers, priorities.

*Perceived value:* Maximum value willing to pay and why.

*Product:* Evaluations of all competing products or services.

*Brand:* Attributes associated with brand.

*Advertising copy:* Comparison of ads.

*Media habits:* Where customers get information.

*Sales calls:* Content of call and effects.

*Pricing:* Likely reactions to prices.

*Buying behavior:* How and where make purchases.

Other studies may focus on:

*Resellers:* For many organizations, resellers may represent the main group of customers, so many of the studies listed under end-users may also be conducted for them as well. In addition, there may be other necessary studies specific to resellers such as how they use sales promotion or what their stocking policies are.

*Suppliers:* Research may focus on comparative costs of various suppliers and the performance of their products and services.

*Competitors:*   Research on competitors needs to determine who they are (often learned from end-users or resellers), their objectives, the strength of their capabilities, and what actions they are likely to take.

*Trends:*   Demographic, social, technological, political/regulatory, and economic trends can all affect the organization. Monitoring and forecasting such trends is also part of marketing research.

## TYPES OF DATA

Data consists of either primary or secondary data. Primary data is what marketing managers or their colleagues collect. Secondary data is what someone else, such as an information service, collects.

Secondary data is often purchased from a research firm and therefore is usually cheaper than if you were to collect the data yourself. The main disadvantage of secondary data is that it may not be exactly what you want. Also you may not know how it was collected, so you may not know how reliable it is. Primary data is tailored to your needs because you define the study and the data to be collected. Usually you will be more aware of any weaknesses of these primary data since you were involved in designing the research.

### Secondary Data

It is very easy to search for sources of secondary data by using the Internet. Sources include: governments, industry associations, companies and other organizations, banks, publications news media, marketing research companies, financial research companies.

The best advice for finding secondary data sources is simply to conduct a search on the Internet for the subject in which you are interested. When you locate what you think might be secondary information that is useful for you, you should try to find a description as to how that information was collected. Then you should evaluate its accuracy using the suggestions following for collecting your own data.

### Primary Data

You may collect data with *random* or *nonrandom sampling*. When you use random sampling, typically the data you obtain can be analyzed with various statistical tests and can be extrapolated to all customers, resellers, suppliers, or competitors.

If you do not use random sampling, then usually you cannot generalize from the data you collected.

Data obtained without random sampling are used primarily to uncover ideas and hypotheses which you can later check with data from randomly selected samples. A common and very useful marketing research tool that often does not utilize random sampling are *focus groups*. A focus group consists of a group of customers or potential customers who are asked questions about a product or service. Their responses can provide insights into how a product or service is used and what are its key attributes. It is often valuable to conduct focus groups before conducting a survey of a large number of respondents to obtain ideas that you can pursue in your larger survey.

## Random and Nonrandom Sampling

There are many activities in marketing research that do not involve sampling, but to understand marketing research, it is necessary to understand sampling and the differences in data collected with random versus nonrandom sampling.

In statistics, a *population* is a group of people—like a target market—or objects—like a collection of competing products—about which you want to know something. For example, perhaps you want to know the average annual income of the members of a target market or the average rating for some performance dimension of your competitors' products.

You could take a *census* of all the members of the group. Unfortunately, often that is very expensive and may not even be possible. Fortunately, in many cases you can obtain almost as much information as a census provides by observing only some of the members of the group—what is called a *sample*. A sample is a group of people or objects selected from the population. The *sample size* is the number of people or objects in the sample.

Generally, there are two possible types of errors in sample information: systematic error (or bias) and random error.

## BIAS

*Bias* means your sample does not represent the population you want to know something about. Possible bias is the main reason it is difficult to generalize from a sample that was not selected randomly.

If your sample is not drawn from the population in which you are interested, it is known as *non-selection* bias. For example, if you choose a sample only from Internet users, you will not have information on people who do not use the Internet. When a sample is selected judgmentally, then the researcher decides which population member will be in the sample and you may have *selection bias*. Generally, people like to talk with people whom they feel are like themselves, which means a judgmental sample is likely biased against inclusion of people unlike the researcher.

When people do not cooperate in a survey, there may be bias called *non-response bias*. People may not agree to be questioned in a mall perhaps because they are too busy. *Response bias* happens when questions may be too difficult ("How many shirts did you buy in the past five years?"), too sensitive ("What is your annual income?"), or too embarrassing ("How many hours a day do you watch game show reruns?") The best way to handle bias is simply to think through your research plan very carefully and hope that you have identified all the possible sources of bias.

---

**The best way to handle bias is simply to think through your research plan very carefully and hope that you have identified all the possible sources of bias.**

---

## Random Errors

Whenever you use a sample, there are *random errors*. Random error occurs because the composition of each sample will likely be somewhat different, leading to somewhat different results. The variation in the results from different samples is measured by random error. The smaller the random error, the more accurate the information from your sample.

You make random error smaller by increasing the size of your sample. However, you should keep in mind that random error does not decrease with the sample size, it decreases with the *square root* of the sample size. That means that to decrease a random error from, say, 0.50 cans of soft drink to 0.25 cans of soft drink—a decrease of 50 percent, you need to quadruple the size of the sample, from, say, 100 to 400 respondents.

## Sample Size

Determining the optimal sample size for a study can be very complicated. However, you can use some rules-of-thumb to help you decide on your sample size.

The *minimum* sample size for any population such as a target market segment should be *30*. The reason that 30 is somewhat of a "magic number" is that with sample sizes of 30, most statisticians would allow the use of the well-known *normal distribution* as an approximation when doing analysis *even* if your target population is not "normal." With data from sample sizes below 30, unless your target population is normal, you may need to use approaches other than the normal distribution to make estimates from your data.

If you can afford it, you would like a sample size larger than 30. Generally, you want a larger sample size:

- *When the target population is heterogeneous:* The more varied your customers, the larger sample size you need. If all your customers are the same or similar, then a smaller sample is sufficient. For example, if you are cooking soup and you stir it well, how many spoonfuls do you need to see how it tastes? Likely just one.
- *When the members of a population are very important:* It is more important for you to survey more large customers than small customers because a large customer's actions will have more of an impact on your sales.

## METHOD OF CONTACT

You may conduct a survey in a variety of ways, for example: mail, Internet, telephone, in-person, observation. Mail is the slowest method with respect to receiving a response and also likely has the highest nonresponse rate. Internet can provide rapid feedback and is especially useful for questions regarding choices. Telemarketing has lowered the response rates in telephone surveys, but telephone can still be used for targeted research. In-person provides the interviewer the opportunity to build a rapport with the respondent, which may allow the asking of sensitive or complex questions. Observation, if unobtrusive, removes nonresponse and response bias.

## DESIGN OF QUESTIONNAIRE

Questionnaire design is part science, part art. An effective questionnaire flows like an interesting conversation. Just as you would start a conversation with an "ice-breaker" question, you start a questionnaire with a question you think the respondent might like to answer. You should never start a questionnaire with demographic questions—how interested would you be in talking with someone who began the conversation with questions about your age and income? Just like a conversation, the questionnaire should move into the topics on which you really want to focus. You finish up with demographics or other information that you might need for your market analyses.

---

**An effective questionnaire flows like an interesting conversation.**

---

*Open-ended questions* require the respondent to write down their answers. They can provide a lot of information but may cut into the response rate for the survey. *Closed-ended questions* offer the respondent specific responses from which to select and are much easier for the respondent to complete but do not allow the respondent much freedom in their replies. You can use open-ended questions in a trial questionnaire, then use responses to those questions to prepare closed-ended questions for the final version of the questionnaire.

## ANALYZING YOUR DATA

After you have collected your data, you will want to "run the numbers"—do some analysis. While there are many sophisticated ways to analyze data, often you can obtain much insight into your market with simple tables.

The first type of table you want to look at consists of just the averages for the questions you have asked in your survey. For example, if you have asked customers of your realty agency to use a 10-point scale to evaluate how important are the dimensions of the service you provide them, such as financial expertise, school expertise, and accessibility (convenient hours and location), then you would want to see the averages for each of those service benefits.

The second type of table you might want to consider is what is called a *cross-tabulation* or cross-tab. That would be a table in which you look at two pieces of information at the same time. For example, you might want to see if there are differences between women and men in regard to how important they consider the various benefits your realty agency provides. If their opinions differ, you would say that perceptions of your services are *associated* with gender and that might be useful for you to know when you are considering market segments.

For example, Exhibit 9.1, page 78, is a two-way cross-tabulation of the answers to the survey question "How important are each of the following benefits to you?" versus different family status situations such as singles, young couples, and young families. Exhibit 9.2 is a three-way cross-tabulation since it includes both family status and gender.

## SURVEYING YOUR CUSTOMERS— ART ASSOCIATION EXAMPLE

Suppose you are the chairperson of the marketing committee of a small not-for-profit arts association and you would like to know more about your members. Your budget for your entire study is just a few hundred dollars. You decide to do a mail survey because it is relatively cheap and you already have the mailing list of your members. You take a random sample of 200 members to whom you will send your questionnaire with a stamped, addressed return envelope.

You develop the questionnaire by first speaking with a few members so you can make as many of the questions as possible closed-ended to increase the response rate.

The first question concerns in what types of visual arts the respondent is interested (Exhibit 27.1). This is the "grabber"—question of relatively high personal interest to the respondent. Then the questionnaire moves into the important areas of reasons for joining, satisfaction with current activities, and interest in future activities. The questionnaire ends with the classification questions such as age, family status, and other associations of which they are members.

## CONCLUSIONS

Without marketing research, you are guessing when you develop your marketing strategy. You can certainly be successful without marketing research because you can be lucky with a product or a service. However, in the long run, you do need consistent and accurate information about your markets if you are going to have continued success. Effective marketing research does not require a large budget or complicated statistical techniques, but it does require thought as to what information is needed and it does require contact with customers.

For review questions for this chapter, log on to www.trumpuniversity .com/marketing101.

## Exhibit 27.1  Sample Questionnaire—Arts Organization

Dear Member,

We would like to know your views as to what we can do for you. We would be very grateful if you might spend just a few moments to let us know what interests you and how you view us. We have designed the questionnaire to be easy, quick (about 4 minutes), and hopefully fun to fill out. Thank you!

1. Please describe your level of interest (please circle):

| | Not very interested | | | | | | Very interested |
|---|---|---|---|---|---|---|---|
| Painting | 1 | 2 | 3 | 4 | 5 | 6 | 7 |
| Graphic arts | 1 | 2 | 3 | 4 | 5 | 6 | 7 |
| Photography | 1 | 2 | 3 | 4 | 5 | 6 | 7 |
| Sculpture | 1 | 2 | 3 | 4 | 5 | 6 | 7 |
| Other_____ | 1 | 2 | 3 | 4 | 5 | 6 | 7 |

2. a) Are you personally involved in one or more of the arts?   yes___   no___

   b) If yes, for each art in which you're involved, how would you describe your level of involvement?

| | Create art but have not exhibited or performed | | Have exhibited or performed | | Have been paid as artist | | Make living as artist |
|---|---|---|---|---|---|---|---|
| Painting | 1 | 2 | 3 | 4 | 5 | 6 | 7 |
| Graphic arts | 1 | 2 | 3 | 4 | 5 | 6 | 7 |
| Photography | 1 | 2 | 3 | 4 | 5 | 6 | 7 |
| Sculpture | 1 | 2 | 3 | 4 | 5 | 6 | 7 |
| Other (please describe) _____ | 1 | 2 | 3 | 4 | 5 | 6 | 7 |

3. About how many years have you been a member? _____ years

4. How did you first hear about us?  (Please check all that apply.)
Storefront sign ___   Storefront window ___   Mailing ___   Flyer___   Letter ___   Newspaper ___
Radio___   Television___   E-mail___   Web site___   Friend/acquaintance___   Don't recall___

*(continued)*

**Exhibit 27.1   Sample Arts Questionnaire—Arts Organization (continued)**

5.  When you joined, how important were each of the following (please circle)?

| | Not very important | | | | | | Very important |
|---|---|---|---|---|---|---|---|
| Exhibit art | 1 | 2 | 3 | 4 | 5 | 6 | 7 |
| Develop art career | 1 | 2 | 3 | 4 | 5 | 6 | 7 |
| Attend openings | 1 | 2 | 3 | 4 | 5 | 6 | 7 |
| Network with artists | 1 | 2 | 3 | 4 | 5 | 6 | 7 |
| Take classes/workshops | 1 | 2 | 3 | 4 | 5 | 6 | 7 |
| Children's programs | 1 | 2 | 3 | 4 | 5 | 6 | 7 |
| Support visual arts | 1 | 2 | 3 | 4 | 5 | 6 | 7 |
| Support our town | 1 | 2 | 3 | 4 | 5 | 6 | 7 |
| Receive discounts | 1 | 2 | 3 | 4 | 5 | 6 | 7 |
| Other (please describe) _____ | 1 | 2 | 3 | 4 | 5 | 6 | 7 |

6.  a) Over the past twelve months, about how often did you do each of the following and, for those events or activities in which you participated, overall how would you rate your experience (please circle)?

| | Number of times | Did not enjoy | | | | | | Enjoyed |
|---|---|---|---|---|---|---|---|---|
| Attend show opening | ____ | 1 | 2 | 3 | 4 | 5 | 6 | 7 |
| Take class/workshop | ____ | 1 | 2 | 3 | 4 | 5 | 6 | 7 |
| Use children's program | ____ | 1 | 2 | 3 | 4 | 5 | 6 | 7 |
| Attend member meeting | ____ | 1 | 2 | 3 | 4 | 5 | 6 | 7 |
| Exhibit art | ____ | 1 | 2 | 3 | 4 | 5 | 6 | 7 |
| Other (please describe) _____ | ____ | 1 | 2 | 3 | 4 | 5 | 6 | 7 |

b)  Which event did you most enjoy?_____
    Why?_____

7.  How do you usually hear about our events? (Please check all that apply.)
Storefront sign ____  Storefront window ____  Mailing ___  Flyer___  Letter ____  Newspaper ___
Radio___  Television___  E-mail___  Web site___  Friend/acquaintance___  Don't recall___

Exhibit 27.1   (continued)

8.  How would you describe us (please circle)?

| Informal     | 1 | 2 | 3 | 4 | 5 | 6 | 7 | Formal       |
|--------------|---|---|---|---|---|---|---|--------------|
| Boring       | 1 | 2 | 3 | 4 | 5 | 6 | 7 | Stimulating  |
| Friendly     | 1 | 2 | 3 | 4 | 5 | 6 | 7 | Unfriendly   |
| Intimidating | 1 | 2 | 3 | 4 | 5 | 6 | 7 | Supportive   |
| Cliquish     | 1 | 2 | 3 | 4 | 5 | 6 | 7 | Open         |
| Traditional  | 1 | 2 | 3 | 4 | 5 | 6 | 7 | Experimental |
| Creative     | 1 | 2 | 3 | 4 | 5 | 6 | 7 | Bland        |
| Playful      | 1 | 2 | 3 | 4 | 5 | 6 | 7 | Serious      |
| Dull         | 1 | 2 | 3 | 4 | 5 | 6 | 7 | Inspiring    |

9.  How interested are you in each of the following (please circle)?

|                            | Not very interested | | | | | | Very interested |
|----------------------------|---|---|---|---|---|---|---|
| More member shows          | 1 | 2 | 3 | 4 | 5 | 6 | 7 |
| More juried shows          | 1 | 2 | 3 | 4 | 5 | 6 | 7 |
| More classes/workshops     | 1 | 2 | 3 | 4 | 5 | 6 | 7 |
| More classes for children  | 1 | 2 | 3 | 4 | 5 | 6 | 7 |
| Artists' resource center   | 1 | 2 | 3 | 4 | 5 | 6 | 7 |
| Professional critiques     | 1 | 2 | 3 | 4 | 5 | 6 | 7 |
| Artist mentor              | 1 | 2 | 3 | 4 | 5 | 6 | 7 |
| Artist business advice     | 1 | 2 | 3 | 4 | 5 | 6 | 7 |
| Other (please describe) _____ | 1 | 2 | 3 | 4 | 5 | 6 | 7 |
| _____                | 1 | 2 | 3 | 4 | 5 | 6 | 7 |

10. Please describe yourself:

Gender: Male__ Female__   Age: Under 16___   16–18___   19–22___   23–35___   36–50___ Over 50___

Family status:   Single___ Living as couple___   Number of children living with you___ (Ages_____)

Member: Northwest Artists Guild ___   Central Art Association___   Other arts associations_____

Thank you very much for your help!

*Source:* "Arrow Guide—Arts Organization Questionnaire," The Arrow Group, Ltd.®, New York, 2004. Used with permission.

# 28

---

# FORECASTING

You have developed your marketing strategy—congratulations. Now you need to forecast what you think will happen when you implement your strategy. You need to make a forecast so you can decide whether or not this strategy is sound and acceptable or whether you need to change it in some way. There are many ways to make forecasts. This chapter gives you an overview of how you might forecast the results of your marketing strategy.

## FORECASTS AND STRATEGY

You compare your forecast to your objectives (Exhibit 28.1). If your forecasts equal or exceed your objectives, then the plan is acceptable. If they do not meet the objectives, then either the objectives need to be decreased or the marketing strategy and tactics need to be revised.

Even if the forecasts do fulfill the objectives, you may be wise—time permitting—to develop one or more other marketing strategies to see if one of them might lead to even more favorable results.

You not only need a forecast for your own decision making, you may also need a forecast for any one you may approach for financial support. Typically they will ask, as they should, what you expect your product or service to achieve in sales revenue and in profits.

**Exhibit 28.1   Developing a Product/Market Strategy**

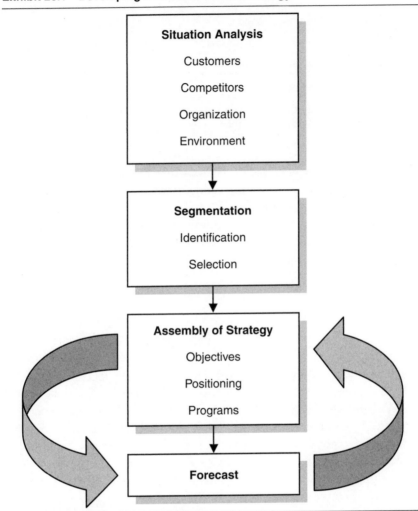

*Source:* "Arrow Guide—Formulating the Product/Market Strategy," The Arrow Group, Ltd.®, New York, 2004. Used with permission.

## POTENTIAL, RESULTS, AND OBJECTIVES

*Market potential* is the maximum sales or profits that you think you might obtain from your target market (Exhibit 28.2). Your sales potential will usually be lower than the market potential because some customers may already be under contract or otherwise loyal to competitors.

**Exhibit 28.2  Forecasts and Objectives**

| Quantity | Your organization | All competitors |
|----------|-------------------|-----------------|
| Potential | Sales potential forecast | Market potential forecast |
| Result | Results forecast | Not applicable |
| Objective | Desired results | Not applicable |

Source: "Arrow Guide—Formulating Sales Strategy," The Arrow Group, Ltd.®, New York, 2004. Used with permission.

*Results* are what you expect to achieve with a given strategy. All forecasts of results must assume a specific marketing strategy—target market, positioning, and marketing programs.

*Objectives* are what you hope to achieve with a given strategy. If your marketing strategy cannot be expected to achieve the necessary results, then you may not want to go ahead with it.

## DETERMINING CURRENT MARKET AND SALES POTENTIAL

You can evaluate the potential of a market with either a direct approach or an indirect approach.

With the *direct approach*, you focus on the sales of existing products or services. If your product or service is new, then you would examine sales for similar products or services or sales of the products or services that would be displaced by your new product or service. For example, if you are introducing a new caffeinated drink, you might look at the sales of coffees and teas that are currently on the market.

With the *indirect approach* you look at characteristics that would be associated with the sale of your product or service. A company that makes cartons to ship apples might estimate the number of cartons needed by a farm by counting the number of apple trees on the farm. The owner of a sporting goods store might estimate the potential in a geographical area by first finding out the number of people who live there, by age and by gender.

You develop the estimate for your *potential sales* by estimating how much sales in the market represent sales to customers who can be expected to remain loyal to competitors. Then you reduce the market potential by those amounts.

For example, if you estimate that there is $5 million of dry-cleaning business in an area but that 40 percent of that is from customers loyal to existing dry cleaners, your sales potential for that area would be the remaining 60 percent or $3 million.

## FORECASTING FUTURE MARKET AND SALES POTENTIAL

When making a forecast, if possible you would like to start with sales potential data over a few years (Exhibit 28.3). Forecasts can be made a variety of ways. Here are some of the most common ways to make predictions:

**Exhibit 28.3   Sales over Time**

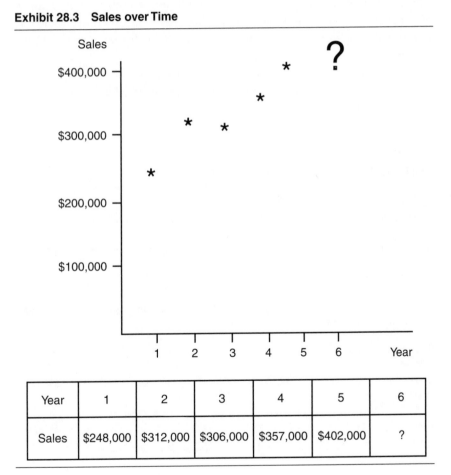

| Year | 1 | 2 | 3 | 4 | 5 | 6 |
|------|---|---|---|---|---|---|
| Sales | $248,000 | $312,000 | $306,000 | $357,000 | $402,000 | ? |

- *Moving average:* Using the average sales for the past few time periods (e.g., the past three years) as an estimate of the sales for the next time period.
- *Exponential smoothing:* Utilizing a weighting scheme for past sales.
- *Regression analysis using time:* Examining the sales trend over time to predict sales for the next time period.

All of these statistical tools are available on Excel. Exhibit 28.4 compares their estimates for year six in the example.

You may have reason to prefer one method over another. In this case, the forecast from the linear regression is highest because there is an upward trend that is the main determinant of the regression forecast. The moving average and exponential smoothing methods tend to dampen out trends. If you do not have reason to prefer one method, then you may use as your forecast the average of the forecasts from the methods you have used.

You may also override these statistically based estimates with your own *subjective estimates* if you feel strongly that your subjective forecast is based on sound assumptions.

**Exhibit 28.4   Alternative Sales Forecasts**

| Year | 1 | 2 | 3 | 4 | 5 | 6 |
|---|---|---|---|---|---|---|
| Actual sales | $248,000 | $312,000 | $306,000 | $357,000 | $402,000 | ? |
| Moving average (3 years) forecast | Not available | Not available | Not available | $288,667 | $325,000 | $355,000 |
| Exponential smoothing (80% damping) forecast | Not available | $248,000 | $260,800 | $269,840 | $287,272 | $390,900 |
| Linear regression forecast | $254,400 | $289,700 | $325,000 | $360,300 | $395,600 | $430,900 |
| Average forecast | | | | | | $392,300 |

## FORECASTING THE RESULTS OF YOUR STRATEGY

*Marketing mix modeling* refers to using techniques such as multiple regression analysis to estimate the impact of changes in the marketing mix involving decisions such as pricing and communications. While promising, marketing mix modeling is not easy to do and is most likely beyond the budget of most smaller organizations.

You can make subjective estimates of the sales you think your strategy will produce. The most straightforward way to approach making such estimates is to estimate what you think your reasonable share of the market will be, then apply that share estimate to your estimate of sales potential. (To do that, you really need to assume that your likely share is not correlated with your potential estimate but that's probably a plausible assumption.)

To make a subjective estimate of your share, follow these six steps:

1. Describe your marketing strategy, including positioning and branding, design, pricing, communications, and distribution.
2. Evaluate your competitors' likely marketing strategies.
3. Identify the highest share you think you will get, the lowest share, and the middle share.
4. Based on your evaluation of your marketing strategy versus those of your competitors, assign probabilities to each of the share alternatives in Step 3.
5. Average your share alternatives by weighting them with the probabilities from Step 4. This average is called your *expected share.*
6. Multiply the expected share times your sales potential estimate to get an estimate of your sales from this particular marketing strategy.

## FORECASTING THE RESULTS OF YOUR STRATEGY— DRY-CLEANING EXAMPLE

Suppose you estimate that the sales potential for your dry-cleaning services is $3 million. You have checked your competitors in the area and believe that the lowest share you will achieve is 10 percent or 0.1, the highest share is 40 percent or 0.4, and the middle share is 20 percent or 0.2.

Based on your assessment of your abilities and strategy versus those of your competitor, you feel that there is a large probability, 0.6, that you will

**Exhibit 28.5   Estimating Your Market Share**

| Possible Market Share | Estimated Probability |
|:---:|:---:|
| 0.1 | 0.6 |
| 0.2 | 0.3 |
| 0.4 | 0.1 |
| | Sum = 1.0 |

Expected share = $(0.1) \times (0.6) + (0.2) \times (0.3) + (0.4) \times (0.1) = 0.16$

obtain only the 10 percent share, a moderate probability, 0.3, that you will obtain the 20 percent share, and a small probability, 0.1, that you will obtain a 40 percent share. Note that your probability estimates must total 1.00 or 100 percent.

According to the calculations in Exhibit 28.5, your expected share is 16 percent or 0.16. Given that your estimated sales potential is $3 million, your sales estimate for this strategy is:

$$\text{Sales estimate} = \text{Sales potential} \times \text{Expected share} = \$3,000,000 \times 0.16$$
$$= \$480,000$$

Finally, to convert this sales estimate into contribution, you would multiply it by your variable margin rate (discussed in Chapter 26). For example, if your variable margin rate was 0.90, your contribution would be $432,000. From that you would need to subtract your fixed costs. If your fixed costs were $240,000, your net profit (before taxes) would be $192,000.

You now need to compare that forecast to your objectives and decide whether you want to proceed with this marketing strategy.

You may want to consider strengthening your marketing strategy. If so, you would change your strategy, then estimate again your likely share, sales, and profits—being sure to include any changes in costs due to your new strategy.

You repeat this process until you find an acceptable marketing strategy or decide that this particular market will not provide you an acceptable return for your efforts.

## Short-Term and Long-Term Forecasts

You can use the entire process mentioned above for forecasting your sales and profits beyond the short-term (next year). To do that you will need to estimate both your sales potential and your market share for each of the coming years.

It is common sense and also sound statistical analysis that forecasts become less accurate the farther out you try to predict. Many finance people say that they look ahead at most five years. You need to decide how far ahead you feel you should try to predict.

## CONCLUSIONS

Going forward with a marketing strategy without trying to make a forecast is risky business. You may win but you may also squander your resources when a somewhat stronger strategy may have succeeded. If forecasting the future were easy, I would not be writing this book—instead I'd be forecasting the spins of roulette wheels in Atlantic City and sleeping late on my yacht. However, you can be systematic in your forecasting—estimate the sales available to you and estimate what portion of those sales you think you can win with your marketing strategy. Then convert your sales estimates into profit estimates.

For review questions for this chapter, log on to www.trumpuniversity .com/marketing101.

# V

## MAKING SURE YOUR MARKETING STRATEGY SUCCEEDS

# 29

---

# THE MARKETING PLAN

Your *marketing plan* summarizes the strategy and all the programs that are designed to achieve your objectives. It describes the outcomes of all the analyses you have done and all the decisions you have made as you have gone through the process of developing your marketing strategy. If you have done all the analyses described in this book—or just the ones you felt were most important—and if you have considered all your alternatives, you will find that your marketing plan basically writes itself. Your marketing plan provides direction for all your marketing actions. You may need to change your plan somewhat as your plan encounters the market, but your plan should provide you with guidance.

## PLANNING AHEAD

How far ahead should you plan? Determining your planning horizon is a lot like driving your car. You need to look ahead on the road at least far enough so that you will have time to brake or turn if you see a problem ahead of you. The same is true of marketing. You need to plan ahead far enough so that you will have time to change your strategy if you need to do so.

## POSITIONING: DONALD J. TRUMP MOBILE CONTENT

Many cell-phone users enjoy having distinctive ringtones—music or voice. How can you position a ringtone? Due to *The Apprentice* reality television show, Donald Trump's voice has become well-known. In addition, Donald Trump has a widespread reputation for business acumen. That combination—voice and advice—differentiate a Trump ringtone. The Trump Organization and Rhino Entertainment, a division of Warner Music Group, developed a collection of voice and video ringtones and ringback tones that consist of messages from Mr. Trump such as:

> "Always stay focused. Also, you're getting a phone call, focus on that."

> "You're getting a phone call and believe me it better be important. I have no time for small talk and neither do you."

> "Why not answer your phone, you could be missing out on some really big business."

The Trump brand and the messages themselves make these ringtones unique and give them a positioning difficult to imitate.

---

You should develop your marketing plan for a time period *longer* than the time it will take you to implement any major changes in your strategy. For example, if it will take you two years to find and train more staff, then your plan should look ahead at least two years. If it will take you four years to change your brand name and brand position, then your plan should look ahead at least four years.

Your marketing plan should reflect what you feel will be changes in your competitive environment during the time bounded by your planning horizon. Because you expect new competitors to enter your market, you may need to change your target competitor and your benefit advantage and competitive advantage. For example, if you operate a restaurant and a new chain restaurant opens in your area, you may need to rethink your strategy—in particular your target market and your positioning which, in turn, would be reflected in your marketing programs.

# THE MARKETING PLAN

Your marketing plan (see the worksheet in Exhibit 29.1) consists of the four main components of your marketing strategy (target market, objectives, positioning, and programs), your forecasts for your main objectives, and a list of your key planning assumptions. You need to determine what objectives are important to you and what marketing programs you will be using and tailor Exhibit 29.1 to your situation.

**Downloadable Exhibit 29.1    Marketing Plan** *

| | | Year | | |
|---|---|---|---|---|
| | | **1** | **2** | **3** |
| Objectives | Share | | | |
| | Profitability | | | |
| | Cash flow | | | |
| Positioning | Target DMU member | | | |
| | Target competitor | | | |
| | Benefit advantage | | | |
| | Competitive advantage | | | |
| Programs | Design | | | |
| | Advertising | | | |
| | Identifiers | | | |
| | Promotion | | | |
| | Selling | | | |
| | Public relations | | | |
| | Pricing | | | |
| | Distribution | | | |
| Forecasts | Share | | | |
| | Profitability | | | |
| | Cash flow | | | |
| Key Planning Assumptions | | | | |

*Source:* "Arrow Guide—Formulating the Product/Market Strategy," Copyright © 2004, The Arrow Group, Ltd.®, New York. Used with permission. ***A blank version of this page can be downloaded from www.trumpuniversity.com/marketing101 and customized for your personal use.** For any other use, contact Don Sexton at Marketing101@thearrowgroup.com.

## THE PLANNING PROCESS

In many chapters, this book provides planning analyses that make your marketing planning easier. They cover important issues such as finding market segments, determining positioning, and developing communications messages. Typically, there are one or more planning analyses available for each step in the planning process. Exhibit 29.2 shows you where each planning analysis fits in the process of formulating a marketing strategy.

If you are stuck in any phase of your planning process, you will find it helpful to use one of the planning analyses for that phase. They often unblock planning logjams and help generate ideas.

**Exhibit 29.2   Marketing Areas and Planning Analyses**

| Marketing Area | Planning Analyses |
| --- | --- |
| Customers | Actual value, perceived value, positioning, communications |
| Competitors | Capability, competitive advantage, strategic theme |
| Organization | Marketing orientation, capability, competitive advantage, strategic theme |
| Environment | Situation |
| Identification | Segment identification |
| Selection | Segment selection, growth strategy |
| Positioning | Competitive advantage, positioning, strategic theme, brand attribute |
| Design | Design, positioning, product space |
| Advertising | Integrated communications, communications |
| Identifiers | Integrated communications, communications |
| Promotion | Integrated communications, communications |
| Selling | Integrated communications, communications |
| Public relations | Integrated communications, communications |
| Pricing | Pricing |
| Strategy | Market strategy, growth strategy, competitive advantage |
| Forecasts | Situation |

*Source:* "Arrow Guide—Formulating the Product/Market Strategy," The Arrow Group, Ltd.®, New York, 2004. Used with permission.

## USING THE PLANNING ANALYSES

You can use these analyses yourself. You can also use them as frameworks for leading discussions with your colleagues. Generally, these analyses work most effectively with groups of from five to seven individuals, although they can be employed successfully with groups of any size. Often the groups include a few people from functions other than marketing, such as finance and operations. That allows the group to have a broader view and builds ownership of your marketing plan across the organization.

If possible, you will find it helpful if two or three of the group members are not responsible for the marketing strategy under consideration but are knowledgeable about the situation. They play the role of "reality-checkers." They often ask questions that ensure the analysis is grounded in reality and not wishful thinking.

If you use the planning analyses with your colleagues, you will find that they:

- Facilitate discussion: Making it easier for people to comment on your marketing strategy, both positively and negatively.
- Help communication among your managers: Especially across functions.
- Utilize current information by providing the opportunity for people to share what they know.
- Spotlight issues that may affect your marketing strategy.
- Identify information gaps that you need to fill.
- Provide the opportunity to evaluate new approaches.
- Lead to your marketing strategy.
- Build ownership of your marketing strategy.

Building ownership is especially important. Without the support of your people, the most brilliant marketing strategy will likely fail. Allowing people to take part in the development of your strategy brings them into the process. You may not use all their ideas or even any of their ideas but they will feel that they have participated in crafting the strategy and that usually results in a sense of ownership.

## FINDING A POWERFUL POSITION

Suppose you assemble your marketing strategy and your forecasts fall short of your objectives. What can you do?

*There are several ways to improve your positioning and strengthen your product/market strategy* (Exhibit 29.3). You should consider them in the following order:

- *Improve your marketing programs:* Make sure that your customers perceive the value you are giving them—especially in terms of your performance of the benefits they most care about. For example, you may have an excellent product or service but your communications are not persuading your customers.
- *Improve your capabilities:* Find the benefits of highest priority to your target customer. Make sure your capabilities are sufficient to provide those benefits at a superior level.
- *Persuade your target customer to value those benefits you already do well and where you have your strongest competitive advantages:* This approach is not as easy as it might sound. Customers usually do not change their priorities unless given very compelling reasons.
- *Add benefits that you think will be of high priority to your customers:* Before you try this approach, be sure you have sound information on what your customers want. Then you must communicate to them that you have these new benefits.
- *Select a different member of the decision-making unit:* You are hoping to find a target member of the decision-making unit who wants the benefits you already provide at a superior level and which are supported by your competitive advantages.
- *Select a different target competitor:* The competitor you select is one you know you are superior to with respect to the benefits your customers want.
- *Select a different target market:* If your superior benefits are not of interest to your current target market, perhaps you can find another target market that will appreciate them.
- *Resegment the entire market:* If you cannot find a target market you can win within your current segmentation scheme, then perhaps you should try another way to segment the market.
- *Redo your situation analysis:* If you are unable to find a target market, target member of decision-making unit, or target competitor that provides you with the opportunity to win, then maybe this market is not for you. Before you depart, however, you may want to reexamine your situation analysis one more time.

**Exhibit 29.3    Improving Your Marketing Plan**

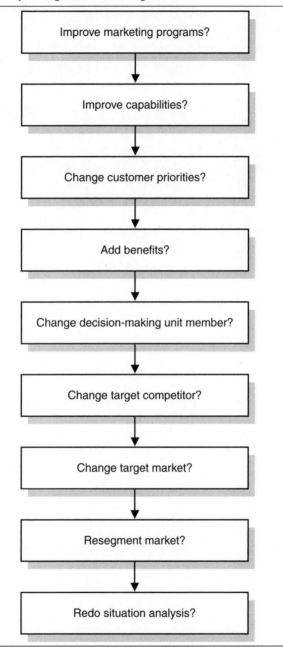

*Source:* "Arrow Guide—Formulating the Product/Market Strategy," The Arrow Group, Ltd.®, New York, 2004. Used with permission.

Every one of these actions has the potential to strengthen your product/market strategy and improve the forecasts of return such as sales, profit, and cash flow. All these actions involve targeting, positioning, or marketing programs. All focus on managing perceived value to your customers.

## FINDING A POWERFUL POSITION—RESTAURANT

Assume you own a small restaurant in the downtown area of a small city. You have a broad menu. You are now faced with new competitors who are specializing in different cuisines. What might you do?

- *Improve marketing programs:* Examine your advertisements to see if they are on strategy—communicating your benefit advantages to your target customers. Perhaps you might want to consider some promotions to attract new customers.
- *Improve capabilities:* You might first evaluate your chef, waitstaff, décor, and food supplies. You may need to improve them in some way.
- *Communicate importance of benefits:* You might find that your menu has many healthy items on it. You may need to communicate that to your customers and raise their health consciousness. You may advertise and spotlight the healthy items on your menu.
- *Add benefits:* You may find that your customers would like to have easier parking. You might arrange with a neighboring business to use their parking facilities, then communicate that to your customers.
- *Target new decision-making unit member:* Perhaps you have not been focused in your advertising. You may want to develop communications that might appeal to either the husband or wife of a family. For example, if you believe that the wives are especially concerned with healthful entrees, you might target them.
- *Target new competitor:* You may want to reevaluate your target competitors. Rather than taking on other local restaurants, you might consider focusing on fast-food or other chain restaurants and emphasize your local presence and support of the community.
- *Target new segment:* If you have been targeting all families, you might want to concentrate your efforts on families with young children. You might provide special meals or drinks for the children, as well as premiums or contests.

- *Resegment market:* If you cannot find a target segment you think you can win, you might try to resegment the market—perhaps by income or by age.
- *Rethink situation:* Finally, if you cannot find a target segment even after you have reexamined your market segmentation, you might want to rethink your situation and decide whether there is room for your restaurant in this market.

## CONCLUSIONS

Your marketing plan is your blueprint for your future actions. It should pull together all your thoughts for your marketing strategy. The target markets and positioning are the heart of the plan. They should coordinate all your marketing programs. Your forecast should validate your plan.

For review questions for this chapter, log on to www.trumpuniversity .com/marketing101.

The concepts and approaches in this book form the basis of the marketing and sales courses at Trump University. If you wish information about those courses and how to enroll, please contact www.trumpuniversity.com.

# NOTES

## Chapter 4: Understanding Your Customers

1. Dave Norton, "Meaningful Brand Experiences," *Brand Experience Newsletter* (May 20, 2005), pp. 3–4.

## Chapter 6: Understanding Your Competitors

1. "Visa Embarks on 1.5 Million Pound Small Business Push," *Marketing Week* (November 20, 2003), p. 9.

## Chapter 8: Understanding Your Overall Competitive Environment

1. Sonia Reyes, "Kellogg Goes Bananas for Healthier Corn Flakes," *Brandweek* (January 5, 2004), p. 4.
2. Amy Garber, "Pizza Hut Rolls Out New Lower-Fat Pie," *Nation's Restaurant* (October 27, 2003), p. 1.
3. Geoff Keighley, "Is Nintendo Playing the Wrong Game?" *Business 2.0,* vol. 4, no. 7 (2003), p. 110.

## Chapter 9: Identifying Your Possible Markets

1. Lisa Sanders, "Verizon Wireless Upsells Youth Via Instant Texting," *Advertising Age*, vol. 75, no. 9 (2004), pp. 3–4.
2. Sonia Reyes, "Campbell Looks to Make a Splash with Hispanics," *Brandweek* (December 8, 2003), p. 9.

## Chapter 10: Selecting Your Key Target Market

1. Lisa Sanders, "Verizon Wireless Upsells Youth Via Instant Texting," *Advertising Age*, vol. 75, no. 9 (2004), pp. 3–4.
2. Jean Halliday, "Toyota Concentrates Marketing on Women to Boost Solara Sales," *Advertising Age*, vol. 75, no. 12 (2004), p. 13.
3. Sonia Reyes, "Kellogg Goes Bananas for Healthier Corn Flakes," *Brandweek* (January 5, 2004), p. 4.

## Chapter 12: Creating Your Most Valuable Asset

1. Deborah Ball, "Advertising: Diageo's Shot at Vodka Rivals Will Revamp the Smirnoff Brand," *Wall Street Journal* (September 5, 2003), p. B-4.
2. Ryan Chittum, "Holiday Inn Is Getting a Makeover," *Wall Street Journal* (September 23, 2003), p. D-4.
3. James Scully, "Louis Vuitton," *Time* (Spring 2004), p. 20.
4. Gary McWilliams, "High Definition Via Mirrors," *Wall Street Journal* (February 5, 2004), p. B-1.
5. Ravi Chandiramani, "Can Kodak Thrive Amid the Digital Revolution," *Marketing* (July 3, 2003), p. 13.
6. Wendy Zellner, "Lessons from a Faded Levi Strauss," *BusinessWeek* (December 15, 2003), p. 44.
7. Neal E. Boudette, "BMW's CEO Just Says 'No' to Protect Brand," *Wall Street Journal* (November 26, 2003), p. B-1.
8. The Conference Board, "Managing the Corporate Brand" (New York, 1998); and American Productivity and Quality Center, "Brand Building and Communication" (Houston, 1999).

## Chapter 15: Increasing Your Customer Satisfaction

1. Jan Carlzon, *Moments of Truth* (New York: HarperCollins, 1989).
2. Kate McArthur, "Wendy's International," *Advertising Age*, vol. 74, no. 50 (2003), p. S-4.

## Chapter 18: Advertising

1. Alfred Hille, "Ikea Turns Beijing Lifts Into Sales Tool," *Media* (March 12, 2004), p. 9.
2. "Mobile Phones Finally Used as Effective Marketing Channel for Consumer Brands," *AGIPNEWS* (January 18, 2006).

# About the Author

**Donald E. Sexton** is professor of business, Columbia University. Don received his PhD and MBA from the University of Chicago in the fields of economics and mathematics. He has been teaching for more than 35 years at Columbia in the areas of marketing, international business, and operations management and is a recipient of the Business School's Distinguished Teaching Award. He is Trump University's subject matter expert and faculty member in the area of marketing and sales.

Don has served as a visiting professor at the China Europe International Business School and at INSEAD. He has also taught at the Indian School of Business, the Hong Kong University of Science and Technology, the Australian Graduate School of Management, the U.S. Business School in Prague, the University of Tehran, and the University of California-Berkeley. His articles have appeared in numerous journals such as the *Journal of Marketing*, the *Journal of Marketing Research*, *Management Science*, and the *Journal of Business*. He is a sought-after conference speaker on issues concerning marketing, branding, and marketing ROI. He is often quoted in media such as the *New York Times*, *BusinessWeek*, and Bejing's *China Economic Daily*.

Don is the founder and president of The Arrow Group, Ltd.® (www .thearrowgroup.com), a firm that provides consulting and training services in the areas of marketing, sales, and brand management. His clients have included companies such as GE, Pfizer, IBM, Kodak, Citigroup, Shell, MetLife, Motorola, Kellogg, AT&T, Wendy's, and DuPont.

He is rated a Master Scuba Diver and is an award-winning painter whose works are in collections in the United States, Europe, and Australia (www.sextonart.com).

You can contact Don at Marketing101@thearrowgroup.com.

# INDEX

# Learn the Trump Way to Market Your Business

**Make no mistake: A Trump University marketing course can give you the knowledge and tools to accelerate the growth of your business — IF you're ready.**

**You will learn how to:**

- ☐ Focus your business on the areas your customers care most about.
- ☐ Expand the scope of your business and acquire new customers.
- ☐ Maximize customer retention rate.
- ☐ Make your products/services irresistible to prospects.
- ☐ Develop an advertising message that works.
- ☐ And much more!

**Trump University has a marketing course that's right for you, including:**

- ☐ **Build a Profitable Marketing Plan:** Proven Marketing Strategies to Understand your Customer and Position your Product
- ☐ **Keep them Coming Back:** Customer Retention Strategies that Work Every Time
- ☐ **Accelerate your Business Growth:** Successful Marketing Strategies for New Products
- ☐ **Develop a *Trump Quality* Image:** How to Create First Rate Branding, Advertising and Public Relations

Each course is created by Don Sexton and features exclusive, cutting-edge content; experiential learning using simulations and realistic scenarios; interactive tools you can use in the real world; and comprehensive support from course facilitators.

Is a Trump University marketing course right for you? There's really only one good way to find out. Just visit **www.TrumpUniversity.com/LearnMarketing**